DARLAN

DARLAN

❧

Admiral and Statesman of France, 1881–1942

George E. Melton

PRAEGER

Westport, Connecticut
London

DC
373
.D35
M45
1998

Library of Congress Cataloging-in-Publication Data

Melton, George E., 1932–
    Darlan : Admiral and statesman of France, 1881–1942 / George E.
Melton.
        p.   cm.
    Includes bibliographical references and index.
    ISBN 0–275–95973–2 (alk. paper)
    1. Darlan, François, 1881–1942. 2. Darlan, François, 1881–1942—
Assassination. 3. Admirals—France—Biography. 4. France.
Marine—Biography. 5. World War, 1939–1945—France—Political
aspects. 6. France—History—German occupation, 1940–1945.
I. Title.
DC373.D35M45   1998
940.54′23′092—dc21
    [B]   97–32541

British Library Cataloguing in Publication Data is available.

Library of Congress Catalog Card Number: 97–32541
ISBN: 0–275–95973–2

First published in 1998

Praeger Publishers, 88 Post Road West, Westport, CT 06881
An imprint of Greenwood Publishing Group, Inc.

Printed in the United States of America

The paper used in this book complies with the
Permanent Paper Standard issued by the National
Information Standards Organization (Z39.48–1984).

10 9 8 7 6 5 4 3 2 1

Contents

Photo essay follows p. 126.

Preface

The author was fortunate to have interviewed and exchanged letters with several Frenchmen, some now deceased, who were close to Darlan. General André Dorange received me in his home and prepared for me several written statements about his experiences in North Africa in 1942. Captain Henri Ballande, Admiral Louis de la Monneraye, and General Jean Chrétien welcomed my wife and me into their homes for long, helpful visits. Their many letters were especially useful. Alain Darlan shared with me by telephone important information and insights about his father. Mme. Hervé Cras, widow of the French naval historian Jacques Mordal, permitted me to examine the papers of her late husband.

Baron Pierre Ordioni received the author more than once in Paris, as did Mme. Francine Hezez, niece of Admiral Darlan. The many helpful letters from Mme. Hezez are much appreciated. I am heavily indebted to Captain Claude Huan, who introduced me to the French National Archives and to the French Naval Archives at Vincennes. Captain Huan also shared with me important documents from his own collection. Other French friends, among them Admiral Alex Wassilieff, Admiral Bernard F. Favin-Levêque, and M. Arnaud de Chantérac, generously shared with me their books and articles.

The late General Mark W. Clark, who kindly welcomed the author and his wife into his home for a long interview, made his personal papers available to me. John Taylor of the United States National Archives was always generous with his time and insights into the documents under his supervision. I appreciate his taking the initiative to inform me of new materials arriving in the military documents section. I am especially indebted to Professor Arthur Layton Funk for his gentle encouragement, his many letters, and his sharing with me numerous documents and other materials from his personal collection.

Among the many friends and colleagues who helped with editing, gave encouragement, and shared insights were Charles Joyner, Larry Addington, Tom

Williams, Jack Roper, and Dean Larry Schulz. My colleague, Professor Charles Clark, lent valuable technical assistance, as did Bill Pfeifer and Billie Adeimy. Bill Loftus and Catharine Neylans were always ready to help with subtle language translations. The editorial suggestions of Katie Chase and Heather Ruland were especially helpful. My visits over several years to French and American archives would not have been possible without the generous financial assistance of St. Andrews Presbyterian College, and before that of Pfeiffer College, and of the Cooperative Program in the Humanities of Duke University and the University of North Carolina at Chapel Hill. Finally, my special thanks to George, Marjorie, and Carrie, patient at the frequent absence of their father, and to my wife Anne Ramsay, who managed our busy travel schedule and helped in many other ways.

Abbreviations

AFHQ	Allied Force Headquarters
DFCAA	*La Délégation française auprès de la commission allemande d'armistice; recueil de documents publié par le gouvernement français*. Paris: Imprimerie Nationale, 1947-1959, 5 volumes.
DGFP	United States, Department of State, *Documents on German Foreign Policy, 1918-1945*, Series D, 13 volumes. Washington, DC: U.S. Government Printing Office, 1949-1964.
DWSTK	German Armistice Commission
EMG/SE	État Major Général/ Section d'Études
FRUS	United States, Department of State, *Foreign Relations of the Untied States, Europe, 1940, 1941, 1942*. Washington, DC: U.S. Government Printing Office, 1957, 1959, 1962.
MGD	Microfilmed German Documents
ONI	Office of Naval Intelligence
OSS	Office of Strategic Services
RG	Record Group
SHM	French Naval Archives, Paris. Château de Vincennes, Service Historique de la Marine
USNA	United States National Archives, Washington, D.C.
VFDM	*Vichy French Diplomatic Messages*

CHAPTER 1

Introduction

The mood of tension hanging over the city of Algiers that wartime Christmas Eve of 1942 had nothing to do with the known presence of Axis agents in the city, or with the military campaign raging in nearby Tunisia. Nor was it connected with the steady march of foreign armies through the city, or with the occasional air raid warning that interrupted daily routines. It wasn't the war that created the tensions; it was instead divided loyalties among Frenchmen and the threat of revolt. The walls of the city bore graffiti summoning men to action. Rumors of conspiracy had reached the authorities. In restaurants near the seat of government, men raised their glasses in toast--to the death of the Admiral.

About midmorning, a lad of twenty met his priest in a deserted street to confess the crime he intended to commit that same day. His confession ended, young Bonnier de la Chapelle rushed off to the Palais d'Ete, presented forged papers, and slipped quietly to a tiny room off the main corridor to await the arrival of Admiral Jean François Darlan, High Commissioner of French North and West Africa. Observing the Admiral leaving the grounds moments later, Bonnier retired to a nearby restaurant, met with his friends, exchanged his weapon for a better one, and returned to the Palace early in the afternoon. He regained entrance to the building the same as before and slipped again to the room near the Admiral's office.

Toward midafternoon, a limousine entered the drive at the south entrance of the Palace. Admiral Darlan, a short, blue-eyed man in his early sixties, stepped from the vehicle and walked briskly into the building. Accompanied by a naval aide, he continued down the corridor toward the office of the High Commissioner. As they paused before the office door, the youthful intruder dashed from the shadows and fired two shots directly into the chest of the older man. Stumbling through the office doorway, Darlan struck his face against the corner of the desk and fell to the floor. Additional shots were fired before the aide and palace guards disarmed the gunman. As the frightened youth was dragged away for interrogation, Darlan was rushed to a nearby hospital where he died in surgery.

WARTIME VIEWS OF DARLAN

That act of violence thrust the name of Darlan into the world's headlines for the last time. Although Darlan was unknown to the American public before the war, his name had appeared regularly in the press after the fall of France in 1940. At the end of 1942, Americans understood that Bonnier's attack had ended the life of an important wartime figure. Americans who kept up with the news knew that Darlan had commanded the French navy, that he had served as Chief of the Government at Vichy under Marshal Philippe Pétain, that he had met personally with Adolf Hitler, and that he had helped the Allies when they occupied North Africa in the autumn of 1942.

Americans of the World War II generation remembered that Darlan appeared in the news as a shady character who hated the British and collaborated with the Germans. During those years the attitude of the press toward Darlan and Vichy did not always coincide with the official position of the American government. Washington maintained friendly relations with defeated France, but that policy was not uniformly popular with the public. Many American newspapers and periodicals lent moral support to the Free French Movement, sometimes picturing Charles de Gaulle, rather than Vichy, as the true spokesman for the French people. Thus, while Washington pursued a friendly but pragmatic policy toward Vichy, the dominant voice of the press viewed the war from an Anglo-Gaullist perspective that saw de Gaulle as hero and Darlan as villain.

To a large extent, then, Darlan was etched into the American mind by the Anglocentric perspective that dominated the press when he first broke into the news. The negative labels that Winston Churchill and Charles de Gaulle assigned to him quickly reappeared in the American press. The August 24, 1942, issue of *Life* magazine, for example, listed Darlan among the leading traitors of France. Nearly all Americans would have read that Darlan was a traitor and a collaborator. Some would have thought of him as a fascist, others as an opportunist or an Anglophobe. Half a century later these labels linger with remarkable persistence wherever Darlan is remembered.

POSTWAR VIEWS OF DARLAN

Darlan's name rarely appeared in the American press after 1942, but postwar historians in France and the United States maintained a lively interest in his wartime career. French historians writing in the tradition of the resistance movement have largely supported the popular Gaullist view of the Admiral. Their work was so successful that historians sympathetic to Darlan struggled against the awesome prestige of de Gaulle, against the natural tendency of Frenchmen to identify themselves with the resistance movement, and against the need of Frenchmen to forget their loyal support of Vichy during the early years of the German occupation.

In the United States, the postwar debate about Darlan unfolded in numerous specialized studies of the early war years. Historians writing in defense of Washington's Vichy policy sometimes argued that Pétain and Darlan had all along played a double-game with the Axis, pretending to collaborate while privately awaiting the Allies. Other historians leaned toward the popular wartime view of him. A common feature of nearly all of these studies, whatever their posture toward Darlan, was their narrow focus on aspects of World War II. Most of the literature about him addressed only the last three years of his life. With his earlier years largely hidden from view, it is not surprising that assessments of Darlan's wartime career often perpetuated old myths about him and failed to unravel the rich complexity of his mind and personality.

In recent years numerous new Darlan materials have emerged from French and other archives, and from private collections. These materials add importantly to our understanding of Darlan's role both before and during the war. It is now possible to view Darlan in fresh perspective and to assess his career with better balance and objectivity. What emerges from these materials is the picture of a French statesman considerably more complex and interesting than that presented to the American public during World War II.

CHAPTER 2

The Future Admiral

Jean-Louis-Xavier-François Darlan was born on August 7, 1881, in the village of Nérac, in Lot-et-Garonne, eighty miles up the Garonne River from Bordeaux. His forefathers had been mariners at Podensac, near Bordeaux, where they manned small river craft. The Darlans had always been identified with ships, so much so that it was said in Nérac that a Darlan had commanded Noah's Ark.

HERITAGE

Admiral Darlan would later claim that his great-grandfather, Antoine Darlan, had served at Trafalgar on the *Redoubtable*, which fired the shot that took the life of Lord Nelson. There is no good evidence for the popular myth that the Trafalgar incident nourished in Darlan a lifelong hatred of the English. But there is no reason to doubt that Darlan's grandfather, Sabin Darlan, served in the French navy and later prospered at Podensac as the owner of seagoing sailing vessels.[1] It was Sabin who provided the Darlan family with the solid middle-class status that was as important for the career of the future Admiral as was his seagoing heritage.

The next generation of Darlans entered new professions and made new connections. The future Admiral's father, Jean-Baptiste Darlan, and his uncle, Xavier, married the Espagnac sisters, daughters of a physician in Nérac, and settled the family there. Neither of the brothers was a mariner. Xavier became a physician, and Jean-Baptiste a lawyer. The brothers prospered. Jean-Baptiste became Mayor of Nérac and later a member of the National Assembly. An able man, he served in 1896 as Minister of Justice in the cabinet of Jules Méline.[2]

The father established in the family a political perspective that influenced the son. Jean-Baptiste Darlan was a man of the political left-center, an active Free-mason, a leader in the Radical Socialist party, a stout defender of the Third Republic, and a secularist opposed to the political ambitions of the Roman Catholic Church.[3] Although the future Admiral did not always adhere strictly to the views of his father, he took seriously the family political tradition. His politics would be more progressive than that of most French naval officers.

Jean-Baptiste Darlan's political connections were helpful to the career of the future Admiral. The most important of these was the family relationship with Georges Leygues, a fellow deputy from Lot-et-Garonne who served for many years as Minister of Marine. Leygues took the lead role in rebuilding the French navy after World War I, nursing the passage of numerous navy bills to build the fleet that Admiral Darlan would later command. After the death of the elder Darlan in 1912, the Leygues and Darlan families remained close. The future Admiral therefore enjoyed a friendly influence at the top of the French navy.[4]

Darlan's childhood was, however, not a happy one. His mother died during his third year. Afterward, his busy father had little time for him. François and his sister, Hélène, three years older, were placed under the care of a governess and an aunt. Small and sickly, François developed at an early age the personality and habits of mind that persisted into adulthood. The most noticeable--a chronic timidity and an innate cleverness--were permanent features of his personality. As a child and as an adult he tended to avoid personal confrontation. He spoke little but wrote voluminously. Despite his timidity, he developed in childhood a keen sense of humor. But in conversation, he often seemed inattentive.[5]

The early education of the future Admiral was similar to that of many French boys from affluent families. His father enrolled him in the lycée de Talence at Bordeaux, where he received instruction in basic subjects. But he remained unhappy. Sensitive, lonely, and too small to defend himself, François did not mix well with his classmates. He did, however, form his first enduring friendship, that of Henri Moysset, later his trusted confidant at Vichy.[6]

As François grew older, his family life improved. At age thirteen, he moved to Paris where he was enrolled in the lycée Henri IV. There he was closer to his father, and to the Leygues family. The special relationship that developed between Georges Leygues and young François later gave rise to the myth that the future Admiral was the godson of the Minister. Darlan was not Leygues' godson, but the two families were so close that the parents often spoke of a possible marriage between François and one of the Leygues daughters.[7]

But it did not happen. On December 6, 1910, at age twenty-nine, he took as his wife Berthe Morgan, daughter of the honorary English consul at Saint-Malo and a descendant of the famed English Admiral, Sir George Rodney. Berthe Morgan Darlan was a woman of good sense and attractive personality. The couple settled into a modest but comfortable home at Saint-Malo where they occasionally entertained small groups of friends. Berthe Darlan was an asset to her husband, popular with his friends, and always loyal to him.[8]

DARLAN'S NAVAL EDUCATION

Darlan's preparation for a naval career began in 1895 when he entered the lycée Saint Louis in Paris. There he developed a second enduring friendship, that of Jean-Pierre Esteva, who rose through the ranks alongside Darlan. In 1898 young Darlan was admitted to the École navale at Brest upon his second attempt, fortunate to be admitted with his ranking only seventy-seventh in a class of one hundred that had been enlarged because of tensions related to the Fashoda Crisis. Among the future Admirals enrolled there, in addition to Esteva, were Midshipmen Marcel Gensoul, Jacques Moreau, Jean Odend'hal, and Jean Fernet, all of whom would later serve under Darlan. Another, Emile Muselier, would command the Free French navy of Charles de Gaulle.[9]

Darlan's years at the École navale were marked by steady academic and personal growth. His scored his best marks in technical subjects--astronomy and navigation, 17.2; marine light infantry, 17.13; naval artillery, 16.58; torpedoes, 16.82; and naval maneuvers, 17.11. His lowest marks were in English, 12.27 and naval planning, 12.29. At the end of his first semester Darlan ranked sixty-fifth out of ninety-nine students. He improved significantly over the next two years, graduating twenty-seventh in a class of ninety-four. His service record describes him as an "excellent student, disciplined, and full of good will."[10] There now followed the traditional overseas cruise to the Caribbean and the Mediterranean. Returning to France in 1902, and scoring nineteenth in his class on his final examinations, he entered the navy as a Midshipman First Class.

DARLAN'S EARLY CAREER IN PERSPECTIVE

The early career of Darlan coincided with dramatic changes in naval and international affairs. A turn of the century diplomatic revolution ended France's isolation and changed importantly the role of the French navy. The Entente Cordiale of 1904, negotiated during the second year of Darlan's professional career, turned the traditional English enemy into an ally. The Entente also served French interests in the Far East, where Britain's other ally, Japan, could now be expected to respect French rights to Indochina. With British diplomacy and naval power underwriting French imperial security, the French navy was liberated for larger service in the Mediterranean. Darlan's early career therefore coincided with the years when the navy enjoyed the benefits of an English alliance.

Darlan's early career also unfolded in the wake of important changes in naval doctrine. During the 1880s, a new generation of French naval strategists, known as the Jeune École (Young School), breathed new life into the concept of *guerre de course*, or commerce raiding. Impressed with new developments in naval technology--mines, torpedoes, submarines, fast destroyers--the Jeune École argued that heavy battleships and naval blockades had become obsolete. These doctrines matched the security needs of late nineteenth century France, a military power with too few resources to compete in the construction of battleships.

At the École navale, young Darlan also learned of more recent concepts of naval warfare developed by Captain A.T. Mahan, an American naval historian. His books nourished the turn of the century's obsession with navalism and imperialism. He wrote that great nations built huge battle fleets to protect their colonies and their channels of overseas trade. These doctrines were popular at the turn of the century when young Darlan received his naval education. He therefore entered into his naval career with a focus on France's empire and with an abiding faith in the decisive influence of sea power on the outcome of war.

Darlan's early career also coincided with a revolution in naval technology. Submarines, torpedoes, and underwater mines were brought to higher levels of perfection, and numerous small, fast warships were added to the fleets of the great naval powers. Light and heavy cruisers were introduced, but the most startling development occurred in the construction of heavier ships. During Darlan's fourth year as a navy officer, Britain launched the powerful new *Dreadnought,* whose 12-inch guns mounted in revolving turrets rendered all other ships obsolete. So Darlan began his career at the dawn of the era of the modern gunship. He would build his professional reputation as a master of that technology.

Another important change was the decline of the French navy. As Darlan advanced through the lower officer ranks, France had no choice but to commit the greater share of her industrial resources to the military defense of the Rhineland frontier, at the expense of the navy. By 1914 France had slipped to fifth place among the naval powers. But France ranked second in terms of the size of her empire. Her colonies, moreover, were scattered around the globe, so that France's imperial defense commitments far exceeded her naval capabilities. France therefore relied upon strong naval allies. During World War I, her colonies remained secure, for France had aligned herself with all of the great naval powers except Germany. But should the wartime alignment of world naval power eventually break down, the new balance would impose prohibitive burdens on the French navy. As young Darlan rose through the ranks, he no doubt gave little thought to that problem. He surely did not know that he would eventually inherit it.

LEARNING TO BE A MARINER

Midshipman Darlan reported to Toulon in October 1902 for his first assignment, a tour of duty in the Far East arranged for him by Georges Leygues.[11] He commanded a gun turret on the cruiser *Montcalm*. His superiors praised him: "Intelligent, enthusiastic, steady. Already in a position of command. Will make a good officer."[12] Returning to France, Ship Ensign Darlan reported in February 1905 to naval artillery school at Toulon, where he graduated first in his class before accepting an assignment as an instructor at the school.[13] His service there was timely, coinciding with the introduction of large caliber guns on the heavy ships then under construction. The stage was set for his becoming an expert in an area vital to naval operations and ship construction.

When Darlan left naval artillery school in the spring of 1906, he took a short leave and departed France on May 30 for Indochina. In Saigon, he joined the Far Eastern Squadron, consisting of three cruisers and four small destroyers. French naval strength in the Far East had been reduced substantially, reflecting a buildup in home waters during the Moroccan Crisis of 1905.[14] Darlan served as second and then interim gunnery officer on the *D'Entrecasteaux* before returning to France in July 1908. His superior wrote that he "fulfilled his duties with great competence and improved the instructional program."[15]

Having served two tours of duty in the Far East, Darlan welcomed his new assignment as instructor at the pilots school based at Saint-Servan, near Saint-

Malo. During these two years he made important contacts. First, he made the acquaintance of a young lawyer, Alphonse Gasnier-Duparc, who later as Minister of Marine would appoint him Chief-of-Staff of the navy. And it was Gasnier-Duparc who brought him into contact with Berthe Morgan, whom he married in 1910, as we have seen.[16]

Early in 1911, Darlan reported for duty as second gunnery officer aboard the battleship *Waldeck-Rousseau*. Afterward, he served on the *Jeanne d'Arc*, which took him on cruises to the Atlantic and Indian Oceans, and the Baltic Sea to Russia. There were brief leaves to Saint-Malo between voyages. When he returned to Brest in late July 1914, on the eve of World War I, Lieutenant Darlan had become a seasoned mariner, and an expectant father.[17]

A MARINER ON THE WESTERN FRONT

Darlan had expected to apply his skills at sea. But with the Royal Navy guarding the North Sea, French naval guns were released for urgent service on the Western Front. Darlan was assigned to the Toul-Nancy sector near the Vosges Mountains, to begin his wartime service as commander of big naval guns adapted for military use.[18] In December, while he commanded his battery near Toul, Berthe Darlan gave birth to a son, whom they named Alain.

Darlan adjusted quickly to the unfamiliar responsibilities of a field command. Mastering the techniques of unit command and gun emplacement, he attracted the attention of his superior officer, who in early 1915 reported him to be an "officer of great courage, with a quick mind...knows very well how to lead his men and has great influence over them. Will command very well. Deserves to receive immediately the Chevalier Cross of the Legion of Honor."[19] Darlan's combat assignment was interrupted briefly in early 1916 when he supervised the delivery of naval artillery to French units operating in Greece. Returning to France in April, he commanded batteries in the Reims-Soisson sector and at Verdun, where he saw heavy fighting. "I consider him one of the best officers in the unit," wrote his commanding officer.[20]

In 1917 Darlan's guns pounded German lines south of the Aisne River and in the Ypres-Passchendale sector in support of a British offensive. The offensive failed, but Darlan's artillery shattered a German counterattack on the British flank. His performance again earned him praise: "Officer of the very best type having all the technical and command skills to merit an exceptional promotion."[21] As the Passchendale campaign ground toward a close in November, Darlan was surprised to receive an urgent telegram summoning him to Paris.

It was from Georges Leygues, now Minister of Marine in the government of Georges Clemenceau. Leygues received the young officer late in the day in his home at 2 rue de Solferino. Entering the apartment, Darlan noticed the familiar furnishings. At first intimidated by the older man, he soon relaxed and spoke freely. Leygues took notes. The Minister was impressed with Darlan's maturity. They talked about armaments, naval affairs, strategic problems, relations with France's allies, and ways to protect American ships bringing reinforcements across the Atlantic. Late in the evening Leygues offered Darlan a safe staff position at the Ministry, where quick promotions were common. But Darlan surprised Leygues. "I am not able [to accept it]," he answered. "If I go with you, I would be thought of as one who shirks his duty."[22] He recommended his friend Esteva, who had been wounded at the front.

So Darlan returned to the war. In 1918 his batteries north of the Oise River caught the full momentum of the final German offensive. In heavy fighting he barely avoided capture. On June 9 his batteries were so badly damaged that his unit was withdrawn from the line.[23] In July he was promoted to Corvette Captain with a glowing citation:

Officer of the highest type, having outstanding leadership abilities: energy, composure, and powers of decision. Commanding a group of naval artillery in regions particularly active, he repeatedly distinguished himself and fired his batteries with great effectiveness from March 21 until June 10.[24]

During the autumn, Darlan's naval guns lent support to American units fighting in the Argonne Forest until German resistance finally collapsed.[25] Darlan could look back with satisfaction at a good record that included four decorations. He emerged from the war with a reputation in the navy as a strong unit leader, a steady performer in combat, and an officer of superior judgment. At age thirty-six, he was in line for greater responsibility.

AT THE DAWN OF CREATION

Following an assignment in the Rhineland, Frigate Captain Darlan departed in early 1921 for his third tour of duty in the Far East. Returning to France in July 1922 he pulled strings with Georges Leygues to receive command of the *Chamois*, a pilots school he had attended before the war.[26] Darlan's career sped forward. In 1925 he graduated from the Center for Advanced Naval Studies in Paris at the top of the class. By late summer he was back at sea on a battleship in the Mediterranean. Promoted to the rank of full Captain, he reported in early 1926 for duty as Chief Adjutant to the Military Cabinet of the Minister of Marine at the Rue Royale.[27] He had finally joined Georges Leygues.

Darlan's service at the Rue Royale was the first of two key assignments for an officer aspiring to the flag rank. The other was a battleship command. Notwithstanding the friendly support of Leygues, Darlan's promotion to the rank of Rear Admiral would be at risk should he perform poorly in either of these assignments. His duty at the Rue Royale coincided with the brisk activity attendant to the rebuilding of the navy. Parliamentary action early in the decade set the stage for a vast construction program that gained momentum during Leygues' long and nearly continuous service as Minister of Marine. When Darlan reported to the Rue Royale, a new French navy was at the dawn of creation. He would to be a part of the renewal of French naval power from nearly the beginning.

Now Darlan was close to the center of naval power. He was involved with numerous administrative reforms and with the beginning of the new construction program, consisting from 1925 to 1927 of an aircraft carrier, three cruisers, and numerous destroyers and smaller craft, including twenty-two submarines.[28] Intelligent and efficient, Darlan impressed his superiors. Rear Admiral Pirot, Director of the Military Cabinet, reported him to be "an absolutely complete type of officer, as good in council as in action...one of the leaders of the navy of tomorrow."[29] Leaving his post as Chief of the Military Cabinet on August 30, 1927, he was ready for a battleship command.

THE RISE TO THE FLAG RANK

Darlan was assigned to the battleship *Jeanne d'Arc*--a command known as a springboard to the flag rank. Two long cruises kept him mainly at sea between the fall of 1927 and the summer of 1929. The first cruise carried him through the Panama Canal to Peru. He returned to the Antilles, across the Atlantic to Dakar, then to the Mediterranean, and finally to Le Havre in July 1928. The second began in October when he departed Brest on the cruiser *Edgar Quinet* with nearly a hundred young midshipmen aboard for the traditional instructional voyage. He steamed across the Atlantic to Argentina, and through the Panama Canal to San Francisco--his only visit to the United States. Back to the Caribbean in early 1929, he crossed over to Dakar and finally to Brest in July.[30]

His letters from these voyages to Admiral Jules Docteur, whom he had met at the Rue Royale, and to Georges Leygues, reveal much of Darlan's mind and personality. The letters to Docteur, whom he regarded as a peer, are informal and full of humor. One of them poked fun at the huge size of the new American aircraft carrier *Saratoga*, which he had seen in the Panama Canal: "The signalmen move about on the flight deck on motorcycles. A pickup truck is provided to move materials from one end of the ship to the other. I suppose there is a subway inside."[31] In contrast, the letters to Georges Leygues are more formal, and they sometimes flatter the Minister.[32]

The letters reveal a first-class mind, one full of curiosity and sensitivity to detail. They contain absorbing discussions of whatever he observed along the way--architecture, native life, tropical weather and vegetation, natural resources, local history, comparative politics, and city planning.[33] More significantly, Darlan emerges from these letters as a remarkably competent naval technician. They reveal his mastery of naval techniques--ship design, mechanical engineering, communications, navigation, and the training of engineers. In a 1928 letter, written in response to Docteur's inquiry about construction needs, Darlan expressed his ideas about the renewal of French naval power. France could renovate its six old battleships, he thought, and still have a fleet superior to those of Germany and Italy. Thinking that France needed light ships, he opposed construction of huge battleships, which he thought too expensive and too demanding of the tactical support of France's lighter ships.[34]

Promoted to the rank of Rear Admiral on November 18, 1929,[35] Darlan entered the flag rank at age forty-nine as an officer of strong technical competence. His early promotion to that rank perhaps benefited from the friendly influence of Leygues, but he would have arrived there in any event. He had an outstanding combat record. In all of his assignments his performance had been exemplary. He had demonstrated exceptional abilities at administration and command. He had mastered the complex techniques of more than one branch of naval service.

Finally, he had taken care at every step to cultivate the good will of everyone around him--his superiors, his peers, and those who served under him.

NOTES

1. Alain Darlan, *L'Amiral Darlan parle* (Paris: Amiot-Dumont, 1952), 12-13, 17. Hervé Coutau-Bégarie and Claude Huan, *Darlan* (Paris: Fayard, 1989), 26-27.

2. Albert Jean Voituriez, *L'Affaire Darlan; L'instruction judiciare* (Paris: Lattès, 1980), 23.

3. Coutau-Bégarie and Huan, *Darlan,* 28-29. Voituriez, *L'Affaire Darlan*, 22.

4. For more on Georges Leygues, see Ronald Chalmers Hood III, *Royal Republicans: the French Naval Dynasties between the World Wars* (Baton Rouge: Louisiana State University Press, 1985), 129-131, 141; and Jacques Raphaël-Leygues, *Georges Leygues, Le "Pere" de la Marine* (Paris: Éditions France-Empire, 1983).

5. Interview with Mme. Francine Hezez, niece of Admiral Darlan, May 6, 1987; Paris. Coutau-Bégarie and Huan, *Darlan*, 17, 30, 155-159.

6. Coutau-Bégarie and Huan, *Darlan*, 31. Darlan, *L'Amiral Darlan parle*, 16-17. Jacques Raphaël-Leygues and François Flohic, *Darlan* (Paris: Plon, 1986), 16.

7. Coutau-Bégarie and Huan, *Darlan*, 31.

8. Darlan, *L'Amiral Darlan parle*, 18. Coutau-Bégarie and Huan, *Darlan*, 41-42. Raphaël-Leygues and Flohic, *Darlan*, 19-20; interview with Mme. Francine Hezez.

9. Coutau-Bégarie and Huan, *Darlan*, 31-32.

10. SHM, Dossier personnel de l'Amiral de la flotte Darlan; Ecole Navale, "Bulletin Individuel de Notes d'Élève"; The author is indebted to Captain Claude Huan for a copy of Darlan's official service record. (hereinafter cited as SHM, Dossier personnel).

11. Coutau-Bégarie and Huan, *Darlan*, 35.

12. Ibid, 33-37; SHM, Dossier personnel.

13. SHM, Dossier personnel, service record. See also Coutau-Bégarie and Huan, *Darlan*, 38; Raphaël-Leygues and Flohic, *Darlan*, 17; Voituriez, *L'Affaire Darlan*, 23.

14. See Coutau-Bégarie and Huan, *Darlan*, 39.

15. SHM, Dossier personnel, service record.

16. Coutau-Bégarie and Huan, *Darlan*, 41.

17. SHM, Dossier personnel, service record; Coutau-Bégarie and Huan, *Darlan*, 45; Raphaël-Leygues and Flohic, *Darlan*, 20; Darlan, *L'Amiral Darlan parle*, 28-29.

18. SHM, Dossier personnel, service record.

19. Ibid.

20. Coutau-Bégarie and Huan, *Darlan*, 47-48; SHM, Dossier personnel, service record.

21. SHM, Dossier personnel, service record; Coutau-Bégarie and Huan, *Darlan*, 48-49; Raphaël-Leygues and Flohic, *Darlan*, 21; *Darlan, L'Amiral Darlan parle*, 29.

22. Raphaël-Leygues and Flohic, *Darlan*, 22.

23. Coutau-Bégarie and Huan, *Darlan*, 50.

24. SHM, Dossier personnel, service record.

25. Darlan, *L'Amiral Darlan parle*, 29; Raphaël-Leygues and Flohic, *Darlan*, 21; Coutau-Bégarie and Huan, *Darlan*, 51.

26. SHM, Dossier personnel, service record; Raphaël-Leygues and Flohic, *Darlan*, 24-25; Coutau-Bégarie and Huan, *Darlan*, 54-55.

27. SHM, Dossier personnel, service record.

28. Coutau-Bégarie and Huan, *Darlan*, 59-61.

29. SHM, Dossier personnel, service record.

30. For details of these cruises, see Coutau-Bégarie and Huan, *Darlan*, 61-68.

31. Amiral Jules Docteur, *La Grande énigme de la guerre: Darlan, Amiral de la flotte* (Paris: Éditions de la Couronne, 1949), 17 (hereinafter cited as Docteur, *Darlan*).

32. See Raphaël-Leygues and Flohic, *Darlan*, 29-38.

33. See Ibid., and Docteur, *Darlan*, 13-23.

34. Docteur, *Darlan*, 18.

35. SHM, Dossier personnel, service record.

CHAPTER 3

Close to the Center of Power

Except for two sea commands, Darlan was attached to the Ministry of Marine during the five years after November 1929. He served as Chief of the Military Cabinet of the Ministry on three different occasions.[1] Close to the center of power, he influenced events and broadened his understanding of the place of the French navy in world naval affairs.

"A VAST FABRIC OF STUPIDITIES"

Rear Admiral Darlan reported to London in January 1930 as technical adviser to the French delegation at the London Naval Conference. He approached the conference with apprehension, as did his senior colleagues, whose memories stretched back to the Washington Naval Conference of 1921-1922. Frenchmen remembered that conference with little affection. The Five Power Treaty had imposed a ratio of 5-5-3-1.67-1.67 for capital ships and had assigned France and Italy the lower figure, with a 175,000-ton limit. Darlan and his colleagues resented Italy's parity status with France, who had two coasts to defend and a much larger colonial empire. Since the limits applied mainly to battleships, vessels over 10,000 tons, France and Italy became locked in a race to build cruisers and other light ships.

By 1930 France had become isolated from her wartime allies, no longer enjoying their naval support, so that Foreign Minister Aristide Briand aimed at forging a political accord with Britain. But Darlan and the French naval delegation opposed trading tonnage for a political agreement that might narrow the French margin of 280,000 tons over Italy. Committed to a ten-year plan to modernize the fleet, Darlan and his delegation worried that the conference would aim at extending downward the Washington ratios to impose limits on the construction of light ships. If so, the French delegation would appeal to the principle of national defense needs to justify the margin over Italy.

Darlan kept in his files the key document containing evidence of France's greater need for defensive armaments, defined as light ships. Comparative national needs were projected in terms of eight factors, with Italy assigned a base figure of one in each case. Three of the factors were area of territory to defend, the length of coastlines, and the dispersion of territories around the globe:

	Territory	Coastlines	Dispersion
British Empire	15.8	9.5	11.2
United States	4	4.6	3.2
Japan	0.3	3	1
Italy	1	1	1
France	4.7	2.3	6.8

These figures, and those of the other categories, suggest that French defensive needs ranked next to those of Britain and were four to five times greater than those of Italy.[2] Darlan used the figures to prove that France needed a fleet larger than Italy's. But the figures also show that the French navy was badly overextended, that France's Far Eastern colonies were nearly defenseless, and that a naval buildup against Italy would solve only one part of a larger problem. In the event of another world conflict, France could not protect her vital channels of trade without the assistance of a strong naval ally.

The conference did indeed turn on the question of extending the Washington ratios downward. Darlan advised the delegation to avoid discussion of tonnage figures prior to an agreement about national security needs. He recommended that the delegation should declare any results of the conference to be tentative, subject to future negotiations at Geneva.[3] He also proposed that any agreement should extend for ten years, to match France's long-term construction plans aimed at maintaining a margin of 280,000 tons over Italy, and to give France more time to replace older ships. Darlan had touched the point upon which Franco-Italian disarmament negotiations finally would turn: that of replacing obsolete ships, which France possessed in larger numbers than did Italy.[4]

Darlan insisted that French defense needs should determine the size and composition of the fleet, with the minimum level to be set by the French themselves at no less than 800,000 tons. He would set no tonnage ceilings for any of the several categories of ships, as France needed to shift tonnage from one category to another in response to changing defense needs. A naval agreement acceptable to France would be one that set a total tonnage figure for each nation, with freedom to shift tonnage from one category to another, or to create new categories.[5] Darlan cautioned the delegation to avoid an overemphasis on battleships, which he thought to be vulnerable to mines, torpedoes, and aerial bombs. He predicted that the next generation of battleships would be smaller and faster, like a new ship then under construction in Germany.[6] He had in mind the 12,000-ton *Deutschland*, the first of three German battle cruisers soon to change the strategic picture for France.

Darlan's letters to his wife reflect his sour attitude toward the conference. On January 21 he described the opening session as a stuffy outpouring of platitudes in the great hall of the House of Lords, whose murals offended him: "On one of the walls, the Battle of Trafalgar; on the other, Waterloo: charming!"[7] His letters of early April reveal his worry about an Anglo-French alliance at the expense of French naval tonnage. Considering an alliance to be worthless, he wrote on April 4 his delight at London's turning down Briand's proposal for a political accord. On the 11th he expressed his satisfaction at France's emerging with no damage from this "sinister comedy."[8]

Darlan described the London Treaty as "a vast fabric of stupidities."[9] When it was finally signed in April, the French and Italian delegations refused to accept the key section that imposed ratios for light ships. Bilateral negotiations between France and Italy were scheduled for a later time at Geneva, where Darlan would play a larger role. His work at the London conference had introduced him to naval policy issues, but his mind continued to focus on the narrow problem of maintaining the margin over Italy. He still discounted the need of an alliance with Britain to address the larger problem of French naval weakness.

THE THREAT OF THE *PANZERSCHIFFE*

Back in Paris, Darlan managed unfinished disarmament business for the Ministry before serving briefly as Naval Commander in Algeria.[10] His ideas about the shape of the French navy shifted importantly in 1930, in response to the threat of the new German battle cruisers, the first of which was near completion. Formidable ships by 1930 standards, these pocket battleships, or *panzerschiffe*, cruised at twenty-six knots to outrun battleships. They carried eleven-inch guns to destroy any cruiser capable of catching them. Three ships--*Deutschland*, *Scheer*, and *Graf Spee*--would be launched between 1931 and 1934. Designed to prowl the high seas and prey upon shipping, they threatened France's overseas communications.

A letter to Docteur during the autumn reveals that both Darlan and the Ministry were now thinking in terms of large French battle cruisers to match the German threat. They had in mind ships of thirty knots at 25,000 tons, mounting thirteen-inch guns.[11] The concept would find life as the two *Dunkerque* class battle cruisers, built in the mid-1930's for the purpose of outperforming the *panzerschiffe*.

Darlan realized that the *panzerschiffe* would increase importantly France's defense needs. He also worried that Germany and Italy might forge an alliance against France, to impose a two-front war on the navy. Italy would attack in the Mediterranean, and Germany would prey upon France's distant trade routes. Thinking that Britain would lend no help, he recommended to the Ministry that the French fleet "must be superior in strength and number in each category of ships of the fleets of Italy and Germany combined."[12] This meant that France would have to maintain her margin of light ships over Italy and build heavy ships to match the *panzerschiffe*.

AN ASSIGNMENT IN GENEVA

Darlan therefore had in mind the German threat when France and Italy entered into a new round of naval disarmament negotiations in late 1930 at Geneva. Heading the naval team, he worked with the chief of the delegation, René Massigli, French delegate to the League of Nations.[13] Massigli was prepared to propose limited tonnage reductions in exchange for an Anglo-French alliance providing for British defense of Atlantic waters and French defense of the Mediterranean.

Massigli's position caused Darlan to think about the value of an Anglo-French alliance, and what France would concede in exchange for it. Massigli envisioned an Anglo-French accord that would require cutbacks in both the French and Italian construction, so that the French tonnage margin over Italy would be preserved.[14] Darlan held that the maximum level of 760,000 tons, representing France's absolute needs, must be maintained in theory should London back away from the alliance. Otherwise, France would be prepared to reduce its maximum level as of December 31, 1936, by 15.6percent, to its current 640,000 tons. In-place construction would continue, and France would replace her obsolete ships.[15]

Darlan moved cautiously toward pursuing an alliance with the English. He realized that the *panzerschiff* and any sister ships threatened France but not Italy. So French defense needs increased while those of Italy remained unchanged. The obvious value of an alliance was that Britain would underwrite the threat of the German battle cruisers and thereby release scarce French funds for the building of light ships to maintain the margin over Italy. But Darlan estimated that London would demand in exchange a reduction of 75,000 tons, which he thought excessive. He wrote that "a superiority of 240,000 tons over the Italian fleet within the limits of total current tonnage is clearly preferable to a foreign assistance always problematical and which certainly would not be given gratis."[16] It turned out that London had no interest in an alliance, so Darlan had no choice but to negotiate to maintain French superiority over Italy in light ships and to match the German threat with heavy ships.

The negotiations at Geneva bore upon the question of the relative size of the French and Italian fleets, and of modernizing the French fleet. Darlan proposed that until the end of 1936 France and Italy continue only with the replacements of overage ships, ton by ton rather than type by type, so that France might shift some tonnage to heavy ships. This plan would protect France's margin over Italy by 240,000 tons, since France had numerous overage ships and Italy very few.[17]

The Italians rejected the proposal, but negotiations continued into 1931. Sir Robert Craigie, the English middleman who shuttled between Rome and Paris after the Geneva talks had recessed, countered with a proposal that would reduce the French submarine fleet to a level below 80,000 tons and would require France to keep in service her obsolete battleships. Darlan rejected it.[18] But he struck an agreement with Craigie for France and Italy to proceed with the completion of ships under construction in clearly defined categories, with 46,666 tons of capital ships for each nation. This proposal would give France a margin over Italy of 242,798 tons for ships in service, and 157,441 in modern ships at the end of 1936. It would lock Italy into a level of capital ships to prevent her burdening French efforts to match the German threat.[19]

Darlan insisted with Craigie that France reserved the right to replace some overage tonnage after 1936, and to begin part of that construction during 1936. He suspected that Craigie, who delivered the proposal to Rome, did not make clear the French position on that key point.[20] When the negotiations were resumed in London on the basis of the Anglo-French agreement, the Italians obviously had not accepted it. After Craigie and the Italians had rejected other compromise proposals regarding replacements, Darlan could see that London and Rome aimed at burdening the French navy with obsolete ships.[21]

The negotiations finally broke down on the question of replacements. In an interview with British First Lord Alexander on March 28, Darlan noted London's refusal to undertake any commitment to aid France in the event of her being attacked by a continental power. France would therefore have to take measures to protect herself. When Alexander answered sharply that Britain could undertake no continental commitments in advance of a European conflict, Darlan could see that an Anglo-French alliance was out of the question. He offered to continue the discussions on the basis of the British demands for reductions if London would support the French proposal to begin replacement of a portion of her overage tonnage in 1936. But Craigie objected. Darlan then suspended the negotiations, refusing a final interview with the First Lord.[22]

Darlan emerged from the negotiations with the reputation as a hard-liner who had refused to compromise when Paris wanted an agreement. But his Ministry realized that Craigie was to blame for the failure of the negotiations. Darlan's minimum figure of 642,000 tons exceeded the combined German and Italian tonnage by only 96,000 tons. These figures represented France's minimum needs to defend two oceans in the event of a war with both powers, with a 96,000-ton margin to defend France's empire and trade routes. But of that margin, 85,000 tons were obsolete. Had Darlan agreed to keep these obsolete ships in service, France's vital trade routes would have been easy prey for the *panzerschiffe*.[23]

Darlan had bargained faithfully within the limits imposed by the Superior Council of the Navy. That body had set the fleet's minimum need at 642,000 tons, on condition that a new distribution of tonnage within the categories be attained, that a superiority of 240,000 tons over Italy be maintained, and that the fleet be composed entirely of modern ships. Darlan had conceded tonnage reductions to nearly the minimum level, including reduction of the French submarine fleet from the projected 125,000 tons to 82,000, and a decrease of modern heavy cruisers from ten to seven by the end of 1936. He had offered future negotiations on the question of replacing only a portion of France's overage ships.[24] Had Darlan made further tonnage concessions, or had he yielded on replacements, he would have exceeded his instructions. And France would have been unable to match the eight modern capital ships that Germany could construct within the restrictions of the Versailles Treaty.

In a letter to Massigli, Darlan insisted that he had worked for an agreement midway between the French and Anglo-Italian positions. He thought that Craigie, biased in favor of Italy, had aimed at gaining for Britain the largest possible margin of superiority over the combined fleets of France, Italy, and Germany, at the expense of France. Darlan's final proposal would have left the Italian fleet at the end of 1939 entirely modern and 46,250 tons larger than her fleet of 1931. The French fleet of 1939, at 621,608 tons of modern ships, would have been smaller than France's total tonnage of 1931.[25] Darlan's position was not unreasonable. But any agreement acceptable to Craigie would have left France's vital overseas communications poorly defended in a two-front war against Germany and Italy.

Darlan had guarded French naval interests, but he did not make himself popular with his English counterparts, or with his own Foreign Office. When disarmament negotiations resumed in Geneva in early 1932, Darlan would not be in charge of them. He had already gone to sea.

IN COMMAND OF FAST SHIPS

In late 1931 Darlan took command of a division of fast ships operating out of Toulon. The division included four new 10,000 ton cruisers, plus light cruisers and assorted lesser craft. With his friend Louis de la Monneraye on his staff aboard the *Foch*, Darlan was pleased with his new assignment, one well suited for an officer interested in the technical capabilities of France's new generation of fast ships. After the squadron had departed Toulon in early 1932 for war games in the Mediterranean, Darlan wrote Docteur that the fresh sea air had revived him.[26]

Darlan commanded the *Foch*, whose role was to prowl the western Mediterranean with the remainder of his ships posing as an Italian fleet in pursuit. Seven cruisers, a dozen submarines, and thirty seaplanes were assigned to intercept her and prevent her reaching Bizerte. Cruising at twenty-seven knots, he was sighted only twice, by a submarine and a seaplane. He easily slipped away to break unobserved through the blockade around Bizerte three times by night at top speed. He pushed the *Foch* to its technical limits, cruising two thousand miles at speeds up to twenty-eight knots.[27]

WORKING BEHIND THE SCENES

Darlan's recall to Paris came in the wake of the elections of May 1932, which brought to power a left-leaning coalition that included the Radical Socialist party. Returning to a familiar post, Darlan would serve for twenty-two months as Director of the Cabinet of the Ministry under Leygues, who died in office on September 2, 1933, and then under Albert Sarraut and François Pietri.[28] The swing to the left in French politics was timely for Darlan's career. His long-time family tie with the Radical Socialist party was an obvious benefit. The final steps in his rise to the top command of the navy would take place under governments of the left-center.

At Geneva, where the World Disarmament Conference had finally opened in February 1932, the French and German delegations clashed sharply on questions of disarmament and security. Despite French misgivings, the British and American delegations recognized the principle of equal rights for Germany.

Back in Paris in July 1932, Darlan worked behind the scenes to prepare the French proposal for naval disarmament discussions scheduled for the 1933 session. The proposal, recognizing the greater defense needs of the larger colonial powers, would maintain the German fleet at 108,000 tons, and the Italian fleet at two-thirds the level of the French fleet. The French delegation would then support tonnage reductions on a scale respecting the existing relative strengths of all the fleets. Called the "constructive plan," the proposal would allow adjustments in response to changing security needs.[29]

Observing that Germany would soon liberate herself from the naval restrictions of the Versailles Treaty, he boldly recommended that France seek collective action to abrogate the Washington and London Naval Treaties. The ability of a sixth power to act independently, he observed, rendered the five-power treaties obsolete. He also suggested that France express support of any proposal to outlaw submarines, on condition that battleships also be outlawed. These proposals and others, amended in detail, were accepted by his Ministry as back-up options.[30]

When the conference resumed its work in 1933, the "constructive plan" was sidetracked by the MacDonald plan, proposed by British Prime Minister Ramsay MacDonald. Its naval terms would narrow the gap between the French and Italian fleets and reduce substantially the French submarine force. Germany would remain under the restrictions of the Versailles Treaty that permitted her to replace her old ships before 1937. Preparing the French response, Darlan objected that the MacDonald plan departed from the conference agreement to maintain the relative strengths of the leading navies. It would perpetuate the London Treaty at the very moment when the naval balance was shifting. The granting of equal rights to Germany in 1932, he argued, rendered the London Treaty obsolete, requiring a new treaty to include Germany.

Darlan's objections reflected his worry that London intended to shift the burden of disarmament to France. He noted that the MacDonald plan required no reduction of the British fleet, that it diminished French naval strength relative to that of the other powers, that it permitted Germany and Italy to gain the advantage in replacing overage ships, and that it undermined French plans to match the panzerschiffe. He charged that London had a double standard for disarmament: one of Franco-German equality on the continent, and another of British superiority around the globe.[31]

Darlan regarded the MacDonald plan as a self-serving instrument of British duplicity, a scheme aimed at protecting Britain from German naval power and stripping France of her defense against German military power. He observed that its naval terms worked to Britain's advantage, with France paying the price for the agreement. He suspected that London intended to permit an enlargement of the German and Italian fleets, at the expense of French tonnage, so that the Royal Navy would emerge superior to the combined might of the three continental navies. He wrote Docteur that acceptance of MacDonald's ideas would lead to aggression and finally to war.[32]

The French delegation finally rejected the MacDonald plan, on grounds that it changed the relative strengths of the world's navies. Hitler's bold move in

October to withdraw Germany from the conference and from the League of Nations ended the negotiations. It also signaled Hitler's intention to rearm independently, which underscored Darlan's point that the five-power treaties were obsolete.

Darlan had clashed sharply with his English opposites, but he was ahead of them in perceiving the new German threat. Even after the rise of Hitler, London clung to the illusion of disarmament. In contrast, Darlan had anticipated the emerging threat in 1930 when London and Paris might have addressed the German problem from a position of strength. Darlan would soon play a new role in mending relations with London. Meanwhile, on December 4, 1932, he was promoted to the rank of Vice-Admiral. At age fifty-one, he was the youngest officer of that rank in the navy.[33]

NOTES

1. SHM, Dossier personnel de l'Amiral de la flotte Darlan, "Récapitulation des services" (hereinafter cited as SHM, Dossier personnel), compliments of Claude Huan.

2. SHM, 1BB2 EMG/SE, Carton 191, "The French Political Position at the Naval Disarmament Conference at London." The other five factors were population, tonnage of merchant fleets, imports and exports, commercial activity in ports, and the fraction of maritime trade to total foreign trade. For an American critique, see USNA, RG 38, ONI, C-10-e, Reg. # 20228-F.

3. SHM, 1 BB2 EMG/SE, Carton 191, "TRAVAUX DE LA CONFÉRENCE," 17 January 1930.

4. SHM, 1 BB2 EMG/SE, Carton 191, "DURÉE DE LA CONVENTION."

5. SHM, 1 BB2 EMG/SE, Carton 191, "POINT DE DÉPART DES DISCUSSIONS," 31 January, 1930.

6. SHM, 1 BB2 EMG/SE, Carton 191, "NOTE SUR LE NAIVRE DE LIGNE."

7. Alain Darlan, *L'Amiral Darlan parle* (Paris: Amiot-Dumont, 1952), 32.

8. Ibid., 34-36.

9. Ibid., 36.

10. SHM, Dossier personnel, service record.

11. Amiral Jules Docteur, *Darlan.* (Paris: Éditions de la Couronne, 1949), 20.

12. SHM, 1BB2 EMG/SE, Carton 208, "Naval Policy," 30 September 1930; Dossiers Amiral Darlan, September 10 1930.

13. In 1943 Massigli escaped occupied France to serve Charles de Gaulle. USNA, RG 226, E97, OSS, Algiers File, Box 239, Folder 2, and Box 5, Folder 77.

14. SHM, 1BB2 EMG/SE, Carton 193, "Négociations Navales de Genève."

15. Ibid.

16. Ibid.

17. SHM, 1BB2 EMG/SE, Carton 196, "HISTORIQUE SUCCINCT DES NÉGOCIATIONS DU 10 NOVEMBRE 1929 AU 20 AVRIL 1931."

18. Ibid.

19. Ibid.

20. Ibid.

21. SHM, 1BB2 EMG/SE, Carton 193, "NÉGOCIATIONS NAVALES, 1 Mars-1 Avril 1931."

22. SHM 1BB2 EMG/SE, Carton 196, "HISTORIQUE SUCCINCT DES NÉGOCIATIONS DU 10 NOVEMBRE 1929 AU 20 AVRIL 1931;" Carton 208, "POLITIQUE NAVALE." Carton 193, document entitled "LETTRE PERSONNELLE ET CONFI-

DENTIELLE ADDRESSÉ À MONSIEUR MASSIGLI PAR L'AMIRAL DARLAN." See also Darlan's letter of March 30 to Leygues in Jacques Raphaël-Leygues and François Flohic, *Darlan* (Paris: Plon, 1986), 49-50.

23. SHM, 1BB2 EMG/SE, Carton 193, "NÉGOCIATIONS NAVALES, AVRIL-MAI 1931."

24. Ibid.

25. SHM, 1BB2 EMG/SE, Carton 193, "LETTRE PERSONNELLE ET CONFIDEN-TIELLE ADRESSÉ À MONSIEUR MASSIGLI PAR L'AMIRAL DARLAN," November 17 1931.

26. Docteur, *Darlan*, 22-23.

27. Docteur, *Darlan*, 24-25; Darlan, *L'Amiral Darlan parle*, 37.

28. See Hervé Coutau-Bégarie and Claude Huan, *Darlan* (Paris, Fayard, 1989), 77-78.

29. Espagnac du Ravay, *Vingt ans de politique navale, 1919-1939* (Grenoble: Arthaud, 1941), 112-113. The author, Louis de la Monneraye, wrote the book in collaboration with Darlan early in World War II. See also Docteur, *Darlan*, 48; and SHM, 1BB2 EMG/SE, Carton 208, "Note sur une Question Posée par le Gouvernement du Reich," 22 January 1934.

30. SHM, 1BB2 EMG/SE, Carton 193, "PROPOSITIONS SUGGÉREES PAR L'AMIRAL DARLAN."

31. Du Ravay, *Vingt ans de politique navale*, 120-124; SHM, 1BB2 EMG/SE, Carton 208, "CONSÉQUENCES LOGIQUES DES DIVERS PRINCIPES POSÉS À GENÈVE," from Dossiers Amiral Darlan.

32. Raphaël-Leygues and Flohic, *Darlan*, 52-53.

33. Darlan, *L'Amiral Darlan parle*, 38; Coutau-Bégarie and Huan, *Darlan*, 77.

CHAPTER 4

Toward a New Balance of Naval Power

Darlan's rise to the top of the French navy coincided with an ominous shift in the world naval balance. The alignment of the great naval powers against Germany had underwritten the defense of the French empire during World War I. But in the 1930s a new alignment emerged as Italy and Japan moved toward Germany.

THE NEED FOR AN ANGLO-FRENCH ALLIANCE

In early 1934 Darlan continued his service at the Ministry of Marine. As he prepared material for the next disarmament conference, he witnessed the great February riots in Paris protesting the breakdown of French security arrangements in Eastern Europe. Darlan viewed the security problem from a mariner's perspective. Documents found in his files--reports that he wrote, edited, or read--betray his focus on global affairs. They reveal his anticipation of a new naval alignment, and his desire for an alliance with Britain.

Darlan realized that the time had come for France to withdraw from the Washington Treaty, which limited cruisers to 10,000 tons and eight-inch guns. It placed France at a technical disadvantage in matching the three German pocket battleships, each mounting eleven-inch guns at just over 10,000 tons. Bound by the treaty, France would have to build three 26,500-ton battleships to outclass them. He would replace the Washington Treaty with a general agreement to set national tonnage limits, leaving each power free to conclude mutual agreements limiting their tonnage to levels below the maximum figure.[1]

The changing world scene worried Darlan.[2] He therefore wanted France to build a navy capable of dealing with unfavorable shifts in the balance of world naval power. He was alarmed that Germany had stretched the naval restrictions of the Versailles Treaty to the limit, building fast battle cruisers capable of prowling the distant seas to threaten French commerce. Germany's large population and advanced economy, he thought, would soon cause the Reich to break out of her frontiers, to seek ports on the North Sea or the Adriatic, and to find overseas colonies to market her industrial goods and relocate her surplus population. He was sure that Germany had withdrawn from the League of Nations because it cramped her aggressive intentions, and he sensed that the Reich was already drawing closer to Japan. He noticed that Rome, though alarmed at German designs upon Austria, took care to avoid any offense to Berlin. "Italy remains--as always--an enigma: she will act according to her interests and with the least risks," he wrote.[3] He worried about a possible Rome-Berlin alliance against France.

He also worried that London would remain aloof and attempt to play the role of arbiter in the event of a German war against France. It distressed him that London's first concern was with her dominions and colonies and with any challenge to her global maritime commerce, at the expense of Europe. Darlan saw connections between Europe's problems and troubles in Asia where Japan, like Germany, needed economic and population outlets. Japanese expansionists would look first, he thought, to China and Siberia, just beyond the narrow waters dominated by the Imperial navy. He saw that Hong Kong and Indochina stood in the way of Japanese expansion, and that Japan, short of fuel to nourish her fleet, would be tempted to seize the rich oil fields of the Netherlands East Indies. "If therefore Japan undertakes an offensive in Asia," he wrote, "military and economic considerations can put her in conflict with England and the United States and perhaps with us."[4]

That observation underscored in Darlan's mind the fundamental problem as he saw it, which was London's attitude toward Europe. He worried that Britain, preoccupied with the Far East, would concede to Germany a free hand in Europe. "Will England be the French ally in the Far East," he asked, "and at the same time remain aloof from a Franco-German conflict? It seems improbable," he wrote in answer to his own question. "But England conducts her policy as if it should be the case."[5] With the thought of a German-Japanese alliance in the back of his mind, Darlan complained bitterly about London's failure to understand the German threat: "the English," he wrote, "are still living in the age of Bonaparte."[6]

Darlan expected that British naval policy, now unclear, would change as the German naval threat mounted. He noted that England "has not yet grasped the German naval danger," and that "her policy is extremely dangerous for us and for her." France, he concluded, cannot define her own naval policy "as long as there is no naval agreement between France and Great Britain."[7] French policy, he now realized, depended upon the conclusion of an Anglo-French naval accord, essential for the security of both powers.

When the preliminary sessions of the 1935 London Naval Conference opened on October 23, 1934, Darlan had already taken a sea command. But the policy studies he had prepared influenced the French delegation, which gave notice in 1935 of France's withdrawal from the Washington Treaty. After Japan and Italy had withdrawn from the London Conference, France joined Britain and the

United States to sign in 1936 a treaty that left France free to continue rebuilding her fleet.[8]

DARLAN'S LAST SEA COMMAND

Darlan reported to Brest in early October to take command of the Second Squadron, a fleet of forty-six ships operating in the Atlantic. Always happy at sea, he had looked forward to this command. The more prestigious First Squadron, operating in the Mediterranean, was commanded by Vice-Admiral Georges Mouget, an officer with a good record who enjoyed a narrow seniority over Darlan, and who stood first in line to become Commander of the Fleet. Darlan, with his political connections, could have pulled strings to get the Mediterranean command. He chose instead to move in orderly fashion to the Atlantic command where he flew his flag on the *Provence*, one of five French battleships of 22,000 tons still in service.[9]

In 1934 he believed that the Atlantic theater would become the more important one, owing mainly to the rapid progress of aviation and the emerging German menace. The narrow Mediterranean, he thought, would soon be dominated by air power. In a German war, the main body of the fleet would be moved to Brest, to intercept German raiders in the Atlantic. Two new battleships, *Dunkerque* and *Strasbourg*, designed to confront the *panzerschiffe*, were scheduled for Atlantic duty upon their completion. Darlan therefore commanded what would soon become France's strongest naval force.[10]

During the winter of 1934-1935, the Second Squadron operated near the coast. The stormy December weather interrupted training exercises. When it finally cleared on a Sunday, he resumed work, confessing to Docteur that "I don't have any special respect for the Lord's Day."[11] The spring cruise of 1935 took him to the Azores, Madeira, the Canary Islands, and Morocco. Returning to France in mid-June, the Second Squadron joined the First in the Channel for combined maneuvers that turned into a competition between the two squadrons, and between Darlan and Mouget. Alain Darlan wrote that his father won all of the competitions.[12]

Darlan continued with his squadron. On January 15, 1936, he departed Brest for the annual spring cruise, rescheduled for the winter months. This time he took his ships to Dakar in West Africa, returning to Brest on February 27.[13] A week later he learned of Hitler's reoccupation of the Rhineland, which he hoped would convince London of the German menace.[14] Following a brief visit to Paris, Darlan rejoined his squadron. When the call came in June for him to return to the Ministry, four months before the scheduled conclusion of his sea command, he was disappointed. He told a young officer on board the *Provence* that his months with the squadron had been among the happiest of his life.[15]

SERVING THE POPULAR FRONT

Returning to Paris in late June 1936, Darlan undertook again his familiar work as Chief of the Military Cabinet of the Ministry of Marine. He had been called there by his old friend, Alphonse Gasnier-Duparc, a cousin of Madame

Darlan, and now Minister of Marine in Leon Blum's government of the Popular Front. Formed on June 5, it was dominated by the left-leaning Socialists and Radical Socialist parties. On the foreign scene, events had changed importantly to influence Anglo-French relations. Spain stood at the brink of civil war, and Benito Mussolini's war against Ethiopia had tempted Britain to flex its naval muscles in the Mediterranean. With the Anglophile Yvon Delbos at the Quai d'Orsay, the Popular Front government settled upon a new policy aimed at concluding an entente with Britain.[16] Darlan welcomed that policy.

Arriving at the Rue Royale in early July, Darlan found on his desk an important policy study. Dated June 9, 1936, it reviewed recent international naval developments. Reading it, Darlan saw that important changes had taken place while he had been at sea. Anglo-French naval relations had changed for the better, and French and British naval staffs were being drawn into a closer relationship. The Ethiopian crisis had stirred London to worry about the Italian threat to British naval communications in the Mediterranean. He must have smiled gently when he read that "for the first time in perhaps 230 years, Great Britain is not able by herself to supervise her maritime traffic, at least not between Gibraltar and Suez."[17] The statement was close to target, for the Royal Navy, neglected since World War I, had declined in quality.[18]

Darlan read that the Admiralty had been anxious to gain the support of French bases and naval forces, that the British government had requested conversations with the view of assuring Anglo-French naval cooperation, and that "an accord in principle with France was finally concluded on the basis of assistance in the event of unprovoked aggression."[19] This was a reference to the Mediterranean Accord of November 1935, which promised naval cooperation and British access to French Mediterranean ports.[20] But Pierre Laval, having signed the accord, had quickly backed away from it.[21] Concerned to appease Mussolini, Laval had withdrawn his only strong card: the threat of combined Anglo-French naval power against Italy.

Darlan now realized that London had taken the initiative to seek French naval support in the Mediterranean. But reading further, he saw that Britain remained insensitive to French continental concerns, refusing to make any commitments beyond the Rhine. If France is to expect a future rapprochement with Great Britain, he read, the French navy must support to the Royal Navy on the seas, where London continued to focus its attention.[22]

Finishing the document, Darlan could see that the Mediterranean naval balance was shifting to France's advantage at the expense of Italy. But while the British Admiralty had turned to Paris for naval support against Italy, the Foreign Office would make no commitment to support France against Germany. The stage was set for Paris to encourage closer Anglo-French naval relations, which Darlan favored.

A MISSION TO LONDON

When the Spanish Civil War broke out in July 1936, the question in Darlan's mind was whether France and Britain would commit their naval power in the Mediterranean to support the left-leaning Loyalist government at Madrid. He realized that France and Britain enjoyed an overwhelming strategic advantage. They could easily concentrate their combined naval power at any point in Spanish waters. But the German and Italian fleets, separated by geography, could not easily come together. He believed that Anglo-French naval power could determine the outcome of the conflict, to the advantage of both France and Britain. He worried that nonintervention would risk the creation of a fascist state on France's southern frontier, and that Italy and Germany might seize the Balearic and Canary Islands.

Not everyone shared Darlan's view. Blum's first effort to send arms to the Loyalists provoked sharp opposition from conservatives in France. General Francisco Franco's Nationalists enjoyed considerable support among French Catholics, and among Catholics in the French navy.[23] Franco also had support among British conservatives. So Blum, faced with right-wing opposition at home and in Britain, moved cautiously away from the policy of intervention.[24]

But Blum did not give up easily. At the end of July two Italian aircraft with mechanical problems landed in French North Africa. Now, with evidence that Italy had already intervened in the Spanish conflict, Blum renewed his initiative to send aid to the Loyalists. One of his schemes was to send Darlan on a mission to London to seek the support of the British Admiralty, which might in turn pressure the cabinet to reconsider its position of nonintervention. Blum knew that Darlan was on good personal terms with the British First Sea Lord, Admiral Ernle Chatfield, and he could see that Italian intrusion into the western Mediterranean threatened British naval interests. Chatfield received Darlan at the Admiralty on August 5. Darlan tried to convince him of the need for Anglo-French naval intervention in the Spanish conflict.[25]

Darlan reported to Chatfield that information received by the French navy indicated Italian and German designs upon the Balearic and Canary Islands, and that Rome and Berlin would be tempted to take these islands by force. He suggested that Anglo-French intervention in Spain could prevent the triumph of the dictators, which he said would damage both French and British interests. He added that a communist victory would also be undesirable, and that Anglo-French interests would be best served by the establishment of a moderate democratic government in Spain.

Chatfield, unsure of Darlan's information, replied tartly that if French authorities had information so important as to require a direct approach to the Admiralty, then perhaps Paris should go to the trouble of addressing London by diplomatic channels. He indicated that he would be grateful to the French navy if future information clearly pointing to a danger might be sent to the Admiralty by way of naval attachés, to save time. Darlan could see that the interview was going poorly. Chatfield remarked that the British cabinet believed that the only solution was one of not becoming involved. Darlan countered that nonintervention would cripple any effort of mediation aimed at establishing a democratic government in Spain. "That result," he insisted, "would be eminently desirable, as much for England as for France."[26]

Growing impatient, Chatfield answered that intervention risked being caught in the middle. But Darlan stood his ground, reminding Chatfield of the Admiralty's duty to protect British citizens caught in a foreign war zone. They discussed the question of protecting English and French nationals stranded in Catalonia, where the war was about to spread. Darlan insisted that France did not want to keep naval units at Barcelona any longer than necessary, and that it would therefore be desirable for the French and British commanders on the scene to work in harmony with each other. Chatfield, however, replied evasively. Darlan could see that the First Lord had no interest in Anglo-French naval cooperation in Spain. Finally, the Frenchman ended the interview, noting that his visit was merely a mission initiated by the Ministry of Marine to share information.[27]

Disappointed, Darlan could see that the Admiralty had no intention of using British naval power to influence the outcome of the Spanish conflict. Nor was it eager to cooperate with the French navy to protect Anglo-French interests in Spanish waters. Now Blum would set aside his policy of intervention, and Darlan would have to await another chance to promote Anglo-French naval cooperation in the Mediterranean.

PROMOTION TO THE TOP COMMAND

With his slight seniority over Darlan, Rear Admiral Georges Mouget stood first in line to succeed Georges Durand-Viel as Chief of the General Staff of the Navy upon the latter's mandatory retirement in March 1937 at age sixty-five.[28] But on October 1, 1936, in a surprising turn of events, Darlan received the appointment, effective January 1, 1937, nearly three months before the expiration of Durand-Viel's term.[29]

Mouget, an intelligent man with broad cultural interests, was a competent seaman and a strong leader. He had also served longer at sea than had Darlan. He had always been promoted early, and there were no blemishes on his record.[30] But with the Popular Front government in power, the mood of the moment was to the left. Darlan, son of a family long identified with the Radical Socialist party, stood politically to the left of most French naval officers. He therefore enjoyed a doctrinal link with the Popular Front. He would be politically safe, a progressive officer who would support the government's reform program and keep the more conservative officer corps in line. Darlan therefore had strong political support, particularly among the Radicals. He could count on the support of his old friend, Gasnier-Duparc, Minister of Marine in 1936.

In choosing Darlan, the Cabinet opted for an officer with a special set of skills. In contrast to the more philosophical Mouget, Darlan was a skilled naval technician, a steady officer who had long played an important staff role in the reconstruction of the fleet. He was therefore better prepared than Mouget to preside over the final phase of the rebuilding program.

Mouget, moreover, was unable to conceal entirely the symptoms of a tragic mental illness that soon led him to take his own life.[31] Any hint of mental illness would have been fatal to the chances of an officer seeking the highest rank in the navy. Mouget appears to have successfully concealed the severity of his mental depression, but not the fact of it. His illness could easily have been a silent factor in his being passed over for the final promotion. Darlan brought to the top command a stability that Mouget lacked.

THE SHIFTING BALANCE OF WORLD NAVAL POWER

In 1936 and 1937 Darlan watched as the world naval balance turned against France. In October 1936, Hitler and Mussolini signed the Rome-Berlin Axis. A month later Berlin and Tokyo negotiated the Anti-Comintern Pact, which Italy joined in 1937. The new alignment, though fragile, shaped the outlines of what would become the Axis alliance. Darlan knew that its weakest link was the Mediterranean, where Britain and France could combine their naval power against Italy.

Darlan's promotion to the top naval rank coincided almost exactly with the creation of the Axis alliance. He therefore inherited a new balance of world naval power that bore heavily to France's disadvantage. Even should the rebuilding program be completed on schedule, Darlan still would not command enough assets to protect France's empire and trade routes in a war against Germany and her allies. The new naval balance created for Darlan an imperial crisis that the French fleet could not manage without the help of the Royal Navy.

London, however, hesitated to tie herself to France, whose eastern alliances might drag her into a costly continental war. Darlan knew that Britain and France acting together could dominate Mediterranean and perhaps also Atlantic waters. But with the Maginot Line serving as a shield against German aggression in the west, and with French naval power already poised against Italy in the Mediterranean, Paris had nothing more to offer London. Darlan had little choice but to promote Anglo-French naval cooperation in the Mediterranean and hope that London would soon see the need of a alliance. If working closely with the Royal Navy in the Mediterranean would draw France and Britain closer together, he was prepared to play the role. Events in that troubled sea would soon give him another chance to push that agenda.

NOTES

1. SHM, 1BB2 EMG/SE, Carton 208, "Dénonciation du Traité de Washington avant le 31 Décembre 1934," 12 January 1934, Dossiers Amiral Darlan.

2. This summary of his view of the international scene is based on SHM, 1BB2 EMG/SE, Carton 208, "Politique Navale," 17 January 1934, Dossiers Amiral Darlan, a document intended to influence the passage of a naval construction bill.

3. Ibid.

4. Ibid.

5. Ibid.

6. Ibid.

7. SHM, 1BB2 EMG/SE, Carton 208, "Note sur une Question Posée par le Gouvernement du Reich," 22 January 1934.

8. Information about the 1936 Treaty is contained in USNA, RG 38, ONI, C-9-d, Reg. 21968, "The London Naval Conference of 1935-1936."

9. Hervé Coutau-Bégarie and Claude Huan, *Darlan* (Paris: Fayard, 1989), 78, 107-109; Alain Darlan, *L'Amiral Darlan parle* (Paris: Amiot-Dumont, 1952), 38; Amiral Jules Docteur, *Darlan* (Paris: Éditions de la Couronne, 1949), 26.

10. Coutau-Bégarie and Huan, *Darlan*, 108-109; Espagnac du Ravay, *Vingt ans de politique navale, 1919-1939* (Grenoble: Arthaud, 1941), 294.

11. Docteur, *Darlan*, 30.

12. Darlan, *L'Amiral Darlan parle*, 38.

13. Ibid., 112.

14. Docteur, *Darlan*, 31.

15. Darlan, *L'Amiral Darlan parle*, 39.

16. See John E. Dreifort, *Yvon Delbos at the Quai d'Orsay* (Lawrence: The University of Kansas Press, 1973).

17. SHM, 1BB2 EMG/SE, Carton 208, "Note pour le Ministre," 9 June 1936.

18. See Correlli Barnett, *Engage the Enemy More Closely: The Royal Navy in the Second World War* (New York: Norton, 1991), 29-30.

19. SHM, 1BB2 EMG/SE, Carton 208, "Note pour le Ministre," 9 June 1936.

20. See USNA, RG 38, ONI, C-9-c, "Confidential Letter No. 82" from the Paris Embassy to the Secretary of State, November 6, 1935.

21. See Anthony Eden, *The Memoirs of Anthony Eden: Facing the Dictators* (Boston: Houghton Mifflin, 1962), 315-316, 526.

22. SHM, 1BB2 EMG/SE, Carton 208, "Note pour le Ministre," 9 June 1936.

23. See Ronald Chalmers Hood III, *Royal Republicans: The French Naval Dynasties between the World Wars* (Baton Rouge: Louisiana State University Press, 1985), 161-162.

24. Dreifort, *Yvon Delbos at the Quai d'Orsay*, 31-41.

25. The minutes upon which this section is based are contained in SHM, 1BB2 EMG/SE, Carton 203, "Entretiens Franco-Britanniques du 5 Août 1936 à L'Amirauté Britannique."

26. Ibid.

27. Ibid.

28. In wartime, the Chief of the General Staff became the Commander-in-Chief of the Navy. See Jacques Raphaël-Leygues and François Flohic, *Darlan* (Paris: Plon, 1986), 59.

29. Coutau-Bégarie and Huan, *Darlan*, 117-118.

30. Ibid., 114-115.

31. Docteur, *Darlan*, 32-33.

CHAPTER 5

Blunting Fascist Aggression

What began in 1936 as scattered clashes between Loyalist and Nationalist ships along the coast of Spain flared in 1937 into indiscriminate violence and piracy throughout the Mediterranean. The scene was set for Darlan to help unleash massive Anglo-French naval power to blunt fascist aggression at sea.

WARNINGS AND PROPOSALS

Naval intelligence services provided Darlan with detailed reports of the volatile Spanish scene.[1] Well informed, he kept his minister, Gasnier-Duparc, posted of events. In early November 1936 he reported that Madrid was about to fall to General Franco's Nationalists. It was a premature judgment, but Darlan was on target when he predicted in the same report that the Insurgents [Nationalists] would impose a naval blockade on Spain's southeastern coast, that the blockade would lead to violations of international maritime law, that the Insurgents would seek the active naval support of foreign powers, and that Germany and Italy would be tempted to extend diplomatic recognition to the Franco faction.[2]

Darlan warned his minister that Germany or Italy, or both, would in time provide Franco with submarines. He noticed that German surface ships, allegedly on training cruises, had already arrived in Spanish waters.[3] But Darlan was more alarmed at the presence of Italian warships at Majorca, recently fallen to Franco.[4] Italian control of that base, he insisted, would be a matter of grave concern for France and Britain, especially France, as it would threaten communications between the Mediterranean and Atlantic squadrons, and between France and North Africa. He warned that Franco would request the support of Italian aircraft at Majorca, to attack ships unloading cargo in Spanish ports. France's best interest, he insisted, was to restrain Italy and keep open the option of French intervention in the Balearics.[5]

Darlan saw the Italian threat as an opportunity to forge closer Franco-British naval cooperation in the Mediterranean. He reminded his minister that French and British naval interests in the Spanish affair were linked together. At the risk of getting out of line, he recommended that Paris approach London to consider sending Rome parallel notes aimed at discouraging Italian activity at Majorca. He also proposed that the French and British Admiralties consult together to take precautions in the event of Axis opposition to any Anglo-French diplomatic initiative.[6]

Darlan's proposal to flex Anglo-French naval muscles in the Mediterranean was premature, for London and Paris were considering peace overtures. But his assessment of the Spanish scene was on target. In mid-November, the Franco faction declared its intention to interdict maritime traffic in Spanish waters and if necessary to bomb foreign shipping in Spanish harbors, as Darlan had predicted. On November 18, again as Darlan had anticipated, Germany and Italy extended diplomatic recognition to the Franco regime. Italian delivery of submarines to enforce the blockade would come later.

PLANS FOR NAVAL INTERVENTION

In any naval war with Italy, the French navy would have to divide its strength between Mediterranean and Atlantic waters. Knowing that the Mediterranean squadron was not equal to the entire Italian fleet, he drafted contingency plans to compensate for that weakness. Summaries of these plans sent to Gasnier-Duparc during the autumn of 1936 reveal Darlan's thoughts about the Spanish conflict. He worried that the two sides had come to depend upon massive deliveries of reinforcements and supplies from the Soviets and from Italy and Germany. He was sure that the military balance would tilt to the side that controlled the sea. He worried that the war would be prolonged, that there would be serious incidents at sea, that the Soviets and the Axis would step up their involvement, and that Paris and London would try to avoid being dragged into the conflict.[7]

Darlan's concerns focused on Italian activity at Majorca, German penetration into Spanish Morocco, and Axis utilization of Nationalist ports, all of which weighed heavily upon French naval and military communications. Confronted with the threat of a two-front naval war, Darlan could not count on the assistance of the Royal Navy.[8] His plans therefore assumed that France would fight alone. He notified the military command that troop movements between France and North Africa could not be assured unless the naval balance in the Mediterranean shifted in France's favor. Should war appear imminent, the navy would attempt a quick transfer of troops to North Africa in advance of hostilities, for a swift conquest of Spanish Morocco. There were also plans for military intervention on the east coast of Spain at ports still under Republican control.[9]

Darlan's plan aimed at seizing control of Atlantic and Mediterranean waters near the Spanish coasts, so that the flow of supplies to the Insurgents could be interrupted. Darlan assumed that the combined Axis fleets in the Mediterranean would be superior to the French Mediterranean squadron. But he knew that the enemy naval forces would be divided and dispersed at the outset of the conflict, making it possible for the French fleet to avoid a clash with combined enemy forces.[10]

His plans for the Mediterranean envisioned the transfer of units based at Toulon to ports further west. The offensive phase aimed at tilting the naval balance in the western Mediterranean toward France. Aircraft, destroyers, and submarines would attack enemy vessels in the Balearics and in Spanish ports controlled by the Insurgents. Minorca would be occupied if it remained under Republican control. Most of the heavy ships of the Mediterranean squadron would be sent to the Atlantic.[11]

The reinforcement of the Atlantic Squadron aimed at blunting the German threat. The strong Second Squadron could operate out of Casablanca and Brest, or the entire squadron could be concentrated at Brest, ideally located to support operations against the flow of supplies from Germany to the Insurgents. Darlan wrote that German ships already in Spanish ports would find themselves "in a delicate situation."[12]

UGLY INCIDENTS IN SPANISH WATERS

But Paris and London had no intention of becoming involved in the Spanish conflict. In late 1936, when Mussolini increased the flow of supplies to the Insurgents, France and Britain worked to end the war by diplomatic means, or at least to control foreign intervention in the conflict.[13] Nevertheless, the tension mounted as naval warfare flared along the southern and eastern coasts of Spain. On January 18, 1937 *The New York Times* reported that Malaga and Almeria were under attack by Insurgent warplanes and that "there are indications that mysterious foreign warships are co-operating in these coastal attacks."[14] Thought to be German, the warships were bombarding the two cities with their heavy guns.

The spread of the naval war to Spain's east coast increased the chances that France might be dragged into the conflict. The first incident involving French ships took place on January 18 when the destroyer *Maille-Breze* was attacked off the coast of Catalonia by an unidentified aircraft. Six bombs were dropped.[15] Responding swiftly, Darlan ordered French warships in the region to return fire should they be attacked.[16] Although the *Maille-Breze* incident involved no damage or loss of life, it foreshadowed events to come.

In March a Nonintervention Committee sitting in London assigned naval patrols to enforce a Nonintervention Agreement among the powers. The Royal Navy and the French navy took responsibility for coastal zones where German and Italian vessels would normally deposit shipments for the Insurgents. Germany and Italy were assigned the eastern coast of Spain, where Soviet deliveries to the Loyalists usually arrived. Italian ships would also patrol near Minorca, still under Republican control.[17]

Darlan could see that the patrol system lent legitimacy to the presence of Axis warships in Spanish waters. On May 24 the Italian cruiser *Barletta*, anchored at the Insurgent port of Palma in the Balearics, was damaged by Loyalist aircraft. The *Barletta* had become a part of the naval patrol, so Italy filed a complaint with the Nonintervention Committee, which passed a resolution deploring the incident.[18] Although Italian warships had operated out of Palma from the beginning of the conflict, the legitimacy accorded them by the patrol agreement obscured the fact that their reason for being in those waters had always been to protect Italian intervention. A similar attack upon the battle cruiser *Deutschland* anchored at the Balearic port of Ibiza provoked the Germans to mount a naval bombardment of Almeria, the town that earlier had been attacked by mysterious foreign ships.[19] But since the German warship had a right to patrol Spanish waters, the discussions in London focused on Spanish aggression rather than on the German bombardment of an innocent coastal town.

Darlan stood by as foreign warships fired angry shots in waters that France and Britain together could dominate. He could see that Axis ships were lending naval support to Nationalist military operations along the Spanish coast. They were using Palma and Ibiza as their bases, and they were exploiting the Nonintervention Agreement to cover their aggression.

RISING TENSIONS IN THE MEDITERRANEAN

During the summer of 1937, after Franco's forces had blockaded Santander and threatened French merchant and fishing vessels in the Bay of Biscay, Darlan sent ships of the Second Squadron into these waters.[20] The incidents in the Bay of Biscay anticipated a higher level of violence that spread throughout the Mediterranean later that summer. Darlan's files contain reports of nearly fifty attacks upon neutral shipping in 1937: bombings and strafings, shelling by surface craft, the planting of mines in busy shipping lanes, and numerous torpedo attacks by submarines. The attacks occurred mainly in the central and western Mediterranean against ships of various nationalities.[21]

Darlan was sure that the Italians had either staged the attacks or had provided Franco the means to mount them. His judgment was on target. Mussolini had agreed in early August to an urgent request from Franco for active naval assistance to interrupt the flow of Soviet shipments to the Loyalists. Il Duce would send Franco submarines and join the attack with his own. The latter would display the Spanish flag should they be forced to the surface.[22]

Darlan kept his government well informed of these indiscriminate acts of violence. With this information in hand, Foreign Minister Yvon Delbos seized the initiative, inviting London to join France in arranging a multilateral conference to address the problem of Mediterranean security. It was scheduled for September 10 at Nyon, Switzerland, with the Mediterranean states, including Italy, and also Germany and the Soviet Union receiving invitations.[23]

By September 7 Darlan had prepared a plan for naval action. Convoys would not solve the problem, and organizing an international force with the delicate question of command would require a detailed study. There was no time for all that.[24] His solution was to divide the Mediterranean into surveillance zones with each power assigned one zone. The ships of each zone would be of the same nationality, under their own command. Within a system of territorial reciprocity, ships might pursue the aggressor into adjacent zones or foreign territorial waters. British ships would be allowed to pursue any aggressor into French waters off

Algeria and to attack them there. Spanish warships fighting each other would go unmolested, and neutral vessels would enter Spanish territorial waters at their own risk.[25]

Defending his plan before the cabinet, Darlan insisted that its acceptance among the Mediterranean powers would stop the piracy. He observed that the violence was mainly the work of four Italian submarines, two of which had been delivered to Franco. The other two were Italian submarines on long-range missions. He recommended the system of surveillance zones and mutual assistance. Of the several navies involved, he said, the French and the British would be able to cooperate most effectively. The French zone would be opposite North Africa and in the region of the Balearics.[26] The plan approved, Darlan departed for Nyon.

THE NYON CONFERENCE

When the delegates assembled on September 10, Germany and Italy were absent, having declined the invitation.[27] So France and Britain had their own way at Nyon, where they hosted delegations from Bulgaria, Yugoslavia, Greece, Rumania, Turkey, Egypt, and the Soviet Union. They would have to move quickly to present Mussolini with a *fait accompli* before he could change his mind and send a representative. With Delbos presiding, the nine powers quickly approved an Anglo-French proposal to blunt submarine aggression. Its essential feature was Darlan's plan for mutual assistance and the division of the Mediterranean into surveillance zones. The original Darlan plan was modified slightly to assure better coverage of the most important trade routes. France and Britain received large zones in the western Mediterranean. Smaller zones were assigned in the Aegean to Greece, Yugoslavia, Turkey, and the Soviet Union.

But at the end of the first day the smaller states, fearing Soviet expansion into the Aegean, balked at cooperating with Russia to patrol the eastern zones. Next morning, however, they accepted Darlan's offer to assign French destroyers to assist with the Aegean patrol.[28] Significantly, the two stronger naval powers had exchanged the original zone system for conference approval to expand Anglo-French naval power into the eastern Mediterranean, and to control the surveillance operation. The way was now open for Darlan and Chatfield to unleash their combined naval power against Italian aggression. Foreign Minister Anthony Eden wrote that it was "a solution more satisfactory than our original plan."[29]

That solution, known as the Nyon Arrangement, authorized warships of the participating powers to destroy any submarines found in waters where aggression had recently occurred. The Arrangement did not abandon Darlan's original plan of dividing the Mediterranean into surveillance zones. It instead authorized France and Britain to proceed with them on a bilateral basis. The Aegean states would request foreign assistance as necessary. French and British fleets would patrol the main traffic routes in both the western and eastern basins.[30] Before the conference ended, Darlan and Chatfield concluded a secret accord to divide the Mediterranean into five surveillance zones.

It was therefore the Anglo-French Naval Staff Accord of September 13, signed by Darlan and Chatfield, rather than the Nyon Arrangement itself, which contained the organizational and technical plan for attacking piracy in the Mediterranean. It resembled Darlan's original plan, except that it rearranged the surveillance zones. The accord divided the western basin into two zones, one under British command extending from Gibraltar to the Balearics and Algiers; the other, a French zone, extended south from France to the coast of North Africa. In the eastern basin, Britain took control of a zone between Sicily and North Africa and another that included the Aegean Sea north of the 38th parallel. The fifth zone, under France, covered the remainder of the Aegean and the Ionian Sea off the western coast of Greece. French and British warships might cross from one zone to another in pursuit of any aggressor.[31]

Darlan and Chatfield wrote into the agreement provisions for Anglo-French naval cooperation and mutual assistance. They allowed French and British warships to put into each others ports without prior notice or diplomatic authorization. The local naval command was expected to offer full services to any visiting vessel. French and British aircraft would overfly each other's territory without notice or authorization. Significantly, the accord brought the British and French Admiralties into consultation with each other for the purpose of carrying out the terms of the Nyon Arrangement. Two Admirals, one from each navy, were made responsible for operations, and for maintaining regular personal contact with each other. They would exchange information about ship locations, establish guidelines for communications, and simplify the formalities of visitation and salutation. They would have the services of a liaison officer from their opposite.[32] Admiral Sir Dudley Pound would command British operations. His opposite was Vice-Admiral Jean-Pierre Esteva. They would operate out of Oran in North Africa.[33]

Delbos kept open the invitation to Mussolini, but events moved too swiftly for him to respond. A large but deserted surveillance zone was reserved for Italy, so that Mussolini, according to Eden, "could then send his warships to hunt his own submarines where it mattered least."[34] A supplementary agreement extended the Nyon provisions to cover acts of piracy committed by surface ships and aircraft.[35] Embarrassed, Mussolini finally authorized negotiations with the British and French naval staffs in Paris, but it was too late for him to undo the damage. The German Chargé d'Affaires in Paris reported to Berlin on September 25 that "political and military cooperation with Britain in the Mediterranean, which Laval had avoided, has now become a fact."[36]

NYON: A TURN IN THE RIGHT DIRECTION

The Nyon Arrangement, a brilliant triumph of French diplomacy, was the only occasion prior to the war that Paris and London used force to blunt fascist aggression. Mussolini suffered a sharp setback. Piracy in the Mediterranean was quickly brought under control. Mussolini would later accept his zone, which extended westward in a point to the Balearics.[37] The Italian zone would not burden the Anglo-French work of keeping peace at sea. Mussolini would have continued his deliveries to the Insurgents in any event, as Nyon was intended to stop piracy rather than commerce.

Nyon underscored what Darlan had known all along, that France and Britain working together could influence events. Eden shared that view, writing Churchill on September 14 his conviction that Anglo-French cooperation could be effective, and "that the two Western democracies can still play a decisive part in European affairs."[38] Nyon upstaged the Axis state that had the best reason to fear Anglo-French power. It proved that Italy was the weakest link in the Axis chain and that the Mediterranean was the area where Paris and London could best employ offensive power.

The French press was nearly unanimous in praise of the agreement. The left press was especially outspoken, pointing out that the combined Anglo-French fleets patrolling the Mediterranean were "a warning to Mussolini that he was not going to have his own way in the Mediterranean forever." Another Paris daily saw Nyon "as a prelude to a stiffening of France-British diplomacy in the foreign field." *Figaro*, however, commented that "England's firmness does not exclude her desire to negotiate with Italy." There was, nevertheless, overwhelmingly favorable comment in the French press supporting Anglo-French naval cooperation.[39]

The success of the Nyon Arrangement bore out Darlan's judgment that France and Britain together could dominate the Mediterranean. The naval staffs at Nyon had agreed that Britain would assign thirty-five destroyers to patrol duty, and France twenty-eight.[40] Within ten days Darlan could count twenty-four French destroyers in the waters between Casablanca and Suez. His records show that Britain had sent to the Mediterranean an equal number of destroyers, plus two battleships, three cruisers, and an aircraft carrier.[41] But it was not merely the number of ships on station that enabled them to call the signals. It was their solidarity, their ability to concentrate their ships at any given place, and their willingness to use them.

The Nyon agreements created an informal Anglo-French naval alliance in the Mediterranean, tilting the balance of power toward the two democratic powers at the expense of Italy. Darlan now presided over a period of cordial Anglo-French naval relations. The two navies began to cooperate on a regular basis, using each other's ports, exchanging information, planning patrols, lending support to each other at sea, and exchanging social visits. Darlan's records indicate a continuing presence of British warships in French Mediterranean and Atlantic ports in 1937 and 1938. In late September 1937, for example, five British destroyers were operating out of Oran. The aircraft carrier *Glorious* was at nearby Arzew, as was the battleship *Barham*. In January 1938 the battleship *Hood* put into Marseilles for several days. British ships arrived at Marseilles nearly every day in late 1937 and early 1938.[42]

Nyon brought the French and British naval staffs into a close relationship not shared by their military counterparts. The naval accord provided a solid foundation upon which London and Paris might build a strong Anglo-French alliance, one that would bring their military and naval staffs together for joint planning. French public opinion clearly favored an alliance.[43] But time was running short for London and Paris to move in that direction. Darlan had done his part to set the stage for a closer relationship. At the end of 1937 the question was whether

London would complete the work begun at Nyon or choose instead to flirt with Mussolini.

NOTES

1. See SHM, 1BB2 EMG/SE, Cartons 202, 203, and 204.

2. SHM, 1BB2 EMG/SE, Carton 203, "Note Pour Le Ministre," 4 November 1936.

3. Ibid.

4. In January 1937 the United States naval attaché in Paris reported that "the French are extremely worried about the future of the Balearic Islands which are now undoubtedly filled with Italians." USNA, RG 38, ONI, C-9-d, Reg. 3636A.

5. SHM, 1BB2 EMG/SE, Carton 203, "Note Pour Le Ministre," 4 November 1936.

6. Ibid.

7. SHM, 1BB2 EMG/SE, Carton 203, "Memento," 20 November 1936.

8. SHM, 1BB2 EMG/SE, Carton 203, "Note Pour Le Ministre," 4 November 1936.

9. Ibid.

10. Ibid.

11. Ibid.

12. Ibid.

13. Hugh Thomas, *The Spanish Civil War* (New York: Harper and Row, 1963), 335.

14. *The New York Times*, January 18, 1937, 6.

15. Ibid., January 19, 1937, 12.

16. SHM, 1BB2 EMG/SE, Carton 203, Ministere de la Marine, État-Major Général, No. 101 E.M.G.3, 27 January 1937.

17. See Thomas, *The Spanish Civil War*, 394-395.

18. Ibid., 439-440.

19. Ibid., 440-441. See also John E. Dreifort, *Yvon Delbos at the Quai d'Orsay* (Lawrence: University Press of Kansas, 1973), 57-58.

20. SHM, 1BB2 EMG/SE, Carton 202, Folder #1, "Protection of the Fleet," 1937. SHM, 1BB2 EMG/SE, Carton 203, "Le Ministre de la Marine à Monsieur le Président du Conseil," 7 July 1937.

21. SHM, 1BB2 EMG/SE, Carton 202, "Dossier Incidents No. 1," 1937-1938 contains record of more than thirty attacks. Other folders in Carton 202 record numerous other incidents in 1937.

22. See DGFP, Series D, III, Nos. 407, 408, 409.

23. Dreifort, *Yvon Delbos at the Quai d'Orsay*, 62-64.

24. SHM, 1BB2 EMG/SE, Carton 203, "Note," 7 September 1937.

25. Ibid.

26. SHM, 1BB2 EMG/SE, Carton 203, "Note pour le Ministre," 7 September 1937.

27. SHM, 1BB2 EMG/SE, Carton 203, "Bulletin d'Information," 10 September 1937. See also DGPF, Series D, III, Nos. 417, 420. Italy refused to sit at the same table with Soviet Russia. Berlin cited Italy's refusal and their common preference to treat Mediterranean matters through the Nonintervention Committee.

28. Anthony Eden, *The Memoirs of Anthony Eden, Earl of Avon: Facing the Dictators* (Boston: Houghton Mifflin Company, 1962), 526-527.

29. Ibid., 526.

30. SHM, 1BB2 EMG/SE, Carton 204, "The Nyon Arrangement," 14 September 1937.

31. SHM, 1BB2 EMG/SE, Carton 204, "ACCORD entre les États-Majors Navals britannique et français," 13 September 1937.

32. Ibid.

33. SHM, 1BB2 EMG/SE, Carton 204, No. 114, E.M.G./S.E., 5 October 1937.

34. Eden, *Facing the Dictators*, 527.

35. SHM, 1BB2 EMG/SE, Carton 204, "Agreement Supplementary to the Nyon Arrangement," 17 November 1937.

36. DGFP, Series D, III, No. 422.

37. SHM, 1BB2 EMG/SE, Carton 204, Dossier #1, "Guerre d'Espagne, Conférence Méditerranenne et accords de Nyon," 1937, containing maps showing the surveillance zones.

38. Eden, *Facing the Dictators*, 528.

39. USNA, RG 38, ONI, C-4-e, Reg. 21555-E, report of the United States naval attaché in Paris, 21 September 1937.

40. Eden, *Facing the Dictators*, 527-528.

41. SHM, 1BB2 EMG/SE, Carton 203, "Situation des Forces Navales," 24 September 1937.

42. SHM, 1BB2 EMG/SE, Carton 203, Dossier No. 8, "Guerre d'Espagne, EMG-2, 1936-1939."

43. In November the American naval attaché in Paris reported that "the entire French press...has come out openly for an encouragement of and maintaining at all cost a close alliance with Great Britain." USNA, RG 38, ONI, C-9-e, Reg. 19447-C, November 1937 report of the naval attaché.

CHAPTER 6

Preparing for War

The new balance of world naval power and swift Axis rearmament imposed a heavy burden on the French navy. In late 1937 Darlan could see that France and Britain together could dominate selected European or Mediterranean waters, but they would be hard pressed to defend their trade routes in a war against more than one Axis power. He also realized that France might have to fight any or all of the Axis without British help.

A TURN IN THE WRONG DIRECTION

In the autumn of 1937 Darlan and Chatfield threatened Mussolini with massive naval power in the Mediterranean: the only area where the democracies could mount enough offensive power to back up their diplomacy. The stage was set for London and Paris to exploit their advantage over Rome. On the continent, Anglo-French military capabilities were limited, as France had no good way to blunt German aggression in Eastern Europe. British rearmament had failed to keep pace, and most Englishmen opposed any military involvement on the continent. With the Maginot Line shielding Britain as well as France, London might be tempted to appease the dictators in hope of reaching a diplomatic settlement. That policy would risk frittering away the advantage Darlan and Chatfield had gained over Italy from the use of combined naval power in the Mediterranean.

The best option was for London and Paris to build upon the Mediterranean partnership Darlan had helped to forge. They would have to bring their military staffs into consultation, avoid negotiations with the dictators, and maintain naval pressure on Mussolini in the Mediterranean. Darlan was in step with Eden and Churchill. Churchill's September 20 letter to Eden expressed hope that the Nyon advantage would be exploited. "Mussolini," he wrote, "only understands superior force, such as he is now confronted with in the Mediterranean," and he added that "Italy cannot resist an effective Anglo-French combination."[1] Eden's reply discussed Anglo-French naval power as the foundation for a stronger European policy. He commented that eighty Anglo-French destroyers patrolling Mediterranean waters "has made a profound impression on opinion in Europe."[2]

Clearly Eden and Delbos, with Darlan and Chatfield, had taken the first step at building an effective policy toward the European Axis. But Eden would have to defend the Nyon policy against Prime Minister Neville Chamberlain and Lord Halifax, who favored negotiations with the dictators and opposed Anglo-French military staff consultation.[3] In early 1938, Chamberlain pressed Eden to open negotiations with Rome. Refusing, Eden resigned his office in February.[4] Now, with Halifax at the Foreign Office, Chamberlain was free to launch a policy of appeasing Mussolini. British policy toward the Axis took a turn in the wrong direction. Chamberlain and Halifax discarded the military and diplomatic trumps that Darlan had helped win at Nyon. The strong Anglo-French alliance that Darlan desired would have to await another day.

PERSPECTIVES, 1937-1938

In 1937 Darlan worried about the security of France's sprawling colonial empire. In his view, these scattered colonies formed a unified system held together by the navy and a network of bases carefully situated to serve the defense and economic needs of the entire system. But he knew that the colonies were too widely scattered to be defended without a stronger fleet.[5] In his speeches and articles, Darlan stressed the wartime role of the fleet in keeping open the vital lanes of supply and reinforcements between France and her colonies.[6] Without supplies from abroad, he wrote, France "would find it absolutely impossible to hold out more than a few weeks against a strong industrial power."[7] He insisted upon the need for allies, which he thought France would find only if she remained strong.[8]

Darlan's view of the composition of the fleet had changed since 1930. "The battleship," he wrote, "is the backbone of the fleet."[9] He shared the conventional view that France had little need of aircraft carriers in the Mediterranean, dominated by land-based aircraft.[10] In his view, the primary function of naval aviation was observation.[11] Darlan realized that protecting the sea lanes would be more difficult than ever before, as modern submarines and surface raiders had longer range and could attack convoys far from port. He insisted that every type of ship in the fleet would have an important specialized task and one common objective: to protect the empire's trade routes.[12]

WAR PLANS

Darlan's 1937 plans for a European war therefore aimed at protecting French maritime traffic. But Darlan could not know in advance whether the enemy would be Germany or Italy, or both, or whether Britain would enter the war. The plans therefore took into account a range of contingencies. They assumed that the enemy would attack suddenly with warships already at sea.[13] Darlan regarded Germany as the probable enemy. Italy would remain neutral at the outset, as would Great Britain. His plans therefore assumed that France would have to fight alone until the moment of British intervention. He concluded that "our initial strategy then should not rest on the hypothesis of that intervention; but it should be capable of adapting itself quickly to it."[14]

His plans assumed that the first German naval attacks would be launched against French maritime traffic near West Africa and Morocco. They would be led by fast raiders capable of striking at widely scattered targets. Supported by supply vessels hidden in the vast expanse of ocean, these raiders would be capable of sustained operations. Should Italy enter the war at the outset, France could expect attacks against the coast of North Africa and against communications in the Mediterranean. These attacks, conducted by light vessels, submarines, and perhaps aircraft, would aim at interrupting the flow of reinforcements from Africa to the military front on France's northern frontier.[15]

Darlan underscored the need to protect communications with the Bay of Biscay, whose ports were best suited to serve the interior. Should Germany be the only enemy, France would protect the Mediterranean sea lanes with secondary units. A squadron would be assigned to the Gibraltar area to guard against German penetration there. A High Seas Force, composed of France's newest and heaviest ships, would be concentrated in the Atlantic to blunt any German incursion from the North Sea. Should Italy enter the war, Darlan would change his plan only slightly. The Mediterranean squadron would be moderately strengthened with light ships to protect what would become a lower volume of traffic in that area. Commerce would be diverted to Atlantic ports. He would keep his High Seas Force in the Atlantic, where he expected the first naval clashes to take place. Its objective was to destroy German commerce raiders. Darlan was haunted at the thought of German surface raiders attacking French troop convoys steaming from West Africa. Expecting the enemy to be situated to intercept the first convoys, he assigned highest priority to their protection. The High Seas Force would therefore provide escort. Should Italy remain neutral, the convoys would be routed through Gibraltar to ports in southern France.[16]

The plan called for communications to be centered in Paris under Darlan's personal authority. He would control all fleet movements, at least at the outset when scattered French naval units would have to be directed to prearranged locations. He would control the movements of the High Seas Force. Two new commands would be created, both reporting directly to Darlan. The first, Commander-in-Chief South, would operate out of Oran with authority over western Algeria and Morocco. The second, Commander-in-Chief North, would establish headquarters at Dunkirk and command operations in the Channel area. All other regional commands would remain in place, reporting to Darlan. Forces and missions would vary, depending upon whether France or Germany would have allies. Should Italy or Britain enter the war, French assets would be shifted toward the Mediterranean.[17]

The plan was conservative and defensive, aimed at protecting the shipping lanes. But it suffered from a shortage of assets. Out of necessity it committed the preponderance of French naval power to Mediterranean and Atlantic waters north of Dakar. There was not much left for patrolling the sea lanes connecting

France with her distant colonies or for the defense of Indochina against Japan. A staff study of November 1937 made clear the point that the French navy remained unequal to its mission. The study noted that "the only solid element around which resistance by the threatened parties can be organized remains a Franco-English alliance, which has become absolutely necessary."[18] But even an alliance would not be enough, the study warned, for Britain had waited too long to start rebuilding her fleet. Therefore, Germany and Japan would hold vast expanses of ocean that Britain and France ought to control. Britain would not be able to lend much help in the Mediterranean since she would have to bear the triple burden of defending against the German and Japanese fleets, and of protecting allied maritime communications around the globe.[19]

Darlan therefore understood that the French fleet, too weak to operate much beyond Dakar, would have to concede to Britain the burden of protecting the remote parts of the French empire and the distant sea lanes. He knew that the tiny French squadron assigned to defend Indochina was no match for the Japanese navy.[20]

"A QUESTION OF LIFE OR DEATH"

In early 1938 Darlan worried that Germany was surging ahead in naval rearmament. France and Britain, he wrote, "...have placed Europe in a critical situation identical to that before 1914."[21] He was sure that the time for action had come, that the French government must decide upon a naval policy to strengthen the fleet. He urgently desired an Anglo-French alliance, complaining that England "prefers to act alone and continue its see-saw policy whose sole effect until now has been to increase German power."[22] Unsure about assistance from Britain, Darlan thought that France would have to redouble her naval preparations in advance of the coming conflict. Otherwise, he thought, Germany would seize French colonies and perhaps portions of the coast of France. In his mind, the solution was the construction of more battleships. Darlan's list of needs included four battleships of 30,000 tons, three aircraft carriers, three 10,000-ton battle cruisers, six cruisers, 270 seaplanes, and standard aircraft for the three carriers. Further, it called for the passage of a naval law in 1938 to finance this construction, a statute of personnel for recruitment of crews, and authorization of government borrowing to cover nonbudgeted construction costs. This program, Darlan wrote, was "a question of life or death."[23]

Darlan used all of his political skills to promote a long-term naval policy to govern ship construction from 1939 until the end of 1942. Although he had to settle for only a part of his package, measures approved by the National Assembly in the spring of 1938 authorized construction of forty warships: two 35,000-ton battleships, two 18,000-ton aircraft carriers, two 8,000-ton cruisers, four heavy destroyers (*contre-torpilleurs*), fourteen destroyers, and sixteen submarines. The two battleships would resemble the powerful *Richelieu* and *Jean Bart*, already under construction.[24] But the German program had already surged ahead, with the *Bismarck* and *Tirpitz* scheduled for launching in early 1939.

The number of ships under construction in 1939 pushed hard against the upper limits of French industrial capacity. The building program moved slowly.

Under construction in French shipyards in the spring of 1939 were three battle-ships, one aircraft carrier, one cruiser, sixteen destroyers, and thirteen subma-rines. Waiting in line for vacant construction slips were a battleship, an aircraft carrier, two cruisers, four heavy destroyers, ten destroyers, twelve submarines, and thirty-four smaller vessels. Total construction authorized under the package was approximately 165,000 tons, averaging just over 41,000 tons annually, a significant increase over the annual average of 32,426 tons for the years 1925-1937.[25]

His success in winning the 1938 construction credits nourished the myth that Darlan was the creator of the modern French navy. But he did not create it. The rebuilding program began under Georges Leygues in 1922, when the National Assembly voted funds for thirty-three new ships. In nearly every year after 1925, additional construction funds were approved. Credits for the construction of France's first modern battleship, the *Dunkerque*, were approved in 1931, and funds for her sister ship, the *Strasbourg*, were voted in 1934. Credits for the two 35,000-ton battleships, *Richelieu* and *Jean Bart*, were approved in 1935.[26] So the modern French ships of World War II were all authorized before Darlan took the top command in 1937. The heavy ships authorized by the naval bill of 1938 re-mained unfinished at the time of the fall of France in 1940. Darlan contributed importantly over a full decade to the restoration of the French fleet. But the creator of the modern French navy was Georges Leygues, who built the fleet that Darlan later would command.

Darlan exercised broad powers over the navy. In 1937 he reorganized it with the intention of concentrating more power at the top command. He brought the Section d'Études Générales under his personal control, centralizing the functions of planning and policy making. Sections were also established for ship construc-tion and for naval personnel, both of which reported directly to the Chief of the Naval General Staff.[27] These measures and others enabled Darlan to exercise personal control over the essential details of naval management, often at the ex-pense of the Minister of Marine.

Darlan also strengthened his grip on the navy by carefully selecting his sub-ordinates, surrounding himself with a cadre of followers whose careers benefited from his. Known informally as the A.D.D. (Amis de Darlan), these men were intently loyal to him. Some of them were old friends such as Jean-Pierre Esteva. Louis de la Monneraye was a good Roman Catholic, the son of a noble family long associated with the navy.[28] Paul Auphan, whom Darlan met in 1926 at the Rue Royale, was, like de la Monneraye, strongly religious. Some of the A.D.D., brilliant young men like Henri Ballande, shared the Admiral's technical interests. Jean-Léon Bourragué, Maurice Le Luc, and Robert Battet would serve as Dar-lan's Chief-of-Staff. There were others, among them Jacques Moreau, Emmanuel Ollive, Marcel Gensoul, and Jean Odend'hal, who were with Darlan at the École navale at the turn of the century.[29]

Outside the service was Henri Moysset. Educated in the Catholic Church, Moysset had served as the tutor to young Darlan at the lyceé de Talence in 1894. He remained in contact with Darlan and eventually served him at Vichy. Moysset, de la Monneraye, and Auphan enjoyed Darlan's special confidence.[30]

All strong Roman Catholics, and one of them an aristocrat, they stood in contrast to the free-thinking, left-leaning Darlan.

THE MUNICH CRISIS

The great summer crisis of 1938, which grew out of Hitler's intention to crush Czechoslovakia, confronted Darlan with the threat of a Franco-German naval war. Tensions mounted during September. On the 22nd, as France and Germany stood poised for war, Darlan ordered full mobilization of the fleet.[31] He saw that France was in no position to wage a naval war against Germany without the active support of Britain. But he suspected that Germany would not attack France immediately, that she would wait until she had seized the Eastern European states and their vast supplies of raw materials and petroleum, and until she had grown strong enough to challenge Anglo-French overseas communications and resources.[32]

Nevertheless, he worried about France's military capabilities. German frontier defenses had grown too strong, he believed, to attack them directly, and French airpower was too weak to risk aerial attacks upon the Reich. Moreover, German naval power had grown so strong as to blunt any attack through the North Sea. He was confident of France's frontier defenses, but he worried that German surface raiders would lay waste to French shipping in distant waters. France, he thought, should fight a defensive war on the northern frontier. Since that line would hold, he expected Germany to seek the active assistance of Italy. France and Britain would then have to stand together to protect their trade routes, to seize Spanish Morocco and the Balearic Islands, and to attack Libya and Italy. Should France and Britain succeed in dominating both the Mediterranean and the Atlantic, he expected that Germany would eventually smother under an Anglo-French blockade. He knew that domination of these waters would not be easy, since France and Britain would have to spread their assets as far as the Pacific Ocean.[33]

In September, Darlan and his staff entered into conversations with their British counterparts. They quickly agreed upon a redistribution of their assets in Atlantic and Mediterranean waters. Since the Royal Navy held the edge in the Channel, French units in the Calais region were pulled back. The Anglo-French staffs also agreed upon the creation of a strong French Raiding Force to help guard Atlantic communications. Most of the remaining units of the French home fleet were sent to the western Mediterranean.[34]

Darlan now divided his fleet into five squadrons. The weakest was based at Dunkirk. Another operated out of Brest to defend mainly the Bay of Biscay. Vice-Admiral Esteva commanded the Mediterranean squadron. The remaining two squadrons were organized around heavier ships capable of carrying battle to the enemy in either Mediterranean or Atlantic waters. The High Seas Force, built around the renovated battleships *Provence*, *Bretagne*, and *Lorraine,* would assure the security of shipping from Africa to France. The Raiding Force, assembled from France's newest and fastest ships, was led by the battleship *Dunkerque*, supported by three cruisers of the *Gloire* class and eight heavy destroyers.[35]

Fast and powerful, this squadron was capable of pursuing and destroying German raiders on the high seas.

Although the Munich crisis was settled peacefully at the end of September, the mobilization of the fleet had been a realistic test of existing plans. Except for the addition of the Raiding Force, the redistribution of the fleet units conformed generally to Darlan's 1937 plan. The experience would serve as a model of efficiency for mobilization when war broke out in 1939. But Darlan understood that efficiency was not enough. He knew that the empire had never been so insecure and that France and Britain would have to stand together if they expected to fight a successful naval war against the Axis.

NOTES

1. Winston S. Churchill, *The Second World War*, 6 volumes (Boston: Houghton Mifflin, 1948-1953), I, 247.

2. Ibid., I, 248.

3. Anthony Eden, *The Memoirs of Anthony Eden, Earl of Avon; Facing the Dictators* (Boston: Houghton Mifflin Company, 1962), 557-558, 565-567. The British military chiefs also had reservations about staff talks with the French. See Churchill, *The Second World War*, I, 250-251.

4. See Eden, *Facing the Dictators*, 666 ff.

5. SHM, 1BB2 EMG/SE, Carton 208, "Le Role Impérial de Notre Flotte," 27 March 1937.

6. SHM, 1BB2 EMG/SE, Carton 208, "Composition et Puissance de la Flotte. Son role dans la Défense nationale," 4 Décember 1937.

7. Ibid.

8. Ibid.

9. Ibid.

10. That France would have no need for aircraft carriers was mentioned in 1935 in naval attaché reports from Paris. USNA, ONI, RG 38, C-9-C, Reg. 15812-H, "Confidential Letter No. 71."

11. SHM, 1BB2 EMG/SE, Carton 208, "Composition et Puissance de la Flotte."

12. SHM, 1BB2 EMG/SE, Carton 208, "Défendons nos routes impériales." The article, signed by Darlan and undated, is filed among 1938 materials.

13. SHM, 1BB2 EMG/SE, Carton 207, "Directives pour les Plans d'Operations," 5 June 1937.

14. Ibid.

15. Ibid.

16. Ibid.

17. Ibid.

18. SHM, 1BB2 EMG/SE, Carton 208, "Des Conditions de la Guerre dans la Situation Internationale Présente," 12 November 1937. The study was drafted by Admiral Bourragué, Darlan's Chief-of-Staff. Marginal notes are in Darlan's handwriting.

19. Ibid.

20. Darlan's records show that only three light cruisers and various lesser craft were in Indochina. SHM, 1BB2 EMG/SE, Carton 205, "Situation des Batiments à la Mer et Prévisions à la Date du 24 Septembre," 24 September 1938.

21. SHM, 1BB2 EMG/SE, Carton 208, "Politique Navale," undated.

22. Ibid.

23. Ibid.

24. Espagnac du Ravay, *Vingt ans de politique navale, 1919-1939* (Grenoble: Arthaud, 1941), 183-184, 296-297.

25. Ibid., 176, 181, 185-186.

26. Ibid., 181.

27. Ibid., 213-214.

28. In an interview with de la Monneraye during the Falkland Island crisis of the spring of 1982, the Admiral took the author to a large map on the landing near his study. He pointed with pride to the Bay of Monneraye in the Falklands that one of his aristocratic forefathers, an admiral of France, had discovered.

29. See Hervé Coutau-Bégarie and Claude Huan, *Darlan* (Paris: Fayard, 1989), 164-169.

30. Ibid.

31. SHM, 1BB2 EMG/SE, Carton 205, "Crise de Septembre 1938, Mesures de Guerre--Marine et Divers," no date. The fleet had been semimobilized since the outbreak of the Spanish Civil War. See SHM, 1BB2 EMG/SE, Carton 208, "Nécessité de la Tranche 40," 5 April 1939.

32. SHM, 1BB2 EMG/SE, Carton 208, "Note au sujet de la Politique Française de Défense Nationale," 26 September 1938.

33. Ibid.

34. SHM, 1BB2 EMG/SE, Carton 205, "Note sur la nouvelle organisation du commandement et de la répartition des forces navales françaises," 28 September 1938.

35. Ibid.

CHAPTER 7

Shifting Strategies of War

The question facing Darlan in 1939 was how to fight a successful naval war against Germany, Italy, and perhaps Japan, and simultaneously defend France's empire and trade routes. He searched for a solution that would enable France and Britain to overcome their naval weakness and win the war.

ADMIRAL OF THE FLEET

In 1938 Darlan held the rank of Vice-Admiral, the highest rank in the navy at that time. He was not, however, the senior officer of that rank. Admiral Jean de Laborde had been promoted to it ahead of him. Darlan commanded the navy by virtue of the fact that he was Chief of the Naval General Staff, a peacetime post that an officer ordinarily held for up to five years before retirement. The rank of Commander-in-Chief of the Navy was reserved for wartime service.

In 1938 President Albert Lebrun issued a secret decree designating General Maurice Gamelin as Commander-in-Chief of the Army, effective in wartime. After Darlan had suggested similar action for the navy, Lebrun on June 9 by secret decree designated Darlan as Commander-in-Chief of French Maritime Forces, effective upon execution of the decree by the Minister of Marine. Darlan would assume that title at the outbreak of war in 1939.[1]

A year later, on June 6, 1939, Darlan was promoted to the newly created rank of Admiral of the Fleet. There were reasons for an upward revision of the rank structure. In 1938 the French hierarchy of ranks was out of step with the international standard, which had become so inflated that foreign officers often outranked their French counterparts. Representing France at the coronation of the King of England in 1938, Vice-Admiral Darlan marched behind the Chinese admiral.[2] He often cited that incident, not to protest English formalities, but to underscore the need to match the French command structure with that of other countries; or, as he wrote a friend, "to prevent our country from marching behind Siam or Equador in international ceremonies."[3]

The promotion, however, was more than a cosmetic change, and it benefited Darlan's career more than he admitted. As France's only Fleet Admiral, he enjoyed greater prestige, outranking his senior in service, Vice-Admiral de Laborde. The promotion also lengthened his tenure as naval chief. Under the old system, Darlan at age fifty-eight in 1939 had already served half of his five-year term as Chief of the General Staff. Under the new law he could not be removed from command except by retirement, so he could now expect to command the navy four more years.[4]

The new command structure created two other flag ranks: Squadron Vice-Admiral, with four stars; and Admiral, with five stars. Fleet Admiral Darlan wore five stars, but his flag displayed in addition the cross-anchor insignia of the French Admiralty.[5] The new law sidetracked de Laborde, who could be promoted to Admiral but would retire ahead of Darlan.

A SOMBER REALISM

In 1939 Darlan worried that France and Britain might stumble into a war they could not win. His private papers from early 1939, which explore that problem, reveal a somber realism on his part.[6] He worried about the Axis naval presence in Spanish ports and the Canary Islands, from which raiders could attack French convoys and tie up huge Entente assets. He knew that the Anglo-French tonnage advantage over Germany and Italy was not enough to protect European waters and also Anglo-French communications stretching around the globe.[7] Japan's entering the war would spread Entente naval power even thinner: "We would have to fight from the Channel to Saigon or Sydney passing by Dakar, the Cape, Diego, Colombo, and Singapore and still keep guard over our Atlantic coast and the two sections of the Mediterranean."[8] American intervention, he added, "would largely restore the naval balance, but nothing permits us to count firmly and immediately on the active assistance of the great American republic."[9]

Darlan had little zeal to fight the Axis. "The war will last a long time," he wrote, and "it will be exhausting.... We must avoid it."[10] For twenty years, he complained, Paris had pursued a continental foreign policy when it ought to have pursued a global one; and France had allowed Germany to rearm, and for eight years Britain had tried to increase Italian naval power and to decrease that of France. France, he added, had always focused her attention on the northern frontier when in fact Germany had already launched a sea offensive by forging an alliance with Italy and supporting Franco in Spain. "Will France," he asked, "continue with a foreign policy that loses ground every day and risks losing the Empire?"[11]

Searching for solutions, Darlan noted the Italian threat to the empire. And he acknowledged German ambitions to expand to the east, which he thought posed no threat to France. Since saving the empire was his most important concern, he concluded that "we must leave Germany free to act toward the east."[12] France and Britain could then defeat Italy and deal later with any German threat. "But if she is engaged in the east," he wrote, "she would not want to turn this way for a long time."[13] His solution would set up a Russo-German war, but Paris and London did not pursue that policy.

BETWEEN PEACE AND WAR

During the spring of 1939 Darlan watched as Europe edged closer to war. In late March, after Hitler had seized Czechoslovakia, London and Paris guaranteed Poland. So the Entente would not give Hitler a free hand in the east. As tensions mounted, Darlan considered a spread of military options, but just how the navy would wage war against the Axis remained unclear to him. There was no easy way to assist Poland, and he could not know how many enemies France and Britain would have to fight.

Throughout the spring and summer Darlan presided over weekly meetings of the "Action Services," which included his Chief-of-Staff and selected department heads. At the session of April 12, he commented that the navy must to be ready to face an aggravation of the international situation. In the event of hostilities, he warned, the navy would be the first service to see action.[14] On June 8 he observed that the signs indicated a new crisis for late July or August, and that the fleet must be ready for combat no later than August.[15] His comments in these meetings reveal his grasp of detail and his interest in every aspect of naval operations. He knew where everything was located and what steps would be necessary to move ships and equipment from one place to another.[16]

Nevertheless, he continued to worry about France's ability to win the next war. He questioned whether the French system of command could match the quick efficiency of the dictatorships. The French system of government responsibility for war and military responsibility for operations did not inspire his confidence. He would prefer a stronger executive body, a "Directory" of civilians and soldiers to manage political and military business until the emergency had ended. He would wage an ideological war against fascist philosophy, and against Nazi race theories, which he thought to be much overblown, even laughable.[17]

Darlan considered the question of how the next war might break out. Should it come as the result of sudden direct attack, France would have no choice but to respond militarily. But how would France carry the war to the enemy? He thought that the western military front, defensive in posture, would not produce a final victory. He therefore concluded that the ultimate decision of war would turn on the clash of arms at sea. The question, then, was how to fight a naval war against the Axis. He had no zeal for the traditional weapon, a slow blockade that would expose France to heavy losses prior to its attaining full effect. It would therefore be necessary to shorten the war by seizing the initiative on the seas. There were, however, only two areas where offensive operations would be possible, on the North Sea coast of Germany and in the Mediterranean.[18]

Darlan understood the perils of attacking the coast of Germany.[19] Although he would not yet abandon that option, he realized that it would be easier to attack Italy. Another option was to occupy Libya as a first step in gaining control of the eastern Mediterranean, where offensive operations could be undertaken in the

Balkans. At the very least, he thought, a campaign to seize Libya would be necessary. He concluded that a war against the European Axis could be won in the Mediterranean.[20]

Darlan's thoughts about the role of the navy in the coming war were moving from a defensive to an offensive posture. As war approached, Darlan's thinking moved beyond his 1937 plan that had stressed the protection of convoys and overseas communications. In 1937 and 1938 he had repeatedly affirmed that the role of the navy was to keep open the sea lanes. In 1939 he was thinking about offensive operations aimed at determining the war's outcome in the clash of arms at sea.

FINAL PLANS FOR WAR

During the spring of 1939 Darlan watched the Entente spring back to life. At the end of March, after Hitler had seized Czechoslovakia, the French and British military chiefs met in London. Although the initial British commitment of four divisions, in contrast to eighty-eight in 1918, appeared small, the Entente was back in business.[21] Similar conversations between the French and British naval staffs took place during the spring and summer. In July, after Darlan had traveled to London for conversations with Admiral Sir Dudley Pound and his staff, the French Atlantic Squadron and the British Home Fleet joined in maneuvers off the coast of Scotland.[22] The French and British naval staffs grew closer during those months, but it remained to be seen whether they could agree on important questions of strategy. As Chief of the smaller of the two navies, Darlan would have to follow the lead of the stronger naval power whose interests did not coincide entirely with those of France.

A Directive of Admiral Darlan, dated August 3, while the Anglo-French staff talks were still in progress, reveals that the Admiral's strategic thinking had come into sharp focus. He continued to regard Germany as the principal enemy, but now he abandoned entirely any thought of attacking her in the north. Germany could be reached only through the Mediterranean, he believed. "It is therefore in the Mediterranean, and even in the central Mediterranean," he argued, "that it is necessary to act. The other theatres are secondary."[23]

Now his ideas fell neatly into place. Germany, he suggested, would not likely leave her warships cooped up in Helgoland Bay. She would instead send them out for operations in the Atlantic. But that threat now seemed not to worry him. Moving quickly to the main point, he insisted that

the Atlantic has less importance than the Mediterranean. As soon as the question of the Mediterranean is settled, everything will be simplified. That will be particularly true for the Far East. In summary, the importance of operations in the Mediterranean will be predominant.[24]

Darlan's strategy would therefore center on the Mediterranean, where France and Britain in concert held the advantage. Darlan would attack the Italian fleet wherever possible. He envisioned naval artillery attacks against Italian port cities. He was also prepared to cooperate with the Royal Navy in operations against

Libya and Sicily. He expected heavy naval engagements in the central and western Mediterranean from Sardinia to the Balearics. He also considered striking eventually at Germany through the Balkans, but he said nothing about the timing of that operation.[25]

But Darlan and his British allies did not agree on every issue. Darlan wanted tight liaison down to the tactical level. The British preferred flexible liaison that went little further than the sharing of codes, the exchange of liaison officers at high command levels, and the assigning of patrol zones and command responsibilities. Nor did the British share Darlan's assumption of the primacy of the Mediterranean and of its importance as a staging area for operations in the Balkans. He thought the British had concentrated too much sea power in the Channel and the North Sea.[26]

Returning to Britain on August 8, Darlan met Admiral Pound at Portsmouth to confirm the agreements already worked out by the two naval staffs. These agreements called for the French Raiding Force to operate out of Brest for service in the Atlantic, as Darlan had desired. The North Sea and the remainder of the Atlantic would fall under British responsibility. Further, the two navies would divide responsibility for patrolling the Mediterranean: the British in the eastern basin and the French in the western.[27] To Darlan's satisfaction, French ships would guard Gibraltar against any Italian threat to the British squadron there. Liaison officers would be exchanged only at high command levels. The agreement included other technical and operational provisions such as the use of each other's harbors and facilities, exchange of codes, and the bombardment of Italian ports in response to any Italian aggression. Darlan raised the question of combined operations against Spain and against Germany through the Balkans, but Pound gave them no support.[28]

London, preoccupied with the defense of British home waters, was not ready to commit large assets against Italy. British naval policy at the outset of war was to take the initiative against the Italian navy only later, after the Royal Navy had completed its buildup. The Admiralty was unwilling to risk its heaviest ships in tactical operations against Italian coastal targets, preferring to withhold the battleships anchored at Alexandria should they be needed in the Far East.[29] London's cautious attitude reflects the fact that the Entente's naval power was stretched so thin that the Alexandria squadron had to serve as a deterrent against both Italy and Japan.

Darlan and his British allies therefore differed in their Mediterranean strategy. But despite his talk of a Balkan campaign, Darlan was on the right track. He understood the problem connecting the Mediterranean to the Far East. And he understood the Entente's overall naval weakness. His solution, brilliant and daring, was to confront both problems simultaneously. He would mount a major combined effort to destroy Italian naval power early in the war. The Alexandria squadron could then be moved to Singapore. He had that solution in mind when he stated in his Directive of August 3 that "as soon as the question of the Mediterranean is settled, everything will be simplified. That will be particularly true for the Far East."[30] Darlan's concept of engaging the Italian navy early in the war to redress the global naval balance was not unrealistic, as Italian naval power was no match for the combined might of the Entente.

Darlan's thinking assumed British control of the Atlantic. He knew that the Entente held a huge quantitative naval advantage over Germany. By 1939 the Reich's three pocket battleships had been reinforced by nine cruisers and the 35,000-ton battleships *Scharnhorst* and *Gneisenau*, which matched Darlan's *Dunkerque* and *Strasbourg*. Still unfinished on the French side were *Jean Bart* and *Richelieu*, and on the German, *Tirpitz* and *Bismarck*. But the combined naval might of the Entente, which included British capital ships and a clear numerical superiority in cruisers and destroyers, far surpassed that of Germany. Although many of the British ships were technically inferior to the Reich's newest ships, Darlan expected the Royal Navy to control the Atlantic.

But London saw it differently. First, the Reich would likely threaten the North Sea with her big ships and send fast raiders into the vast Atlantic to prey upon shipping and to tie up large Entente assets. Second, Japan held a clear naval advantage in Asia. The combined effect of these two threats led London to concentrate large assets in home waters and spread the remainder around the globe. Faced with the urgent responsibility of maintaining the economic life of the British Isles, and protecting the Empire, London placed highest priority on guarding near and distant sea lanes, rather than attacking the Italian fleet.

In contrast, Darlan's strategy assumed that geography afforded the Entente an opportunity to concentrate its naval power against the Axis at its weakest point. He was confident that the Entente could strike a fatal blow against Italy early in the war. With the Italian navy no longer a threat, the problem of Entente naval weakness would be largely solved. Darlan's strategy was not without merit. It was risky only because London had neglected the fleet between the wars in pursuit of naval disarmament. His strategy also hinged upon Italy's being in the war at the outset.

COUNTDOWN TO WAR WITH THE REICH

Returning to Paris after his meeting with Admiral Pound, Darlan threw himself into the work of making the final preparations for war. He no longer took leisurely weekends at Saint-Malo. Although the tensions of the Danzig crisis had already settled over Europe, Parisians took their customary August vacations, so that the capital was nearly closed down when French reservists passed through the city toward the military front. During these weeks Darlan usually arrived in office about 9:30 following a brief walk in the Bois de Boulogne. The communications of the previous night, already sorted by his staff, awaited him.[31]

The news of the Hitler-Stalin Pact of August 23 prompted Darlan to take the final measures to prepare the fleet for war. Each morning during the last week of peace he met with his Chiefs-of-Staff in his second floor office at the navy building on Rue Royale. Captain C. S. Holland, British naval attaché, sat in. Captain Henri Ballande, a brilliant young officer recently assigned to Darlan's staff, recorded on the 24th that the Admiral ordered his theater operational staffs to take their positions. He sent warning messages to merchant ships at sea, ordered aerial surveillance of the waters opposite Brest, Toulon, Bizerte, and Oran, and ordered French naval attachés to report to their assigned posts with the British navy. The navy was put on full alert. Reservists had already been ordered to report to their stations.[32] At the end of the month, combined naval maneuvers were held in the Far East, to impress Tokyo with Anglo-French unity.[33]

On Sunday, the 27th Darlan assumed the function of Commander-in-Chief of French Maritime Forces. He announced the appointment and confirmed his headquarters staff in their posts.[34] Among them were Rear Admiral Maurice Le Luc, Deputy to the Commander-in-Chief, and Rear Admiral Jean-Leon Bourragué, Chief-of-Staff. Other members of his headquarters staff were Captain Paul Auphan, Deputy Chief-of-Staff, Captain Henri Ballande, member of the cabinet, and Chief of the Secretariat, Louis de la Monneraye.

When France went to war with Germany on September 3, Darlan had already learned of Italian and Japanese neutrality.[35] Darlan now would have to endure the frustrations of standing by as the Italian fleet sheltered itself behind an unfriendly neutrality. He could not afford to reduce significantly his Mediterranean squadron, as the Italian fleet remained capable of striking a powerful blow. Darlan could see that Italian neutrality had deprived the Entente of the only naval war that afforded it an opportunity for quick victories.

Mussolini had chosen neutrality because he expected the Entente to confront him with precisely the kind of war Darlan had wanted to wage. In his message to Hitler of August 25, Il Duce backed away from war, demanding that Germany send at once "military supplies and materials to resist the attack which the French and English would predominantly direct against us."[36] A message of the next day insisted that "the French and British would attack Italy in full force by land, sea, and in the air, immediately war broke out."[37] And three days later, German Ambassador Hans Mackensen informed Berlin of Mussolini's motives, reporting that "in the event of war Italy would have to bear the whole brunt of a naval attack, because Germany is practically invulnerable, or only slightly vulnerable, thanks to her favorable geographical position."[38] Mussolini's motives reflect exactly what Darlan had long understood: that Italy was vulnerable to combined Anglo-French naval power in the Mediterranean.

The war at sea opened in the manner that Darlan had dreaded. The *Graf Spee* and the *Deutschland* were already at sea. On the first day of the war a German submarine sank the British passenger liner, *Athenia*. The British declared a blockade of the German coastline. Neutral Italy, however, constituted a huge hole in the blockade. Within days a pattern of the naval war was set as the ships of the Entente began the onerous duty of manning the blockade, escorting convoys, searching for German raiders in the Atlantic, and keeping watch on the Italian fleet. It was the kind of war Darlan had planned in 1937 but not the kind he wanted to fight in 1939.

NOTES

1. SHM, 1BB2 EMG/SE, Carton 218, "Décret VA Darlan, CEC des FNF, à la couverture," 9 June 1938.

2. Amiral Jules Docteur, *La Grande énigme de la guerre: Darlan, Amiral de la flotte* (Paris: Éditions de la Couronne, 1949), 36.

3. Alain Darlan, *L'Amiral Darlan parle* (Paris: Amiot-Dumont, 1952), 39.

4. Jacques Raphaël-Leygues and François Flohic, *Darlan* (Paris: Plon, 1986), 64-65.

5. Ibid.

6. SHM, 1BB2 EMG/SE, Carton 208, "L'Angleterre et la France pouvent-elles soutenir un Conflit contre l'Allemagne et l'Italie," 24 January 1939.

7. In February 1939 the United States naval attaché in Paris reported articles from the French press expressing the same thought. *Excelsior* reported opinion that the French fleet is not strong enough to protect simultaneously the homeland and the colonies. It also reported that the Royal Navy was not large enough to protect Britain's global maritime interests. USNA, RG 38, ONI, C-9-e, Reg. 19447-C.

8. SHM, 1BB2 EMG/SE, Carton 208, "L'Angleterre et la France pouvent-elles soutenir un Conflit contre l'Allemagne et l'Italie."

9. Ibid.

10. Ibid.

11. Ibid.

12. Ibid.

13. Ibid.

14. SHM, 1BB2 EMG/SE, Carton 213, "Conférences des Services d'Action," 12 April 1939.

15. Ibid., 8 June 1939.

16. In August 1938 he had prepared a personal study to govern French ship movements in the event of war against Germany or Italy or both. See SHM, 1BB2 EMG/SE, Carton 214, "ÉTUDE sur la RÉPARTITION des FORCES NAVALES FRANÇAISES en TEMPS de PAIX et leur UTILIZATION en TEMPS de GUERRE."

17. SHM, 1BB2 EMG/SE, Carton 207, "Réflections sur la Situation Actuelle," June 1939.

18. Ibid.

19. Ibid. He had studied that option earlier at the Center for Advanced Naval Studies. See Hervé Coutau-Bégarie and Claude Huan, *Darlan* (Paris: Fayard, 1989), 147.

20. SHM, 1BB2 EMG/SE, Carton 207, "Réflections sur la Situation Actuelle."

21. Henri Ballande, *De l'Amiruté à Bikini* (Paris: Presses de la Cité, 1972), 25-26.

22. Ibid., 13-14.

23. SHM, 1BB2 EMG/SE, Carton 208, "Directives de l'Amiral de la Flotte, Chef d'État-Major Général; Comment se Déroulera la Guerre Maritime?" 3 August 1939. This document is a summary of his remarks in a staff meeting.

24. Ibid.

25. Ibid.

26. Ibid.

27. French warships had begun to concentrate at Gibraltar during the spring of 1939. See USNA, RG 38, ONI, Reg. # 21555-P, April 21 report of the United States Naval Attaché in Rome.

28. Coutau-Bégarie and Huan, *Darlan*, 150-151; Jacques Mordal, *La Marine à l'Epreuve* (Paris: Plon, 1955), 17; Darlan, *L'Amiral Darlan parle*, 40; SHM, 1BB2 EMG/SE, Carton 182, "Résumé de la Conférence tenue le 8 août 1939 à bord de l'Enchantress entre l'Amiral de la Flotte F. Darlan et l'Admiral of the Fleet Sir Dudley Pound," 8 August 1939; SHM, 1BB2 EMG/SE, Carton 182, "Mémento," 8 August 1939.

29. Viscount Cunningham of Hyndhope, *A Sailor's Odyssey*, 2 volumes (London: Arrow Books, 1961), I, 153-153.

30. SHM, 1BB2 EMG/SE, Carton 208, "Directives de l'Amiral de la Flotte.

31. Ballande, *De l'Amirauté à Bikini*, 37.

32. Ibid., 39.

33. USNA, RG 38, ONI, C-9-e, Reg. # 21555 q, Naval Attaché report from Rome, 25 August 1939.

34. SHM, 1BB2 EMG/SE, Carton 233, "Instruction No. 1," 27 August 1939.

35. Ballande, *De l'Amirauté à Bikini*, 41.

36. DGFP, Series D, VII, 286.

37. Ibid., 326.

38. Ibid., 431.

CHAPTER 8

Strategy of Coalition Warfare

As the war on the French frontier settled into a pattern of inactivity, Darlan watched the naval war flare into action. On September 2, 1939 he recorded in his diary reports that five German capital ships had slipped into the Atlantic.[1] But only the *Deutschland* and the *Graf Spee* had gone there. Nevertheless, two raiders at sea tied up large Allied assets. Darlan shifted the Raiding Force toward the Azores and moved units of the Mediterranean Squadron from Toulon toward Gibraltar.[2] The Raiding Force made no contact with enemy surface ships. Darlan recorded on September 18 that twelve German U-boats had been destroyed or damaged by Allied action, and that the British carrier *Courageous* had been sunk by a German submarine.[3]

In early September, Darlan moved his headquarters to Maintenon, a town about forty miles southwest of Paris where underground telephone and telegraph lines from the south and the west converged. From there he could communicate directly with his principal naval bases, with Algiers by underwater cable, and with overseas posts by short-wave radio.[4]

CLASHING STRATEGIES OF WAR

The naval war put the alliance to its first test. Britain, already under naval attack and dependent upon overseas trade, had adopted a defensive strategy of escorting convoys and searching the Atlantic for prowling U-boats and surface raiders.[5] In contrast, Darlan was more interested in the Mediterranean, and in the Balkans. Impatient to get on with the war, he wrote in his diary on September 8 that "it is urgent...to determine the manner by which the war ought to be conducted."[6]

On September 20 the French War Committee, chaired by Premier Edouard Daladier and including Darlan, General Maurice Gamelin, and several others, considered the risks that a strong Italian presence in the Mediterranean imposed on any Balkan venture. They agreed on the necessity of military aid to Turkey, Greece, and Yugoslavia. Paris would launch a diplomatic effort to keep Italy neutral, and Daladier would request a meeting of the Interallied War Committee for September 22.[7]

When the committee met as scheduled, Anglo-French differences on war strategy quickly emerged. Daladier proposed the sending of an expeditionary corps to Salonika or Istanbul, to blunt any German advance toward the Mediterranean. Prime Minister Neville Chamberlain, observing that the Germans could invade the Balkans in any event, replied that the British military staff had already made known its position on the question of a Balkan operation. Following a lively discussion that amplified Anglo-French disagreements, they decided to submit the question to their military staffs and to approach Turkey and Italy through diplomatic channels to see if they would cooperate.[8] So Darlan's Balkan strategy was shelved without the embarrassment of rejecting it outright.

As British reinforcements arrived in France at a painfully slow rate, Darlan stretched his mind to find a way to gain victory through sea power. The problem remained that the Reich could not easily be reached by sea. His October diary entries reveal his growing discontent with the management of the war.[9] He was convinced that France must fight on to victory, but he dreaded the thought of a long war and a burdensome blockade that would test the endurance of both sides. He thought the Germans would be tempted to strike into Scandinavia, or perhaps the Balkans.[10]

In early November, Darlan received Winston Churchill, First Lord of the Admiralty, and a delegation of British naval officers at Maintenon. They talked navy business, including the importance of rushing to completion the *Jean Bart* and *Richelieu.* Churchill offered to fit French warships with Asdics, sonar submarine detection equipment used on British ships.[11] The meeting was cordial, except for Darlan's awkward explanation of the absence of Churchill's civilian opposite, Minister of Marine Cesar Campinchi, who under the French system did not join naval professionals to discuss operations.[12] Despite this affront, the first meeting between Darlan and Churchill established a cordial relationship. But Churchill brought nothing new about carrying the war to the Germans.

In November the Anglo-French staffs considered launching aerial attacks against Germany, but the idea was abandoned on grounds that France would suffer heavy reprisals. Knowing the weakness of French aviation, Darlan had no zeal for an aerial war. He still had not abandoned the idea of a Balkan campaign. The plan was discussed again with the British chiefs at Vincennes on December 11 with no decision.[13] The talks with Italy and Turkey continued without results. Moreover, the British Mediterranean command opposed a Balkan venture.[14]

Toward the end of 1939 Darlan's morale began to sag. He complained of German propaganda sapping the morale of French troops, of communist mischief on the home front, and of sagging civilian morale. He complained that the generals had prepared the army poorly for war. The British, too, were unprepared, and "after having done all they could for twenty years to prevent France having a navy, they are hanging on to my shirttail so that the French fleet will help them meet their responsibilities." He added that *we must conquer* if we wish to remain free, and afterwards we will have to put down communism."[15]

TWO FLAWED PLANS

Darlan's growing anti-Bolshevism was nourished by a December 22 staff report hinting of the enlistment of another ally, Italy, reportedly miffed at Berlin's cozy relations with communist Russia.[16] The study posed options for waging economic warfare against Germany and Russia. French aircraft, overflying Turkish territory with Ankara's permission, would strike at the Caucasus oil fields from bases in Syria. With Russian oil production interrupted, Soviet agriculture would grind to a halt, the Soviet regime would collapse, and Russian wheat shipments to Germany would cease.[17]

The other option was Allied intervention in the Russo-Finnish war. Allied troops would embark at the Norwegian port of Narvik, advance to the Swedish city of Lulea on the Gulf of Bothnia, and capture the iron ore mines near Gallivare, which supplied the Reich with iron ore for her war industry. From Lulea the Allied armies would move into nearby Finland, where they could expect to encounter Italian volunteers fighting communism.[18] On the same day that Darlan read the report, London considered a proposal to plant mines in Norwegian waters to blunt the flow of iron ore from Narvik to the Reich while the frozen Bay of Bothnia closed the eastern route.[19]

Additional staff studies of the Caucasus and Scandinavian options guided Darlan's thinking in early 1940. He turned increasingly hostile toward the Soviet Union, who continued to flood France with propaganda.[20] With the Allies barely able to manage a war against Germany, it seems incredible that Darlan would have contemplated a Soviet war. But as Finland's stout resistance to Russian aggression rekindled anti-Soviet sentiment in France, the Daladier government came under heavy public pressure to help Finland.

In January Darlan drafted a plan to seize the Soviet oil fields. It projected the sending of a strong naval force to the Black Sea. A military force would land near Armavir, seize the city and its pipeline, and thereby deprive Russia of the greater part of its motor fuel. He decided that Baku could easily be taken: "Isolated from the rest of the U.S.S.R. by this action, the region of Baku, after an interval, would fall like a ripe fruit--and perhaps also its installations intact--into the hands of whoever occupies ARMAVIR."[21]

A northern strategy, which Darlan outlined toward the middle of January, also went beyond the staff proposal. Daladier had asked him to plan an Anglo-French operation against Petsamo, the Finnish arctic port recently taken by the Soviets.[22] Accordingly, Darlan modified the northern strategy to include the seizure of Petsamo. An Allied naval force would defeat any Russian ships there. Finnish troops would recapture the city, and an Allied expeditionary force would occupy it. It would be necessary, he noted, to have a base in Norway, which would require diplomatic arrangements in advance.[23]

Darlan reasoned that the alternatives to these operations would be either a costly attack against the Siegfried Line or a protracted war of attrition. In either case the war would be longer and more costly. He concluded that the Entente should strike at the Soviets, either through Scandinavia or the Black Sea.[24] He favored the latter, thinking it easier to reach the Caucasus and more important to deprive Germany of Russian oil than Swedish iron.[25] In either case, the Allies would find themselves at war with the Soviets.

London had already expressed its opposition to a Soviet war.[26] Nevertheless, Darlan submitted a study of France's options to Daladier and Gamelin on January 23. The next day, Daladier received Darlan and the other service chiefs to review the study. They agreed, in view of the urgent need to help Finland, to request a meeting of the Interallied Supreme Council.[27]

FOCUS ON SCANDINAVIA

When Darlan met with the Interallied Supreme Council in Paris on February 5, 1940 the stage was set for serious Anglo-French misunderstandings. Daladier, willing to accept the risks of a Russian war, proposed Darlan's plan to seize Petsamo and simultaneously interdict the flow of Swedish iron to Germany. But the British, opposed to a Russian war, pressed for an operation through Norway to seize the Swedish mines and later push on to Finland. The Supreme Council finally settled upon the British plan. The expedition would embark at Narvik and move by rail toward the mines. Scheduled for early March, the operation would follow an Allied request for free passage through Norway and Sweden.[28]

Daladier intended to send aid to Finland, but the British aimed only at seizing the Swedish mines. Since the operation would proceed under British command, Daladier would have to trust his British allies to move afterward into Finland. Darlan supported the British plan, as he was eager to seize the Swedish mines. But what the Entente would do in the likely event of Norwegian and Swedish refusal to grant free passage remained unclear.[29] London, cautious about any violation of neutral rights, assumed that free entry would have to be gained before launching the expedition. Daladier and Darlan, less sensitive to neutral rights, began their preparations with the view that the project would be undertaken in any event, or if necessary redirected toward Petsamo.[30]

Returning to London, Chamberlain soon learned that the Allies would not likely gain free entry into Scandinavia, which raised doubts about continuing with the project.[31] In France, however, Darlan rushed forward with preparations for the Narvik expedition. Impatient, he was willing to force Norway's hand. On the 6th he ordered warships to assemble at Brest, and he arranged for troopships and cargo vessels to proceed toward ports of embarkation. When British destroyers captured the German ship *Altmark* in Norwegian territorial waters on February 16, Darlan thought that London ought to have exploited the incident to force entry into Norway.[32]

Darlan noticed that the British chiefs seemed to hesitate. On February 19, London notified Paris that the British force could not put to sea until March 12. Since the Russians had already launched a new offensive, Darlan could see that any help for Finland would have to be sent soon. Accordingly, he wrote Gamelin on the 22nd suggesting that French units be sent ahead to arrive at Narvik on March 12.[33] Nothing came of the proposal, but Darlan continued his preparations until Finnish resistance finally ended on March 13. By that time he had assembled a sizable fleet. With British preparations nearing completion, he would continue the Narvik project despite the collapse of Finland. But on the 15th Daladier ordered the force dispersed.[34] Four days later he fell from office.

INTERVENTION IN NORWAY

Darlan's relationship with the new Premier, Paul Reynaud, got off to a poor start. In a March 24 letter to Campinchi, Darlan complained that Reynaud had failed to notify him of a meeting of the War Committee and had discussed naval business in his absence.[35] Although the letter headed off future incidents, Darlan would have no confidence in Reynaud. Further, the Admiral's confidence in Gamelin steadily eroded. Stresses within the French leadership and growing tensions between London and Paris hampered Allied efforts to find an effective war strategy.

Meanwhile, Darlan had kept alive his plans to seize Russian oil and Swedish iron.[36] But when the Interallied Supreme Council met on March 28, it adopted instead British plans to lay mines in Norwegian waters and to mine German canals and rivers. Known respectively as Operations "Wilfred" and "Royal Marine," these projects would be launched April 4 or 5. Darlan supported both projects, expecting them to provoke a German reaction that would justify an Allied occupation of Narvik.[37] But two days later, the French War Committee, fearing reprisals, rejected "Royal Marine." "Wilfred" remained on schedule for April 8.[38]

On March 28, after the decision to lay the mines, Darlan remarked to Gamelin that the German reaction would be swift, and that the Allies must quickly assemble an expeditionary force to counter any enemy military action.[39] Two days later, in a letter to Daladier, he predicted that Germany would react the day after the laying of the mines. He proposed that a Franco-British expeditionary force stand by to strike into Norway in April.[40]

Only later did Darlan learn that Berlin's Scandinavian plans had been drawn independently of "Wilfred."[41] But he was on target to anticipate German intervention in Norway. He therefore moved promptly to prepare another Scandinavian expedition, informing Gamelin on April 2 of measures he had taken to assemble four fast cruisers at Brest to deliver the first units. Three days later Reynaud ordered preparation of a French response to any German action against Norway. Darlan immediately ordered cargo ships to assemble at Brest, and he contacted the British Admiralty to arrange the details of a combined operation.[42]

The German invasion of Denmark and Norway on April 9 came as no surprise. At a War Cabinet meeting that morning, Darlan supported Reynaud's proposal to strike into Norway, and he proposed implementation of a plan held in reserve to advance into Belgium. The War Cabinet decided in principle to go forward with both plans. Early that same afternoon, Darlan informed Gamelin that the four cruisers remained at Brest, ready to move troops to Norway, and that other ships would be ready three days later.[43] The Belgian option, which made more sense than a counter-attack in Norway, would have shortened the front to correct a weakness in the defensive line opposite Germany. It fell easily within the limits of Allied military capabilities. And the German aggression in Scandinavia would have justified Allied violation of Belgian neutrality.

The Frenchmen rushed off that afternoon to London where the Supreme Council agreed that the Norwegian expedition must be pushed forward swiftly. But implementation of Darlan's proposal to move into Belgium was subordinated to receipt of an invitation from Brussels.[44] The Allies therefore responded in the area of relative weakness, as opposed to that of greatest military capability. It dispersed Allied assets and wasted an opportunity to improve positions on the most important front.

Geography imposed a heavy burden on the Norwegian operation. When British and German naval forces clashed in the North Sea on April 9, Darlan's heavy ships were too far away to intervene. By April 13, only one French cruiser had arrived on the scene.[45] And despite Darlan's efficient preparations, the Allies were unable to establish strong beachheads. The first French echelon departing Brest on April 12 proceeded without its heavy equipment. Darlan figured that it would require twenty-seven ships to transport one full division to Norway, and that he could deliver only one division per month.[46] The British could send but eleven battalions.[47] In contrast, the Germans sent six divisions at the outset to seize key Norwegian airfields.[48]

The Allied counteroffensive moved slowly. The first French units arrived in Norway on the 19th, ten days after the German landing. British forces landing north and south of Trondheim, and at Namsos and Andalsnes, were hard-pressed from the beginning. Darlan wrote on May 2 that the British had only carrier aircraft to oppose German land-based airpower.[49] Next day, the Allied force was withdrawn from Namsos and Andalsnes. Farther north, a small Allied force had landed near Narvik. On May 8 Darlan wrote optimistically that if the Allies could lay hold to Narvik and move against the Swedish iron ore, the "balance of the affair will stay clearly in our favor."[50] He noted that the French navy had committed eighty-eight ships to the Norwegian campaign. Between April 12 and 23 a French infantry division had been shipped out of Brest, and delivery of another would be completed by May 10.[51]

The Allies finally occupied Narvik in late May, but they could not hang on in Norway. The campaign failed, not because of poor management, but because the Allies worked at a huge logistical disadvantage. German supply lines were short, enabling the Reich to deliver reinforcements quickly. German aircraft flew directly from Denmark to bases in Norway. For Darlan, the problems of logistics were formidable. He observed on May 10 that the distance between Brest and Narvik was three thousand kilometers.[52] He and his allies had chosen to fight in an area where the enemy held the advantage of interior lines.

The struggle for Norway tested Darlan's confidence in his allies and his government. Although Darlan maintained a correct posture toward the British chiefs, he commented in his diary on April 27: "The British Admiralty, totally depressed, lacks offensive spirit." And on May 3 he noted that "the political situation, in France and in England, is very troubled. The two governments are very shaken; that of Chamberlain because it is soft and hesitant, that of Reynaud because it is divided, disorganized, and impotent."[53] Reynaud held on, but the Chamberlain Government gave way on May 10 to a National Government under Churchill.

A VISIT FROM MARSHAL PÉTAIN

Darlan blamed Allied war failures on inefficiencies and overlapping responsibilities within the French, British, and Interallied command structure. On May 5 he expressed his views to Marshal Philippe Pétain, Ambassador to Spain, who visited the Admiral at Maintenon. The Marshal was impressed with naval efficiency: "At last I see something that works."[54] And he commented, "We must back up one another, I am counting on you."[55]

In a letter to the Marshal, Darlan proposed reform of the wartime committee structure. He would retain the Supreme Council. It would delegate operations to a smaller Military War Committee headed by the Premier, who by law would be Minister of National Defense.[56] To Darlan, organizational efficiency was the key. He was not the only Allied leader who held that view. Winston Churchill complained in his memoirs about the endless delays in making decisions, and of the futility of waging war by committees.[57]

Organizational problems were not, however, the main cause of the weak war effort. Allied war strategy was badly flawed, failing to match the military capabilities of the Entente. Instead, it dispersed Allied assets and contributed to the greater disaster yet to come. Entente war planners were too confident about the security of the front opposite Germany. Darlan had been on the right track in 1937 when he drafted plans to protect the sea lanes to assure a steady volume of supplies and reinforcements to the military front. Easily within the Entente's capabilities, that strategy might have mobilized the full industrial and manpower resources of the French and British empires to support the war in France. But Darlan turned instead to wasteful offensive ventures on the periphery, all of which were strategic dead-ends. The weak war effort was the result of poor strategic judgment on the part of the entire Allied command, including Darlan.

NOTES

1. SHM, 1BB2 EMG/SE, Carton 208, Darlan Diary, 2 September 1939 (hereinafter cited as Darlan Diary).

2. Ibid.

3. Ibid., 18 September 1939.

4. Henri Ballande, *De l'Amirauté à Bikini* (Paris: Presses de la Cité, 1972), 49-50. See also Jacques Raphaël-Leygues and François Flohic, *Darlan* (Paris: Plon, 1986), 71-74; and Hervé Coutau-Bégarie and Huan, *Darlan* (Paris: Fayard, 1989), 171 ff.

5. Winston S. Churchill, *The Second World War,* 6 volumes (Boston: Houghton Mifflin, 1948-1953), I, 426-434.

6. Darlan Diary, 8 September 1939.

7. Ibid., 20 September 1939.

8. Ibid., 22 September 1939.

9. Ibid., 30 September--10 October 1939.

10. SHM , 1BB2 EMG/SE, Carton 208, untitled document, 11 October 1939.

11. Darlan Diary, undated entry; Churchill, *The Second World War*, I, 499-504.

12. Churchill, *The Second World War*, I, 499-500.

13. Darlan Diary, 24 November and 11 December 1939.

14. Viscount Cunningham of Hyndhope, *A Sailor's Odyssey*, 2 volumes (London: Arrow Books, 1961), I, 161-162.

15. Darlan Diary, 14 December 1939.

16. SHM, 1BB2 EMG/SE, Carton 207, Untitled Report, 22 December 1939.

17. Ibid.

18. Ibid.

19. Churchill, *The Second World War*, I, 538-548.

20. See SHM, 1BB2 EMG/SE, Carton 207, "Note," 12 January 1940; and Carton 207, "Conditions d'une Intervention Éventuelle Allié dans les Pays Scandinaves," 3 January 1940.

21. SHM, 1BB2 EMG/SE, Carton 207, "Note sur les moyens d'arrêter les pétroles du Caucase," 26 January 1940.

22. See Coutau-Bégarie and Huan, *Darlan*, 195.

23. SHM, 1BB2 EMG/SE, Carton 207, "Opérations Sous la Finlande du Nord," undated.

24. SHM, 1BB2 EMG/SE, Carton 208, Untitled note, 22 January 1940.

25. SHM, 1BB2 EMG/SE, Carton 207, "Note Complémentaire sur l'Arrêt du Minerai de Fer Suédois et du Pétrole du Caucase," undated.

26. Coutau-Bégarie and Huan, *Darlan*, 195.

27. SHM, 1BB2 EMG/SE, Carton 207, "Note sur l'étude du 23 Janvier 1940 et les décisions de la première expédition B.K.," 15 January 1940.

28. SHM, 1BB2 EMG/SE, Carton 207, "Première Tentative d'Expédition Scandinave," 10 March 1940; Churchill, *The Second World War*, I, 560-561.

29. Churchill, *The Second World War*, I, 561.

30. See Sir Llewellyn Woodward, *British Foreign Policy in the Second World War*, 5 volumes (London: Her Majesty's Stationery Office, 1970), I, 80.

31. Ibid., 83ff.

32. SHM, 1BB2 EMG/SE, Carton 207, "Première Tentative d'Expédition Scandinave," 10 March 1940.

33. Ibid., and SHM, 1BB2 EMG/SE, Carton 207, "Note sur la Possibilité d'Accélérer l'Opération," 22 Février 1940.

34. SHM, 1BB2 EMG/SE, Carton 207, "Première Tentative d'Expédition Scandinave."

35. SHM, 1BB2 EMG/SE, Carton 208, "No. 32 F.M.F.O.," 24 March 1940.

36. Coutau-Bégarie and Huan, *Darlan*, 200-201.

37. SHM, 1BB2 EMG/SE, Carton 207, "Mouillage De Mines Dans Les Eaux Norvégiennes," 10 May 1940.

38. Darlan Diary, 30 March--8 April 1940.

39. SHM, 1BB2 EMG/SE, Carton 207, "Mouillage De Mines Dans Les Eaux Norvégiennes."

40. SHM, 1BB2 EMG/SE, Carton 207, "L'Amiral de la Flotte F. Darlan...à Monsieur le Ministre de la Défense Nationale...," 30 March 1940.

41. SHM, 1BB2 EMG/SE, Carton 207, "Conséquences des Mouillages de Mines dans les Eaux Scandinaves," 10 May 1940.

42. SHM, 1BB2 EMG/SE, Carton 207, "Avril 1940. Résumé Succinct" [of governmental decisions and correspondence with Gamelin], April 1940; and Carton 207, "Histoire de l'Expédition B.K. bis," 11 April 1940.

43. Darlan Diary, 9 April 1940; SHM, 1BB2 EMG/SE, Carton 207, "Résumé Succinct." See also Paul Reynaud, *In the Thick of the Fight*, trans. James D. Lambert (New York: 1955), 270, 283; and Maurice Gustave Gamelin, *Servir la guerre*, 3 volumes (Paris: Plon, 1947), III, 315.

44. Churchill, *The Second World War*, I, 599-600.

45. SHM, 1BB2 EMG/SE, Carton 207, "L'Amiral de la Flotte Darlan...à Monsieur le Ministre de la Défense Nationale," 13 April 1940.

46. Ibid., 12 April 1940.

47. Churchill, *The Second World War*, I, 599.

48. Larry H. Addington, *The Patterns of War Since the Eighteenth Century* (Bloomington: Indiana University Press, 1984), 186.

49. SHM, 1BB2 EMG/SE, Carton 207, "Amiral de la Flotte à Monsieur le Président," 2 May 1940.

50. SHM, 1BB2 EMG/SE, Carton 207, "La Situation Maritime," 8 May 1940.

51. Ibid.

52. SHM, 1BB2 EMG/SE, Carton 207, "Conséquences des Mouillages de Mines dans les Eaux Scandinaves."

53. Darlan Diary, April 27 and May 5, 1940.

54. Alain Darlan, *L'Amiral Darlan parle* (Paris: Amiot-Dumont, 1952), 50.

55. Darlan Diary, 5 May 1940.

56. Darlan, *L'Amiral Darlan parle*, 51-52.

57. Churchill, *The Second World War*, I, 580.

CHAPTER 9

The Failure of Coalition Warfare

The great German offensive against France in May of 1940 thrust the naval war into the background. Only toward the end of that campaign did the focus shift back to Darlan and the navy. During several critical days in June, Darlan's loyalty to his government was put to the test.

WAR IN THE WEST

When the offensive opened on May 10, Darlan noted in his diary that the German attack was strong.[1] Anglo-French armies plunged into Belgium toward the Demer and Dyle Rivers. But as the Allied armies advanced, strong German armored divisions struck through the Ardennes Forest, punching through the thin French line along the Meuse River near Sedan. Moving swiftly, they threatened to trap the Allied armies advancing into Belgium.

Darlan's diary entry of May 14 reveals his reaction to the tragedy unfolding before him. "There is no inspiration," he wrote, "no esprit de corps, neither among the officers waxing like bad bureaucrats, nor among the men rotted by pacifist theories taught by communist teachers." He wrote that panic reigned in Paris, that "the Quai d'Orsay is burning, burning its papers. Grotesque and disgusting."[2] His letter that day to his wife expressed satisfaction at the formation in London of a government under Churchill.[3]

On the 17th he noted in his diary the turning of the German offensive toward Calais, to encircle the Allied flank in Belgium. He noted Marshal Pétain's appointment as Minister of State, and on the 20th he recorded that General Maxime Weygand had succeeded Gamelin as military Commander-in-Chief.[4] Encouraged at the appointments, he thought that the situation would soon improve.[5] But he was mistaken. When the critical battle was fought near Arras, German panzer divisions were already nearing the Channel. Allied attacks both north and south of Arras were poorly coordinated. In the confusion, Lord Gort, commander of the British Expeditionary Force, undertook a defensive maneuver that the French mistook as the beginning of a general retreat toward the Channel. The German corridor held, and the Allied flank was trapped.

On May 25 Reynaud ordered a bridgehead around Dunkirk, and Weygand decided to form a front along the Somme. Expecting the bridgehead to hold, Darlan next day sent Auphan to Dover to coordinate efforts with the British to reinforce it. But Weygand telephoned that sending reinforcements would be impossible.[6] He had decided to evacuate the troops and to concentrate all French assets on the Somme.

DUNKIRK EVACUATION

Misunderstandings about the Dunkirk evacuation emerged on May 28 when Auphan reported from Dover that the British had been preparing for eight days to evacuate their armies. "That," Darlan concluded, "explains Gort's move to retreat, despite Weygand's orders, and the British premeditation to pull everything out of the north without advising us of it."[7] But in fact Gort did not make the decision to advance toward the sea until May 26. Auphan's report of British preparations beginning as early as May 20 was correct, but London had not yet decided to evacuate the Expeditionary Force.[8]

The Dunkirk evacuation, usually regarded as a British affair, was an Allied operation with important French participation that began on May 28. Darlan's first act was to create a separate command for the Pas de Calais flotilla with responsibility for sending ships north. When the Interallied Supreme Council met in Paris on Friday, May 31, Darlan had already ordered Admiral Jean Abrial, Commander North, to evacuate the British troops first. Churchill intervened, insisting that the armies be evacuated on equal terms and that the British form the rear guard. By this time the operation was well under way, with fewer French troops being evacuated. The British armies held positions to the west, closer to the coast. Three French army groups, more distant from the bridgehead, formed the important rear guard.[9]

Another misunderstanding concerned the defense of the bridgehead. Darlan wrote that the French expected to defend it stoutly, to gain time for Weygand to prepare the front along the Somme. His diary entry of May 31 suggests that the British seemed not to understand the reasons for defending Dunkirk.[10] He wrote his wife that "the British lion seems to sprout wings when it's a matter of getting back to the sea."[11] And he told Reynaud that the British "wished at any price to precipitate the evacuation while leaving the French to defend the place."[12] But when he spoke to Sir Edward Spears, British liaison officer in Paris, he commented tactfully that the French and British had misunderstood each other on the possibility of defending Dunkirk.[13]

Darlan wrote on June 2 that the British armies had been evacuated. In a letter to Admiral Emmanuel Ollive, he complained that he had had to kick the backside of the British Admiralty for three days before the ally agreed to return for French troops near the beaches.[14] The two navies, exploiting a pause in the German offensive, evacuated nearly 80,000 additional troops. Darlan recorded that 335,000 troops had been evacuated, of which 110,000 were French.[15] But the nine-day evacuation had not bought Weygand enough time to form a strong line along the Somme.

DARLAN AND REYNAUD

On June 5 strong German forces struck against the thin French lines along the Somme near Amiens. Darlan's diary entry of the ninth indicates that the German attack had spread all along the front. Next day he noted that German units had crossed the Seine at several points, and that the government had decided to abandon Paris. He ordered the Admiralty to relocate at Montbazon, near Tours. He noted briefly the entry of Italy into the war.[16]

Now an armistice faction emerged. Led by Weygand and Pétain, it clashed with Reynaud, who insisted upon continuing the war in Brittany or North Africa. Weygand rejected outright the proposal to defend Brittany, calling it "a joke in very bad taste."[17] In late May Darlan had told Reynaud that he thought Brittany could be defended.[18] But on June 10, after studying the problem, he sent a memorandum to Under Secretary of State Paul Baudouin claiming Brittany to be indefensible. German air superiority would make it impossible to deliver adequate supplies through French ports.[19] With both Darlan and Weygand opposed to defending Brittany, Reynaud abandoned the plan.

On June 11, as the government moved to Tours, Pétain solicited Darlan's support. En route to a meeting of the Interallied Supreme Council at nearby Briare, the Marshal expressed his displeasure with the Reynaud government. He said that France needed a strong government, a consulate, and that he was prepared to recommend Darlan as First Consul.[20] Darlan thanked the Marshal, replying that "I'm not at all desirous of it."[21]

At Briare, Darlan heard that organized resistance was ending, that Britain had no divisions to send, that Churchill would hold back his last twenty-five fighter squadrons to defend the British Isles, and that Britain would continue the war in any case. Shortly thereafter, Churchill pulled the Admiral aside: "DARLAN, if you request an armistice it is not necessary for you to deliver your fleet to the Germans." Darlan answered "there is no question about it...we would sink the fleet before we would deliver it."[22]

Reynaud, having made a commitment in May not to seek a separate peace, searched for a way to continue the war in Africa. On June 12 General Charles de Gaulle, en route to London as Assistant Undersecretary of State for War, asked Darlan at Rochefort to study the problem of transporting 900,000 troops and 100,000 tons of supplies to Casablanca within forty-five days.[23] Darlan therefore learned of his government's interest in Africa just as he turned his attention to Italy.

When he established headquarters at Rochefort on the morning of June 12, Darlan had already planned a naval bombardment of the harbor facilities of Genoa, to take place upon Italy's entering the war.[24] Carried out on the night of June 13, the operation had little impact on the war. But it underscored the fact that the French navy, unlike the army, had not been defeated.

Next day Reynaud summoned Darlan. When the Admiral entered Reynaud's office at Bordeaux early in the morning of Saturday, June 15, he discovered that the timetable for moving 800,000 troops to North Africa had been reduced from forty-five days to ten. Darlan pointed out the impossibility of assembling at Bordeaux on such short notice the two hundred ships necessary to move an army that large. The ships, he observed, were scattered over the ocean. Reynaud later charged that Darlan refused to cooperate because he had already decided to support the armistice faction and to become First Consul in a new government under Pétain.[25]

But Darlan's report of the meeting tells a different story. When Reynaud reported that the schedule had been reduced to ten days, Darlan answered that he could not assemble two hundred ships in such a short time. But he indicated that he had ten transports in the harbor at Bordeaux. "Each of them," he said, "can handle 3000 persons: 30,000 men will therefore depart this same afternoon, if they are ready to embark."[26] Reynaud then admitted that he could not rally even that many troops to Bordeaux.[27]

When he met Reynaud that morning, Darlan had not decided to support the armistice faction. He was instead undergoing an agonizing crisis of conscience arising from the thought that an armistice might require the surrender of the fleet. He was not the type of officer to disobey his government. Nor would he dishonor the fleet. He faced a terrible dilemma at the moment of France's greatest agony.

Reynaud, weak and without fresh ideas, mismanaged his relations with Darlan. The Premier continued to quarrel with Weygand, who had nothing more to offer. He might instead have issued a firm order for Darlan to take the fleet and the loyal part of the government to North Africa. That option, more realistic than delivering nearly a million troops in ten days, was within Darlan's capabilities. Reynaud never explored with Darlan any realistic options for continuing the war overseas.

CRISIS OF CONSCIENCE

As French resistance wound down, the question of the navy shifted to center stage. Darlan could see that his government might consider surrendering the fleet in exchange for a lenient armistice. The time grew near when he might have to make a hard decision. He thought the fleet would obey orders to rally to North Africa or Britain, but he would exhaust every alternative before disobeying his government.

Nevertheless, he was prepared to disobey any order to surrender the fleet, as a note of May 28 to Admiral Le Luc indicates: "In case military events should lead to an armistice whose conditions would be imposed by the Germans and if these conditions should include the delivery of the fleet, *I have no intention of executing that order*."[28] And later, just before he departed Rochefort in the early predawn hours of June 15, he issued new orders to Le Luc that show clearly his intention to continue the war rather than to accept a post in any government that would surrender the fleet. The first of these ordered French warships, in case of armistice terms involving the fleet, to take measures to avoid falling into enemy hands, to flee to French colonial or British ports, or to destroy themselves. This option would be executed upon receipt of new orders from the Admiralty under the signature of "Xavier 377." He also instructed Le Luc to move the Admiralty to Marseilles. Darlan would go directly there from Bordeaux. The instruction indicated his intention to send the *Jean Bart* and *Richelieu* to England no later than June 20.[29]

Therefore, when Darlan arrived at Bordeaux early in the morning of Saturday, the 15th, he was still full of fight. And after he had concluded his interview with Reynaud, he remained determined to continue the war.[30] Shortly afterward he told Edouard Herriot that he would flee with the fleet should Pétain and Weygand conclude an armistice.[31]

When Darlan decided late that Saturday to consider an armistice, it was not out of political ambition. That evening the cabinet accepted a proposal of Minister of Marine Camille Chautemps that an armistice be requested with the private understanding that it would be rejected should it require the delivery of the fleet. Darlan could accept that solution. Nevertheless, he still wrestled with his conscience. Yves Bouthillier, who talked with him afterward, noted that the Admiral's hand trembled, that he was "undergoing a violent crisis of conscience."[32] He added that Darlan had been tempted to rally the fleet to the British, but he saw that this course would ruin any chance for an armistice. That same evening he spoke with Baudouin, expressing his support of the decision to request an armistice, which he now thought to be "inevitable in an extremely short space of time."[33] Darlan therefore came over to the armistice faction on the evening of June 15, after he had heard assurances that his government would not require him to surrender the fleet.

FOCUS ON THE FLEET

The Reynaud government fell late in the afternoon of Sunday, the 16th, after receipt of two notes from London releasing France from her commitment to continue the war, on condition that the fleet be sent to British ports pending the outcome of the armistice negotiations. But Darlan knew he could not expect Berlin to consider an armistice if he sent his fleet to British ports.

The newly formed Pétain government affirmed unanimously its intention to accept a settlement only if the fleet remained under French control. Darlan accepted the post as Minister of Marine, which signaled that the government had no intention to surrender the fleet. For the next four days, while he waited impatiently for Berlin's response to the armistice proposal, Darlan was solicited by Americans and Englishmen, now keenly interested in the fate of the fleet.

On the 17th he received the American ambassador to the Polish government in exile, who invited him to sail with the fleet to the United States. Darlan assured him it would remain French.[34] Next day he read a message from President Roosevelt threatening the empire should France not take care to safeguard the fleet.[35] The President's message confronted him with the bitter fact that France's defeat exposed the empire to possible Anglo-American aggression. That Tuesday afternoon Darlan received at Bordeaux the British First Lord of the Admiralty, A.V. Alexander, and the First Sea Lord, Sir Dudley Pound, who invited him to send his ships to British ports. Darlan assured them "that there was by no means any question of delivering our fleet to Germany and that if the armistice required its surrender, which would be contrary to honor, we would destroy the fleet." He added "that the fleet would belong to no country except France."[36]

PROTECTING THE FLEET

Darlan took great care to protect the fleet. On the evening of June 18 he ordered the continental outposts to prepare for the withdrawal of all ships to North Africa, and to destroy any ship at risk of falling into enemy hands.[37] At about the same time, he informed Admiral François Michelier that he had ordered the fleet to continue fighting, adding that he would not surrender it.[38]

Unsure of German intentions, the government made plans to depart for North Africa should the terms be unacceptable. Pétain would in any case remain in France. Darlan would remain commander of the fleet.[39] He would be responsible for moving the government to North Africa, and possibly for taking the fleet to Dakar.[40] On the 20th, as a French armistice delegation departed for Tours to receive the German terms, Darlan ordered the fleet to continue fighting, to disobey all foreign governments, and never to abandon a ship to the enemy.[41] Afterward, he assured the British Ambassador that the fleet "would remain French or else perish." He added that he had "already taken the necessary precautions."[42]

Late on the 21st, when the German terms were telephoned to Bordeaux, Darlan learned that Article VIII required that the fleet be demobilized and disarmed under German or Italian supervision, in their peacetime ports. The German government would not make use of any French ships in ports under German supervision, excepting those needed for coastal patrol and mine sweeping, and would not make any claim on the fleet at the conclusion of peace. All ships, excepting those assigned to colonial defense, would be recalled to France.[43]

Meeting with the cabinet during the night, Darlan saw that the naval clauses required his heaviest ships to return to Atlantic ports occupied by the Germans. He therefore spoke sharply against the armistice. The ministers decided to reject the clause requiring the ships to return to their home ports. At Baudouin's suggestion, Darlan agreed to order the fleet to steam to Oran. The meeting finally adjourned about 3:00 a.m., but discussion continued in a committee of Darlan, Weygand, Bouthillier, and Baudouin. At 8:00 Saturday morning, when the cabinet again met, it approved a Darlan proposal that the fleet, after being demobilized and disarmed, would steam with reduced crews to North Africa.[44]

Later that day, General Charles Huntziger presented the Germans a list of proposed amendments, pointing out that French warships demobilized in Atlantic ports would be exposed to British air attack. German General Wilhelm Keitel rejected the proposal to anchor the fleet in North Africa, but he indicated that the question of safeguarding the fleet from air attack would be discussed in the armistice commission.[45] Darlan could accept that interpretation, which implied future negotiations.

Darlan kept his officers informed. His order of the afternoon of June 22 explained that "resistance in North Africa would be without any practical significance and would abandon our country to invasion without moral defense of the government. Little local support to wait for England or the United States." And he added: "No effective support from the United States expected for a long time."[46] After further explanations, he ordered that a resolute crew be hidden away on each ship to destroy it should the enemy or any foreigner attempt to seize it.[47]

When the armistice was signed on June 24, Darlan sent a final coded order to the fleet that would remain in force regardless of any future orders to the contrary, even if sent over his signature. He reported the armistice provision that demobilized warships would remain under French flag with reduced crews in home or colonial ports. Should the armistice commission arrive at a different interpretation, he ordered, the ships should be taken without further orders to the United States. Failing that, they should be scuttled to prevent their falling to the enemy. He ordered secret preparations for sabotage so that neither the enemy nor the former ally seizing a ship might use it. He insisted that in no case should a ship be left intact to the enemy, that no ship be used against Germany or Italy without further orders, and that no commander obey a foreign admiralty.[48]

There was, however, considerable unrest in the navy, as some officers and crews wished to continue the war. But Darlan kept it in bounds, insisting that the naval clauses were honorable and that continuing the war would result in the total occupation of France, and perhaps also North Africa.

ARMISTICE DECISION: AN ASSESSMENT

Once the government had made up its mind not to surrender the fleet, Darlan's decision to support an armistice fell into place. It was in keeping with his basic nature, one of discipline and loyalty to the legal civil authority. His decision matched that of the overwhelming majority of officers in all three French military services. There were practically no defections among officers holding command responsibilities. Darlan, loyal by habit of mind, acted predictably at the time of the armistice crisis.

Darlan later justified the armistice decision on grounds that continuing the war would have led to the Axis conquest of French Africa. He first made that argument on June 24, when General Auguste Noguès in Morocco threatened to continue in the war.[49] He repeated the argument many times afterward. At Bordeaux, however, the issue was not whether resistance in Africa was possible, but whether it would serve any useful purpose. He chose the armistice because he believed that continuing the struggle there would be pointless. That was the argument he made to the navy in his order of June 22, before the armistice had been signed. He believed that continuing the war in Africa was a deadend that offered no reasonable prospect of returning to drive the Germans from France. His claim that North Africa could not be defended was an afterthought, a useful argument to justify the armistice to Frenchmen who wanted to continue the war.

Nor did Darlan agree to the armistice in the expectation that North Africa would later become a base for the Americans to liberate France. He had no reason in 1940 to think that the Americans would enter the war. He believed instead that the war on the continent was over, that Britain soon would seek peace, and that France would enter into a long period of recovery following a diplomatic settlement.

NOTES

1. SHM, 1BB2 EMG/SE, Carton 208, Darlan Diary, 11 May 1940 (hereinafter cited as Darlan Diary).

2. Ibid., 14 May 1940.

3. Alain Darlan, *L'Amiral Darlan parle* (Paris: Amiot-Dumont, 1952), 53.

4. Darlan Diary, 17, 18, and 20 May 1940.

5. Darlan, *L'Amiral Darlan parle*, 55.

6. Darlan Diary, 25 and 26 May 1940.

7. Ibid., 28 May 1940.

8. See Winston S. Churchill, *The Second World War*, 6 volumes (Boston: Houghton Mifflin, 1948-1953), II, 58-59, 83-84.

9. Darlan Diary, 28, 31 May 1940; Churchill, *The Second World War*, II, 110-111.

10. Darlan Diary, 31 May 1940.

11. Darlan, *L'Amiral Darlan parle*, 56.

12. Paul Baudouin, *The Private Diaries of Paul Baudouin*, trans. Charles Petrie (London: Eyre and Spotteswoode, 1948), 75.

13. Sir Edward Spears, *Assignment to Catastrophe*, 2 volumes (London: William Heinemenn Ltd., 1954), II, 11-12.

14. Darlan Diary, 2 June 1940; Letter of Darlan to Admiral Emmanuel Ollive, July 7, 1940, compliments of Claude Huan.

15. Darlan Diary, 4 June 1940; see also Churchill, *The Second World War*, II, 115.

16. Darlan Diary, 9, 10 June 1940.

17. Baudouin, *The Private Diaries*, 94.

18. Ibid., 64.

19. Ibid., 99-100.

20. Darlan Diary, 11 June 1940.

21. Amiral Jules Docteur, *La Grande enigme de la guerre:; Darlan, Amiral de la Flotte* (Paris: Éditions de la Couronne, 1949), 74.

22. Darlan Diary, 11 June 1940.

23. Henri Ballande, *De l'Amirauté à Bikini* (Paris: Cité, 1972), 314.

24. Interview with Henri Ballande at Parc Isthmia, Toulon, May 26, 1982.

25. Paul Reynaud, *In the Thick of the Fight,* trans. James D. Lambert (New York: Simon and Schuster, 1955), 512.

26. Ballande, *De l'Amirauté à Bikini*, 315.

27. Ibid.

28. SHM, 1BB2 EMG/SE, Carton 208, "Note pour l'Amiral Le Luc," 28 May 1940.

29. Hervé Coutau-Bégarie and Claude Huan, *Darlan* (Paris: Fayard, 1989), 235.

30. France, Assemblée Nationale, *Les Événements survenus en France de 1933 à 1945*, 9 volumes. (Paris: Assemblée Nationale, 1947), I, 2344, testimony of Paul Bastid.

31. Edouard Herriot, *Épisodes, 1940-1944* (Paris: 1950), 64-65; Haute Cour de Justice, *Le Procès du Maréchal Pétain*, 2 volumes (Paris: 1945), I, 340, testimony of Edouard Herriot.

32. Yves Bouthillier, *Le Drame de Vichy,* 2 volumes (Paris: Plon, 1950), I, 26.

33. Baudouin, *The Private Diaries*, 114.

34. Darlan Diary, 17 June 1940.

35. SHM, 1BB2 EMG/SE, Carton 208, "Message du Président Roosevelt à l'Amiral Darlan," 18 June 1940.

36. Darlan Diary, 18 June 1940.

37. Coutau-Bégarie and Huan, *Darlan*, 239.

38. Jacques Raphaël-Leygues and François Flohic, *Darlan* (Paris: Plon, 1986), 108.

39. Darlan Diary, 19 June 1940.

40. Coutau-Bégarie and Huan, *Darlan*, 241.

41. Docteur, *Darlan*, 81-82.

42. Darlan Diary, 20 June 1940.

43. DGFP, Series D, IX, 673.

44. See Baudouin, *The Private Diaries*, 130-135; Bouthillier, *Le Drame de Vichy*, I, 103-107; DGPF Series D, IX, 665; and Maxime Weygand, *Recalled to Service: Memoirs* (London: William Heinemann, 1952), 195-199.

45. DGPF, Series D, IX, 666.

46. Raphaël-Leygues and Flohic, *Darlan*, 112-113.

47. Ibid.

48. Docteur, *Darlan*, 82.

49. Hervé Coutau-Bégarie and Claude Huan, *Lettres et notes de l'Amiral Darlan* (Paris: Economica, 1992), 211-212.

CHAPTER 10

Empire in Crisis

Darlan was correct in his view that Britain could not defeat Germany, but he underestimated the endurance of the island kingdom. The wartime alliance that had enlisted the Royal Navy to underwrite the defense of the French empire collapsed at the defeat of France. Much of the empire now lay nearly defenseless against foreign powers, including the former ally.

THE FIRST INDOCHINA CRISIS

Since Indochina could not easily be defended, France had maintained friendly relations with Japan. There had been talk in 1932 of Paris and Tokyo forging an alliance that would secure Indochina and lend Japan support in Manchuria.[1] But Paris backed off, and Tokyo turned to the Axis for support of her ambitions in Asia. With the collapse of France in 1940, Indochina hung as ripe fruit to be picked.

On June 19, even before the armistice was signed, Japan presented Governor General Georges Catroux at Hanoi with demands for concessions that included the opening of Japanese control missions in Tonkin. Without consulting his government, Catroux agreed to the demands. That concession enabled Japan to turn the Tonkin region into a base of operations against China. Learning of Catroux's unauthorized concession on June 25, and suspecting his loyalty, the Marshal's government dismissed him and, upon Darlan's suggestion, replaced him with Vice-Admiral Jean Decoux, naval commander at Saigon.[2]

The Indochina crisis raised the specter of dissidence in the empire. Realizing that his colleagues were unsure of Catroux, Darlan guaranteed Decoux's loyalty. In a message of June 25 to Decoux, Darlan underscored the imperative of loyal service.[3] With that appointment, Decoux became the first of several Admirals to receive posts under Vichy because of Darlan's ability to keep his officers in line.

But neither Decoux nor Darlan could keep the Japanese from seizing French airfields near China. Vichy finally signed on August 30 a political agreement with Tokyo that confirmed French sovereignty in Indochina and opened the door for further Japanese penetration. By the end of the summer Japan was firmly entrenched in northern Indochina. Darlan could see that France had no way to resist Japan. In a private note he acknowledged that the agreement was the best available solution for France.[4]

TENSIONS WITH LONDON

London's decision to continue the war amplified the importance of the French fleet, which held the balance of naval power in the Mediterranean. Sentiment in the French navy remained friendly to the former ally, so that a British policy of courting Darlan and his fleet might have been productive. Darlan hoped to remain on good terms with the British.[5] In his memoirs, Churchill admitted that Darlan had given him repeated assurances that the fleet would never fall into the hands of the enemy.[6] The fleet, moreover, was entirely secure. The unfinished battleships *Jean Bart* and *Richelieu* were at Casablanca and Dakar, beyond the Axis reach. And at Mers el-Kébir near Oran were the modern battleships *Dunkerque* and *Strasbourg*. Nevertheless, London remained uneasy.

The text of Article VIII of the Armistice Convention, reaching London on June 22, did nothing to ease apprehension there. The English chiefs misinterpreted the French word *controle* in the first sentence, reading it as the English word *control*, rather than *supervision* or *inspection*. But the text clearly required the fleet to return to home ports, some of which were under German occupation. Addressing the House of Commons, Churchill declared that "from this text it is clear the French war vessels under this armistice pass into German or Italian control while fully armed."[7]

Darlan did not expect the British to attack his ships. Admiral Jean Odend'hal, head of the French naval mission in London, reported that the former ally might blockade the French coast and seize French vessels still in British harbors. On the 23rd he asked Darlan for permission to give the British authorities additional assurances. Darlan wired the next day that he should inform the British that the fleet would remain in French ports under French control. Afterward, he warned French naval stations of British efforts to lure French ships and colonies back into the war. With London forbidding the departure of French vessels from British ports, a dangerous situation had developed. On the 25th Odend'hal requested assurances that the fleet would remain in unoccupied ports.[8] Franco-German negotiations on this point, however, had not yet begun. Darlan therefore did not give these assurances.

In the meantime, a delicate situation had developed at Alexandria where *Force X*, four French cruisers and an old battleship under the command of Admiral René-Emile Godfroy, lay anchored alongside a British squadron. Under orders from London, Admiral Andrew Cunningham had demanded the demobilization of the French squadron. Godfroy and Cunningham were able to negotiate a "gentlemen's agreement" whereby the French ships would not leave the harbor without giving notice. But tensions there continued to rise. On the 25th Darlan instructed Odend'hal to prevent the gulf between France and Britain from widening, and to remind London of his promise to Admiral Pound to keep the fleet out of German hands.[9]

On June 27 Darlan renewed his assurances and asked Odend'hal to urge London to withhold judgment on the French fleet until the conclusion of negotiations between the French and German governments. He explained that France would try to persuade the Axis to permit the ships to remain in Africa.[10] But Darlan did not know that the Churchill government had decided that same day to confront the Mers el-Kébir squadron with an ultimatum and if necessary to use force against it.[11]

On the next day London asked specifically whether the French warships would be interned in French or in African ports.[12] But the question still had not been settled. The first meeting of the German armistice commission at Wiesbaden on June 29 dealt mainly with organizational questions and a German demand that the French recall their ships from British ports. On the 30th the French delegation raised the question of the ports in which the fleet would be anchored, but the matter was relegated to an undercommission for naval affairs.[13]

At Turin, however, the Italian armistice commission accepted the French proposal that the ships be interned in either Toulon or North African ports. Darlan informed Odend'hal of that decision.[14] On July 3 the German commission agreed to relegate to the Italian commission all questions concerning the French Mediterranean fleet.[15] But that concession came too late.

BRITISH AGGRESSION AT MERS EL-KÉBIR

The crisis moved swiftly to a climax. On the morning of July 3, Sir James Somerville's powerful *Force H* appeared off Oran. A British destroyer steamed into the harbor with an ultimatum for Admiral Marcel Gensoul, Commander of the French squadron. Delivered by Captain C. S. Holland, former naval attaché in Paris, it confronted Gensoul with harsh options: (a) sail out of the harbor to continue the war against the Axis, (b) sail with reduced crews under British control to a British port, (c) sail to a French port in the West Indies or to the United States, or (d) scuttle the ships. Failing all of these, the British squadron would use force to prevent an Axis takeover of the French ships.[16]

Seeking a compromise settlement, Gensoul expressed his willingness to disarm his ships on the spot. He sent Darlan a summary of the ultimatum, but he omitted the third option, which might have permitted the fleet to leave the harbor under pretense of going to Martinique or the United States. Darlan wired Gensoul his approval of the offer to disarm the ships.[17] As tensions mounted, Gensoul tried to convince Somerville that the fleet would never be delivered to the enemy. But Somerville had his orders. Wishing to avoid bloodshed, he extended the time limit of the ultimatum. At 4:30 p.m. Captain Holland signaled Somerville that Gensoul would take his ships to Martinique or the United States, if threatened by the enemy. But that solution was unacceptable.[18] Just before six o'clock the British ships opened fire on the French ships in the harbor. After fifteen minutes, Somerville withdrew.

Although the British attack caused serious damage, it fell far short of achieving its objective of destroying the French fleet. Churchill later wrote that "the elimination of the French Navy as an important factor almost at a single stroke by violent action produced a profound impression in every country."[19] But the French navy was not eliminated as an important factor. The only battleship sunk outright was the ancient *Bretagne*, which capsized with a loss of 977 men. Another old battleship, the *Provence*, was badly damaged. The modern battleship *Dunkerque* was run aground with light damage that did not prevent her later slipping over to Toulon. The *Strasbourg*, with several cruisers and destroyers, escaped to Toulon, as did a squadron of cruisers at Algiers. Nearly 1,300 Frenchmen were killed, but the attack hardly destroyed the fleet.

SETTLEMENT AT ALEXANDRIA

In the meantime, the two Admirals at Alexandria negotiated a sensible compromise. Following the "gentleman's agreement" of late June, London warned Cunningham that he might be ordered to use force against the French squadron. Cunningham realized that there was little chance of the French ships going over to the enemy. On June 30, five days before the attack at Mers el-Kébir, he urged London to avoid the use of force at Alexandria, and also at Oran, on grounds that an attack upon the fleet would alienate friendly Frenchmen, who might be useful for later operations in North Africa.[20]

Cunningham was on target. Nevertheless, the Admiralty ordered him to present Godfroy with an ultimatum intended to force a showdown by nightfall, July 3.[21] During the day, while the two Admirals negotiated, Darlan ordered Godfroy to bolt from the harbor. But Godfroy saw the futility of that option. And Cunningham disobeyed his orders to force a showdown by the end of the day. The next day the two Admirals reached a settlement. Godfroy would disarm his heavy guns, discharge the fuel from his tanks, and continue discussion of the reduction of crews. They therefore avoided a bloody clash.

The restraint exercised at Alexandria was not matched elsewhere. Two dozen French warships detained in British home ports since June 18 were seized in the night by British boarding parties. There was loss of life on both sides. Moreover, aircraft from the carrier *Hermes* attacked and damaged the *Richelieu* at Dakar.

RESPONDING TO BRITISH AGGRESSION

The British aggression of July 3 jolted Darlan out of a brief siege of depression.[22] It also caught him in a rare moment of disorder. After the armistice, he had moved the Admiralty headquarters temporarily to Nérac. On July 2 he motored to Clermont-Ferrand in search of permanent office space. Darlan had already opened an office there when Gensoul's summary of the ultimatum reached him late on the morning of the 3rd.[23]

Darlan immediately sent out an alert, ordering French ships to attack any British ship they encountered and to seize British merchant vessels.[24] That afternoon he rushed to Vichy where the government had begun to requisition hotels for office space. That same day, following a French request, General Otto von

Stülpnagel, president of the German armistice commission, agreed that the execution of the naval clauses of the armistice would be suspended until the situation cleared up. The commission agreed to permit French ships to pass by Gibraltar, hitherto forbidden by the armistice. The Germans also liberated the French naval staff captured earlier at Maintenon.[25]

It was only the next day, the 4th, that the full impact of the British aggression struck Darlan. Ballande noticed that the Admiral, usually level-headed, had lost his sense of proportion and had become intent upon gaining revenge.[26] When the Marshal summoned him, along with Laval and Baudouin, early that morning, the Admiral could not conceal his anger. His voice trembling, he lashed out at the British, declaring that he had been deceived and betrayed by his brothers in arms. He announced that he had ordered the *Strasbourg* to attack the British fleet. But Baudouin persuaded the Marshal to forbid for the moment any military reprisals.[27] Later that morning the cabinet approved Baudouin's proposal to sever diplomatic relations with Britain.

The crisis persisted while the British continued to attack French ships, including the *Dunkerque* on the morning of July 6. His anger renewed, Darlan urged Pétain to permit a combined French-Italian operation to liberate the French ships interned at Alexandria. But Baudouin blocked this plan.[28] After the British attack on the *Richelieu* at Dakar on the 8th, Darlan renewed his demands for reprisals, this time by aerial bombardment of Gibraltar. The Marshal approved, but Baudouin later persuaded him to change his mind.[29]

THE TRAGEDY OF MERS EL-KÉBIR

Mers el-Kébir was more than an aggravation of growing Anglo-French tensions at the time of the armistice.[30] It was instead a sudden, unprovoked act of aggression, a dramatic departure from previous relations. It was a tragic error that poisoned Anglo-French relations for many years. But it was a tactical failure. No modern French ships were destroyed. The attack relieved Darlan of any moral obligation to the British, and it risked his unleashing his massive submarine fleet against British shipping.[31]

Importantly, the attack alienated the French naval and colonial establishment. Mers el-Kébir therefore burdened the future, forfeiting British influence among patriotic Frenchmen who later would be in the best positions to resume the war against the Axis. It wiped out in one stroke the huge psychological advantage the British had enjoyed in French Africa. The attack impoverished Churchill's French connections, leaving him nothing better than Charles de Gaulle. Afterward, he had little choice but to accept the strong-headed General as the symbol of continuing French resistance. In turn, Churchill would label those he had attacked as traitors. Mers el-Kébir set the stage for the troubled Anglo-Gaullist partnership that burdened London's relations with Washington throughout the war.[32] It strained the alliance and hampered the war effort. Churchill's attack was a costly blunder, not at all his finest hour.

Mers el-Kébir brought an abrupt end to the friendly relations Darlan had maintained with the British navy since the mid-1930s. Now he emerged as France's foremost Anglophobe. But Darlan was only the first of the overwhelming majority of French naval and colonial officers to undergo a sharp transformation of sentiments. After the attack, these officers turned bitterly anti-English, many of them to remain so for the rest of their lives.[33] Darlan's Anglophobia was therefore only one part of a larger pattern of anti-British sentiment that reigned throughout the navy and empire after Mers el-Kébir. It ran deepest in North and West Africa where the attacks had occurred, where vital Allied interests would later converge, and where the Allies would have to enlist French support.

Mers el-Kébir underscored the fact that France stood alone. In an atmosphere of crisis, sentiment against the republic ran strong and deep. Moving skillfully among the parliamentarians, Pierre Laval persuaded the National Assembly on July 10 to vote sweeping powers to Pétain. The Marshal reformed his cabinet, designated Laval as his eventual successor, assumed a royalist posture, identified his regime with the Catholic Church, and governed France by executive decree. Darlan, remaining as Secretary of State for Marine, never let his republicanism and secularism come between him and the Marshal. He felt at home with the new emphasis on order and discipline.

TROUBLES WITH THE REICH

Now Berlin moved to test Vichy's grip on North Africa. Realizing that the use of force might provoke the fleet and the government to flee the country, the Reich applied diplomatic pressure aimed at gaining a foothold in Africa. On July 15 Wiesbaden confronted the French delegation with a stern note demanding access to African ports and other facilities.[34] This was the first of many demands for concessions in Africa that Berlin would deliver to Vichy during the next thirty months.

The German demands, exceeding the terms of the armistice, ushered in the first crisis in Vichy's relations with the Reich. Fearing that an outright rejection might provoke a German military move against France, the cabinet agreed to evade the German demands but to leave open the door for future discussions. Accordingly, they drafted a letter from Pétain to be sent through the armistice commission to Hitler. It affirmed France's intention to abide strictly by the terms of the armistice and suggested that Franco-German differences could best be settled by direct negotiations between the two governments.

Darlan understood the letter to be a way of evading the German demands and of advancing the French view that any agenda beyond the terms of the armistice should be discussed at a higher political level. He wrote in his diary that "the demands not being included under the armistice, it is advisable that new negotiations take place."[35] He was surprised when no German reprisals followed.

The events of July pointed to trouble in French relations with Germany. On a visit to Vichy from his post as head of the French armistice delegation, General Charles Huntziger reported on the 27th that the German armistice commission appeared to be trying to cut all communications between the two zones, to gain economic control over all of France.[36] Baudouin therefore raised with Pétain the question of a possible German invasion of the free zone.

On Sunday evening, August 4, Pétain received in his office Baudouin and Darlan. They agreed that in case of a German invasion of the free zone, Darlan would take the fleet to North Africa and continue the government there in the name of the Marshal, who would refuse to leave France in any event. Insisting upon a secret oral agreement, Pétain would not sign the order Baudouin had drafted.[37] Baudouin's diary is the only contemporary account of the meeting. But there were good reasons for emergency arrangements, and Darlan, as commander of the fleet, was the logical choice for the assignment.

The Japanese occupation of Tonkin, the attack at Mers el-Kébir, and the German demands upon North Africa were but the first rounds of the struggle for control of the French empire. Darlan, however, wanted peace in Europe. In a short paper he placed in his files on July 16, he wrote of peace negotiations and an early end to the European war.[38] But the peace conference he so earnestly desired would not be on Europe's agenda for 1940. Instead, the war continued, and the stage was set for Darlan to preside over an era of imperial decline.

NOTES

1. USNA, RG 38, ONI, C-9-E, Reg. 15084-A, naval attaché report from Paris, February 1942.

2. Paul Baudouin, *The Private Diaries of Paul Baudouin* (London: Eyre and Spottis-woode, 1948), 146.

3. Amiral Jean Decoux, *A la barre de l'Indochine* (Paris: Plon, 1949), 55.

4. Alain Darlan, *L'Amiral Darlan parle* (Paris: Amiot-Dumont, 1952), 306-307.

5. Baudouin, *The Private Diaries*, 114. See also France, Assemblée Nationale, *Les Événements survenus en France de 1933 à 1945*, 9 volumes. (Paris: Assemblée Nationale, 1947), VII, 2344.

6. Winston S. Churchill, *The Second World War*, 6 volumes (Boston: Houghton Mifflin, 1949), II, 229.

7. Great Britain, *Parliamentary Debates* (5th Series), CCLXII, 304. See also Churchill, *The Second World War*, II, 231.

8. Albert Kammerer, *La Passion de la flotte française, de Mers el-Kébir à Toulon* (Paris: Fayard, 1951), 110-111, 120.

9. Ibid., 132.

10. Ibid.

11. Correlli Barnett, *Engage The Enemy More Closely* (New York: Norton, 1991), 173. Barnett reports that Admiral Pound insisted stoutly upon attacking the French fleet.

12. Kammerer, *La Passion de la flotte française*, 133.

13. DFCAA, I, 10-13, 20.

14. Paul Auphan and Jacques Mordal, *The French Navy in World War II*, trans. A.C.J. Sabalot (Annapolis: United States Naval Institute, 1959), 120.

15. See DFCAA, I, 27.

16. Churchill, *The Second World War*, II, 235.

17. *Les Événements survenus en France*, VI, 1902, 2343.

18. Kammerer, *La Passion de la flotte française*, 169.

19. Churchill, *The Second World War*, II, 238.

20. Viscount Cunningham of Hyndhope, *A Sailor's Odyssey*, 2 volumes (London: Arrow Books, 1961), I, 184-185.

21. Ibid.

22. Darlan wrote in his diary that "July 2 is an empty and despairing day during which I was seized with depression." See SHM, 1BB2 EMG/SE, Carton 208, Darlan Diary, 2 July 1940 (hereinafter cited as Darlan Diary).

23. Auphan and Mordal, *The French Navy in World War II*, 130; Albert Kammerer, *La Tragédie de Mers el-Kébir* (Paris: Éditions Médicis, 1945), 114-115; Henri Ballande, *De l'Amirauté à Bikini* (Paris: Cité, 1972), 104-106.

24. Darlan Diary, 3 July 1940.

25. DFCAA, I, 38-39, 41- 42, 49.

26. Ballande, *De l'Amirauté à Bikini*, 107.

27. Baudouin, *The Private Diaries*, 157.

28. Ibid, 161-162; Yves Bouthillier, *Le Drame de Vichy*, 2 volumes (Paris: Plon, 1950), I, 152.

29. Bouthillier, *Le Drame de Vichy*, I, 153; Baudouin, *The Private Diaries*, 168.

30. Anglo-American views often discount Mers el-Kébir as just another incident among growing Anglo-French tensions.

31. A French naval officer later reminded the American naval attaché at Vichy of the French ability to wage an undersea war against the British: "We cannot hope to successfully fight them on the seas but we have quite a few submarines left and they could play havoc with the African trade." USNA, RG 38, ONI, C-9-E, Box 439.

32. The files of Admiral William D. Leahy attest repeatedly to the heavy burden de Gaulle imposed on Anglo-American relations. See USNA, RG 218, Joint Chiefs, Geographic File, and RG 218, Joint Chiefs, Chairman's File.

33. Interview with Captain Henri Ballande, 26 May 1982, at Toulon.

34. DFCAA, I, 463-464. See also DGFP, Series D, X, 215.

35. Darlan Diary, 16 July 1940.

36. Baudouin, *The Private Diaries*, 183. See also DGFP, Series D, X, 292-294.

37. Baudouin, *The Private Diaries*, 190-191.

38. SHM, 1BB2 EMG/SE, Carton 208, "La Marine Doit Garder Son Indépendence Et Sa Liberté D'Action," 16 July 1940.

CHAPTER 11

Keeping France Neutral

Darlan was disappointed that the European war dragged on. More than half of France lay under a burdensome German occupation, and the empire was threatened by the British, who imposed a blockade on both French coasts. France was trapped between the warring camps, and Frenchmen at Vichy in 1940 were not of one mind about protecting French interests.

Vice-President Laval entered into private discussions with Otto Abetz, German diplomat in Paris representing the foreign ministry to the German military commander. Laval promised Abetz that Vichy stood ready to collaborate. But Foreign Minister Baudouin, Finance Minister Bouthillier, and others had misgivings about any dealings with Germany that went beyond the armistice terms. They preferred to mend relations with London, not because they thought that Britain could liberate France, but because they wished to avoid an Anglo-French war.

IN THE WAKE OF MERS EL-KÉBIR

Darlan clashed with Baudouin on the question of the blockade. Enforced only selectively, the blockade nevertheless threatened vital commerce between France and Africa. In early August Darlan insisted upon armed escorts of French convoys, but Baudouin persuaded the cabinet to authorize contacts with London through the French and British embassies at Madrid, to find a peaceful solution.[1] Baudouin also enlisted the aid of Robert Murphy, American chargé d'affaires at Vichy, who was persuaded to urge Washington to intervene with London on behalf of France.[2]

London's militant attitude played into Darlan's hands. On August 16 de Gaulle publicly accused Pétain of treason, and on the 20th Churchill spoke harshly of Vichy and confirmed the imposition of the blockade.[3] Baudouin's public response calling for moderation set the stage for Darlan to test the blockade. On the 23rd the cabinet authorized him to send past Gibraltar a merchant ship escorted by one small warship.[4]

While Darlan prepared the operation, the French and British naval attachés at Madrid met in secret on September 3 at the home of the American naval attaché, Commander Ben H. Wyatt. The French officer proposed that the British allow French merchant ships to pass through the blockade with food for unoccupied France. In return, Vichy would hold the French fleet "in readiness for action on behalf of England, if and when the proper moment arrives," and should the Germans seizes these foodstuffs, "then the present French Government will remove to the colonies."[5]

On September 7 the two French ships steamed through the strait, and Vichy concluded that London now recognized the right of passage through the blockade. The French Ambassador in Madrid notified British authorities there that Vichy would keep them informed of French naval movements in the Mediterranean.[6] Darlan now began to think in terms of regular passage through Gibraltar. The British, however, had made no commitment to relax the blockade.

CLASH OF ARMS AT DAKAR

In early September the Italian armistice commission at Turin served notice that the naval disarmament clauses suspended in July would be reimposed on September 30. The protest note of September 5 that Huntziger delivered to Wiesbaden was no doubt the same document Darlan had submitted to the cabinet on the 3rd.[7] Observing that Turin's action weakened French defenses just after Gaullist forces had seized Equatorial Africa and Chad, it asked Wiesbaden to keep the suspension in place. On the 17th Wiesbaden answered that the clauses would remain suspended to the extent that the French Mediterranean squadron would consist of four cruisers and nineteen lighter ships.[8]

Meanwhile, with cabinet approval, Darlan had unleashed his cruisers to recover the dissident African colonies.[9] He sent three fast cruisers to steam past Gibraltar to Dakar. They would join the old cruiser *Primaguet* to attack Libreville. The *Primaguet*, escorting a tanker, departed Dakar on September 15, followed by the three fast cruisers on the 18th. But the *Primaguet* stumbled onto the powerful British *Force H*, en route to attack Dakar. Facing overwhelming British strength, the entire French force turned back. Two of the cruisers finally reached Dakar, the others Casablanca.[10] Darlan's effort to recapture the colonies ended in a display of French ineptitude.

But the Anglo-Gaullist attack at Dakar on September 23 found the French holding higher cards. The strong British naval squadron that appeared offshore early that morning was accompanied by a Gaullist landing force. But the Vichy forces ashore enjoyed the advantage of fighting from well-prepared positions, and they were strongly motivated to stand their ground. During the morning two Gaullist officers went ashore to invite Governor-General Pierre Boisson to lead West Africa into the Gaullist camp. Stoutly loyal, Boisson promptly jailed his two visitors. Early in the afternoon the British squadron opened fire. The great battleship *Richelieu*, immobile but capable of firing two of its fifteen-inch guns, led the vigorous French defense. The cruisers *Georges Leygues* and *Montcalm* joined in, as did ancient but effective shore batteries placed at Gorée and Cape Manuel. As the battle raged over three days, French submarines entered into the action, and French military units engaged the Gaullist force coming ashore at nearby Rufisque.

Although the French suffered the loss of two submarines, a destroyer, and further damage to the *Richelieu*, they won a clear victory. Shore batteries scored hits on the cruisers *Delhi* and *Cumberland*. The *Resolution*, flagship of Vice-Admiral John Cunningham, was badly damaged. French range-finders aboard the *Richelieu* charted the course of the big British ship and radioed it to Captain Lancelot, commanding the submarine *Beveziers*. A single torpedo found its mark. Lancelot, later to serve under Cunningham, was the hero of the Battle of Dakar.[11]

On September 25 London withdrew the squadron and began evacuation of the Gaullist troops. Significantly, the defenders of Dakar had remained loyal to Vichy. Meanwhile, Darlan had gained cabinet approval for aerial attacks against Gibraltar. Staged from Algeria and inflicting little damage, the raids were suspended when Cunningham disengaged at Dakar. Nevertheless, the raids demonstrated French ability to threaten a spot vital to the British war effort. But in the wake of the Dakar incident, de Gaulle seized the French Cameroons.[12] Despite the victory at Dakar, Darlan could see that he could not recover the dissident African colonies, or defend any French colony beyond Dakar.

IMPROVING RELATIONS WITH BRITAIN

Anglo-French relations took a surprising turn for the better after Dakar. Rumors reached London that an impending Franco-German agreement would permit Axis penetration into French Africa and that Darlan would enter the French fleet into the war on the Axis side.[13] Darlan had no such intentions, but London could take no chances. During October, German U-boats took an awesome toll of British shipping, sinking sixty-three ships. The Admiralty could see that a rupture with Vichy would risk Darlan's unleashing his submarines against British shipping.[14] In November, Churchill wrote de Gaulle in Libreville: "We are trying to arrive at some *modus vivendi* with Vichy."[15]

In October the first steps of an informal settlement were marked out in conversations between Professor Louis Rougier and Churchill.[16] Similar discussions in Madrid between the French and British ambassadors focused on the pressing question of whether France would attempt to reconquer the dissident colonies. The British were willing to allow French ships to pass Gibraltar if the French would promise to make no move against de Gaulle in Africa.[17] London worried that Darlan would again send his ships to recover the colonies, which might lead to an unwanted Anglo-French war. On November 11 the French chargé d'affaires at Madrid handed the British ambassador a note affirming Vichy's position "that they had never taken the initiative in an attack against Great Britain and did not intend to do so," but it went on to say that Vichy "would try to safeguard the unity of their Empire by every means in their power."[18] Despite the obvious inability of France to recover the colonies, Vichy would not forfeit the right to attempt to recover them.

Discussion continued at Vichy in early December with the Canadian chargé d'affaires, Pierre Dupuy. In an interview with Darlan on December 6, the Admiral assured Dupuy that France would resist German pressure to attack the colonies at least until February.[19] In his report to London, Dupuy indicated that Darlan had also promised formally that the French fleet would not attack the British fleet or the dissident colonies.[20] Darlan may not have been so explicit, but he knew the futility of sending his ships on another mission to recover the colonies.

Vichy and London finally settled upon a tacit understanding reflecting the realities of the moment. Dupuy's report that Darlan would not use the fleet against the colonies appears to have relieved London's anxiety. And London's relaxing the blockade met Vichy's pressing economic needs. French maritime traffic increased noticeably in late 1940, and passage of French ships through Gibraltar became a common occurrence.[21] The British relaxed the blockade in the interest of reducing the risks of provoking Darlan's submarines back into the war.

MEMORANDUM OF NOVEMBER 8

London's fears about a Franco-German settlement had not been entirely groundless, for France came under considerable pressure to close ranks with the Reich. In October, Hitler journeyed to the small border town of Hendaye for conference with the Spanish dictator Franco. En route, he received Laval on October 22 at the French village of Montoire. Promising a lenient peace settlement if France would help Germany defeat Britain, Hitler asked for a meeting with Pétain.[22]

Hitler went on to Hendaye. With the conquest of Gibraltar in mind, he hoped to enlist the active military aid first of Spain and then France in reducing the British stronghold. But Franco's price for aiding the Axis--French Morocco and Oran--was incompatible with French participation.[23] So Hitler had no clear agenda for France when he received Pétain at Montoire on October 23. After explaining his general plans to create a broad European community against Britain, Hitler asked if France would cooperate. But the Marshal made no specific commitment, insisting that he "was in no position at this time to define the exact limits of French cooperation with Germany. All he could do was to express himself in favor of the principle of such cooperation."[24] Nevertheless, the Montoire summit created the impression in Vichy that Laval was leading France into the German camp, an impression that was strengthened early the next week when Laval supplanted Baudouin as foreign minister. As Laval moved confidently toward closer relations with Germany, the stage was set for Darlan to offer a sober proposal to keep France on the narrow middle ground between Britain and the Reich.

Laval's German policy caused much anxiety at Vichy. While London and Washington continued to view Darlan and Laval in much the same light, the Admiral in early November had already settled onto more moderate ground. He moved toward Baudouin and the others who worried that Laval might drive Vichy back into the war when France could not easily defend her African possessions. Boldly seizing the initiative on the 8th, Darlan handed the Marshal a long memorandum recommending a policy of neutrality.[25]

At the outset Darlan noted that the policy of collaboration the Marshal had accepted in principle at Montoire ought to be defined clearly in terms of German and French expectations. The country, he noted, was nearly empty of economic goods, and industry suffered from heavy burdens imposed by the demarcation line that seperated Vichy's free zone from the occupied zone. He observed that many Frenchmen in both zones remained sympathetic to Britain. He reminded the Marshal that France, nearly devoid of armed forces, was incapable of staging any sustained offensive operations. He wrote that the navy was incapable of operations in remote parts of the empire. Darlan insisted that the French armed services were unwilling to collaborate with the former enemy. The navy would resist any further British aggression, but it was not inclined to attack the former ally.

Continuing, Darlan wrote that France would profit from Britain's being expelled from the Mediterranean and Gibraltar. The Americans, he added, desired to seize French colonies in the Caribbean. As for the Germans, he deplored their interdiction of commerce across the demarcation line, their political and financial pressures on France, and their exploiting the armistice to their advantage. All of that, he insisted, had created an atmosphere unfriendly to Franco-German collaboration. Assessing the war, Darlan wrote that Britain would find it difficult to take the offensive except in peripheral areas such as central Africa, and that neither the United States nor Russia would intervene in the European conflict for a long time. He moved quickly to the main point:

> Militarily, we should remain neutral, because we are not ready either morally or materially to re-enter the war--either in one camp or the other--and because we ought to avoid an open break with the Anglo-Saxon powers. We would be the first victims of that rupture: we would lose the Antilles, Saint-Pierre and Miquelon, Madagascar, Réunion. We would be attacked at Morocco, at French West Africa and probably in unoccupied France without having the power to offer effective resistance to England.[26]

Darlan observed that France would have to collaborate economically with Germany, just to keep the country alive. Political collaboration would also be necessary, he thought, because Germany would create a European bloc over against an American bloc. There followed a list of concessions that France might demand in return for collaboration. Among them were reduction in the size of the occupation zone, suppression of the demarcation line to the level of a purely military barrier, and reduction of occupation costs. He added that Vichy might demand an increase in armaments for imperial defense, release of French war prisoners, and the restoration of French sovereignty in the occupied zone, subject to the rights of the occupation authority. In return, France would defend the African empire with its own forces but would not take offensive action unless attacked. French industry would provide materials to the Axis, and domestic and colonial goods would be traded to them. Finally, France would participate in the establishment of a new European order.

Darlan shared his memorandum with Bouthillier, who had already engaged others in the cabinet to blunt Laval's German policy. The memorandum, with its stout defense of neutrality, made it easier for Bouthillier to invite the Admiral to join the conspiracy against Laval. It also marked an important shift in Darlan's thinking. He had come to realize that military restraint and prudent diplomacy would best serve French interests.

MILITARY DISCUSSIONS WITH THE REICH

While Darlan pressed for neutrality, Laval negotiated with the Germans to enter France into the war, when British forces opposed French efforts to recover the dissident colonies, or when British aircraft bombed French factories working for the Reich.[27] Toward the end of November, he summoned Huntziger and Darlan to Paris to review plans to recover the dissident colonies. Hitler had already issued a directive ordering his military staff to prepare for Operation FELIX, the conquest of Gibraltar and Atlantic islands near Africa. Laval's program fitted neatly into the German plans, for Hitler's directive indicated that France would remain neutral only until the time when a French offensive against the dissident colonies would draw her into a war with Britain.[28]

Neither Darlan nor Huntziger shared Laval's zeal for a military operation that might spark a war with Britain. On November 30, when they joined Laval in Paris for conference with General Walter Warlimont, Huntziger dragged his feet, declaring that a campaign to recover Equatorial Africa could not be launched until the autumn of 1941. Darlan insisted repeatedly that he could protect the supply route to Dakar only if the armistice commission would permit France to rearm the navy. He warned that the British would intervene, and that France could win a clash of arms at sea only if the Reich would liberate the entire French fleet from the armistice restrictions.[29]

When they met again on December 10, Warlimont pressed for an operation in the near future.[30] The German record reports that Darlan indicated he would use French warships against Freetown should the British interfere with Vichy's efforts to recover the colonies.[31] But Huntziger reported to the Marshal next day that it was Laval who had supported that action.[32] And Darlan told Bouthillier on the 11th that he would not commit the fleet in any event.[33] Throughout these discussions, Huntziger and Darlan projected the campaign safely into the future. In contrast, Laval insisted that Vichy intended to undertake military action at the earliest possible moment, even at the risk of war with Britain.

THE CONSPIRACY OF FRIDAY THE THIRTEENTH

Meanwhile, the conspiracy against Laval gained momentum. The Marshal, influenced by Darlan's November 8 memorandum and losing confidence in Laval, favored a policy of prudent neutrality.[34] Bouthillier and Baudouin, now a secretary of state, and interior minister Marcel Peyrouton, quickly emerged as the leaders of the conspiracy. They needed Darlan's support.

When Bouthillier received Darlan on November 24, the Admiral was worried about Laval's risky plans to recover the dissident colonies. Bouthillier commented that Laval would not change his mind and that the only solution was to force him out of office. Darlan agreed. "Count on me," he said, "I will take the risk with you."[35] Darlan therefore joined the conspiracy. "Darlan was one of us," Bouthillier wrote, "because he thought as we did."[36]

In early December, with Laval in Paris, the conspiracy moved forward. At the council meeting of the 2nd, after Huntziger reported German pressure to attack the dissident colonies, Bouthillier revealed that Laval had agreed to deliver to the Germans the Belgian gold on deposit with the French government. There was unanimous agreement that Laval's German policy could not continue much longer. Baudouin then met with the Marshal, who agreed that Laval must go. He also met with Bouthillier and Peyrouton. They would step up their pressure on the Marshal to dismiss Laval quickly.[37]

Two days later, Darlan received Bouthillier at Toulon aboard the *Strasbourg.* The Admiral agreed to await a signal to move against Laval. As they shook hands, Darlan said "Old friend....upon a sign from you, I will march into the abyss."[38] The conspiracy turned on the 12th when Laval phoned from Paris that Hitler expected the Marshal to participate on the 15th in ceremonies at Les Invalides honoring the return of the remains of the Duke of Reichstadt, son of Napoleon. The Marshal had already expressed himself privately against appearing in Paris with German officials, but Laval, arriving at Vichy on Friday, the 13th, persuaded him to change his mind.

The conspirators would have to act quickly, for Pétain would leave for Paris that same evening. Meeting in the gardens near the Hôtel du Parc in midafternoon, Bouthillier and Peyrouton decided to force Laval's dismissal before the end of the day. About four o'clock they summoned Darlan, Huntziger, and several others to the office of Henri Du Moulin de Labarthète, director of the Marshal's civil cabinet. They decided that Darlan would take the lead in making their case to the Marshal. Shortly thereafter they entered Pétain's office, where Darlan in simple, direct terms denounced Laval's policies and insisted that the Marshal must not appear with him in Paris. Others joined in, and Pétain promised he would dismiss Laval at the cabinet meeting that evening. When Peyrouton said that the foreign minister would be arrested and taken to his estate at Châteldon, Darlan suggested that he be treated with dignity befitting his years of public service.[39]

At the eight o'clock meeting, Laval noticed nothing unusual. But Peyrouton had taken care to cut telephone connections. Trusted policemen were brought into the Hôtel du Parc. The ministers assembled, Pétain asked for the resignation of the cabinet. Departing, he returned shortly to announced acceptance of resignations that included Laval. Visibly shaken, Laval asked for an explanation. Pétain answered that the foreign minister no longer had the confidence of the cabinet, nor of himself. Minutes later Laval was escorted to Châteldon.

These events influenced the direction of the war. On the 12th, Madrid informed Berlin that "Spain could not enter the war within the immediate future."[40] The purge of Laval the next day signaled that France would be equally uncooperative. So Hitler shifted his attention from the Mediterranean to the east. A week later he issued the final directive for an invasion of the Soviet Union in the spring of 1941.[41] In the meantime, Darlan and his colleagues at Vichy braced themselves for the German reaction to the purge of Laval.

NOTES

1. Paul Baudouin, *The Private Diaries of Paul Baudouin* (London: Eyre and Spottiswood, 1948), 199.

2. Robert D. Murphy, *Diplomat Among Warriors* (New York: Doubleday, 1964), 63-64.

3. Yves Bouthillier, *Le Drame de Vichy*, 2 volumes (Paris: Plon, 1950), I, 158.

4. Baudouin, *The Private Diaries*, 212-214; Bouthillier, *Le Drame de Vichy*, I, 158-161.

5. USNA, RG 38, ONI, C-9-e, 19447-C, secret reports of naval attachés.

6. Bouthillier, *Le Drame de Vichy*, I, 161-162.

7. See SHM, 1BB2 EMG/SE, Carton 208, Darlan Diary, 3 September 1940 (hereinafter cited as Darlan Diary).

8. DFCAA, I, 257-258, 261-262, 286.

9. Darlan Diary, 29 August 1940.

10. See Hervé Coutau-Bégarie and Claude Huan, *Darlan* (Paris: Fayard, 1989), 322-333.

11. Meeting Lancelot, Cunningham greeted him with the terse "good shot." See Henri Ballande, *De l'Amirauté à Bikini* (Paris: Cité, 1972), 117-119.

12. See Baudouin, *The Private Diaries*, 246-248; and Winston S. Churchill, *The Second World War*, 6 volumes (London: Houghton Mifflin, 1948-1953), II, 492-494.

13. Sir Llewellyn Woodward, *British Foreign Policy in the Second World War*, 5 volumes (London: Her Majesty's Stationery Office, 1970), I, 413-414.

14. Churchill, *The Second World War*, II, 513-515; Correlli Barnett, *Engage the Enemy More Closely* (New York: Norton, 1991), 196.

15. Churchill, *The Second World War*, II, 517.

16. Louis Rougier, *Mission secret à Londres, les accords Pétain-Churchill* (Genève: Éditions du Cheval Aile, n.d.), 75-76.

17. Woodward, *British Foreign Policy in the Second World War*, I, 420-421.

18. Ibid., I, 421.

19. Ibid., I, 429-430. See also Coutau-Bégarie and Huan, *Darlan*, 326-327.

20. Coutau-Bégarie and Huan, *Darlan*, 328.

21. Bouthillier, *Le Drame de Vichy*, I, 186.

22. DGPF, Series D, XI, 354-361.

23. Ibid., 371-377.

24. Ibid., 389.

25. For the text of Darlan's memorandum, see Bouthillier, *Le Drame de Vichy*, I, 301-304.

26. Ibid.

27. DGPF, Series D, XI, 401-402.

28. See Ibid., 527-531.

29. Ibid., 752-753, 760-762.

30. Bouthillier, *Le Drame de Vichy*, I, 253.

31. DGFP, Series D, XI, 840.

32. Baudouin, *The Private Diaries*, 285.

33. Bouthillier, *Le Drame de Vichy*, I, 253.

34. See Maxime Weygand, *Recalled to Service: Memoirs*, trans. E.W. Dickes (London, 1952), 436.

35. Bouthillier, *Le Drame de Vichy*, I, 227.

36. Ibid.

37. Baudouin, *The Private Diaries*, 280-281.

38. Bouthillier, *Le Drame de Vichy*, I, 245.

39. Ibid., I, 253-256; Haute Cour de Justice, *Le Procès du Maréchal Pétain,* 2 volumes (Paris: 1945), I, 553.

40. DGFP, Series D, XI, 853.

41. Ibid., 899-902. See also DGFP, Series D, X, 373.

CHAPTER 12

Darlan versus Laval

December 13 opened the door to the rise of Darlan, and a new kind of leadership. Whereas Laval had focused his attention narrowly on German relations, Darlan had a broader view, one sensitive to the connections between France and the empire. As Commander-in-Chief of the navy, the Admiral enjoyed a power base that Laval had lacked. And the more pragmatic Darlan had no ideological commitment to Franco-German collaboration.

At the end of 1940 Darlan believed that neither Germany nor Britain could invade the other, and that however the war ended, Germany would dominate the European continent. He would defend the empire against any Anglo-Gaullist aggression, but he was prepared to cooperate with London for reasons of state. He would welcome American economic aid for France and North Africa, but he did not expect an American liberation of France.[1]

APPEASING ABETZ

Darlan quickly emerged as the Marshal's spokesman in negotiations with the Reich. In Paris on December 15, he represented Pétain in the ceremonies returning the remains of the Duke of Reichstadt. When he met with Otto Abetz, the Admiral reported that Laval might be recalled at a later time, but not immediately. Furious, Abetz announced abruptly that he would go to Vichy to see Pétain.[2] Rushing to Vichy ahead of Abetz, Darlan warned Pétain that the German would come to demand Laval's inclusion in a Directorate. Abetz, escorted by armed motorcyclists, made an impressive entry into Vichy late on the 16th. Next morning, when he met with Pétain and Darlan, Abetz charged that Laval's dismissal was a personal affront to Hitler, who would withdraw his offer to collaborate. But the Marshal stood firm, declaring that he would resign if

Berlin insisted upon Laval's return. Abetz then asked that Laval be brought to Vichy for discussions.[3]

Arriving about noon, Laval demanded the Ministry of Interior, but Pétain offered him instead his choice of two minor posts. Laval refused, lost his composure, and spoke disrespectfully to the elderly Marshal.[4] With this evidence of personal antagonism between Pétain and Laval, Abetz could see that the immediate restoration of Laval would be impossible. They finally agreed that Darlan would preside over a Directorate, to include Pierre-Étienne Flandin and General Huntziger. Laval might be added later. The Marshal would also dismiss Peyrouton and other ministers whom the Germans thought to have instigated Laval's dismissal. Abetz accepted the plan, thinking that Laval would return after a brief interval.[5]

Impressed with Darlan, Abetz saw the Admiral as a temporary alternative to Laval. In his report to Berlin, he praised Darlan as the only man at Vichy with qualities of leadership. He recommended that the Admiral be accepted as head of the Directorate. He would later replace Pétain as Chief of State, to make room for Laval as Premier.[6] Abetz accepted Vichy's explanation that Laval had been dismissed for domestic political reasons related to opposition that included the army.[7] Hitler, quick to pick up on that theme, blamed the sudden chill in Franco-German relations on General Weygand, now the Marshal's personal representative in North Africa.[8] This was not the last time Weygand would absorb the blame for Darlan.

INTERVIEW WITH HITLER

Although Pétain had already made explanations for Laval's dismissal, he asked Abetz to arrange for Darlan to see Hitler. Accordingly, Hitler received the Admiral on Christmas day in his private coach near Beauvais. The Chancellor, accompanied by Abetz and interpreter Paul Schmidt, was in a bad mood when Darlan arrived an hour late.

The Admiral insisted that Pétain and Laval had been in personal conflict for some time. Pétain, he said, had hoped to patch up his relations with Laval, but when they grew worse, he had no choice but to dismiss him. Darlan added that the Marshal had asked him to assure Hitler that the French government would remain faithful to the policy of collaboration.[9] Darlan explained that the Directorate would centralize the powers of the government and make it more harmonious. It would advise the Marshal on political questions, especially those concerning foreign policy and cooperation with Germany. If Hitler would approve the French plan to reorganize the government, Darlan suggested, the ministers responsible for the events of December 13 would be replaced by men who would not repeat that kind of mistake.[10]

Responding, Hitler railed at Darlan for a full half hour.[11] But as for Vichy's governmental reorganization, he would not intervene. "If relations between France and Germany were to remain the same as before," he declared, "it was actually quite immaterial who represented the French Government."[12] He pointed out that he had always favored good Franco-German relations, but that his effort since the armistice to improve relations with France would be absolutely his last. Hitler praised Laval, hinting that General Weygand was responsible for his downfall. The French government, he charged, appeared to be "setting out again onto the same road which had led it to Vichy."[13]

Darlan maintained his composure, answering that Hitler's granting an armistice was proof of the Führer's intention to assign France a place in the reconstruction of Europe. The Admiral reminded Hitler that he could have sailed with the French fleet to America at the expense of an armistice. But he decided instead that France's future lay in cooperating with Germany in the framework of a new European order. That is why, he explained, he had ordered the fleet to follow the Marshal. But on the question of Laval, Darlan stood his ground, insisting that English propaganda would exploit Laval's return and impose a burden on Franco-German relations. Laval, he said, should remain in the background, at least for a time. Concluding, Darlan noted that cooperation involved the participation of both countries, including the stronger. He urged Hitler to continue to cooperate with France.[14] Hitler brought the meeting to a close, shaking Darlan's hand and indicating his intention to respond in writing to Pétain.[15]

Schmidt, who journeyed back to Paris with Darlan, was impressed with the Admiral's calm response to Hitler's blunt manner. He wrote that "the whole scene had slid off the back of this creator of the modern French navy like a breaker off the oily skin of an old walrus."[16] The Admiral had reason to be pleased. Hitler had made no specific demands upon France, nor had he insisted upon Laval's recall.

Darlan's star had begun to rise. Reporting to Washington on December 27, H. Freeman Matthews spoke of Darlan as the new *Dauphin*. He noted that Darlan had become more important politically, "as the fact that he has twice been sent by the Marshal to Paris to treat with German leaders in the past week already shows."[17]

THE STRUGGLE FOR POWER

Absorbed with planning the invasion of the Soviet Union in early 1941, Berlin assigned a lower priority to French affairs. But in Paris, Abetz decided that the time to restore Laval had come. He had the support of collaborationist circles in Paris, led by the journalist Marcel Déat and Fernand de Brinon, the Marshal's representative in the city. The collaborationist press regularly sniped at Flandin, whom they wished to unseat as foreign minister. Darlan had no reason to think that Paris spoke only for itself.

Meanwhile, the Marshal went ahead to create informally the Directorate. He did not, however, announce it to the public, nor did he proceed with the reorganization of the government, as he still expected a message from Hitler. As the Paris press continued to demand Flandin's resignation, Pétain began to weaken on the question of restoring Laval. Toward the middle of January, Darlan informed Abetz that Vichy might restore Laval as minister of state without specific administrative responsibilities.[18]

Pétain continued to think that Berlin desired Laval's restoration. Accordingly, he met with Laval on the 18th at La Ferté-Hauterive, near the demarcation line. If we are to believe Abetz's report of the meeting, Pétain and Laval cleared up their personal misunderstandings. Abetz reported that the Marshal promised that Laval might later be admitted to a cabinet post, pending receipt of Hitler's letter, and that Pétain would issue a statement to prepare public opinion for a possible governmental reorganization.[19]

On the following day, Darlan wrote in a private memo that Hitler might agree to the temporary exclusion of Laval if the Marshal would reorganize the government in a manner friendly to the Reich. He considered that the Marshal might wish to constitute formally the Directorate and admit Laval later as its fourth member. Darlan would remain President of the Directorate and take control of four key ministries. On January 30, as the pressure from Paris mounted, Darlan again wrote privately of his willingness to admit Laval to the Directorate without a portfolio. But when he returned to Paris February 3, Abetz made no demands for the immediate return of Laval.[20]

THE SHELVING OF LAVAL

Unknown to Darlan, Berlin had already decided to put Laval on the shelf, to keep him in Paris where his availability to head a rival French government might be used to influence Vichy. He had also decided to limit French relations strictly to the armistice.[21] Hitler could see that Darlan had more to offer than did Laval. With his imperial connections, the Admiral represented stability in French Africa at a time when Berlin's strategic interests required the status-quo behind the Italian front in Libya. A note from Hitler to Mussolini in late 1940 expresses German worries about the threat of secessionism in French North and West Africa:

> I have always believed that there does not exist a put-up game between the French Government and General de Gaulle. Nevertheless, the circumstances require great prudence. Already the slightest counterstroke could cause North Africa and West Africa to become insecure and--separating themselves from Vichy--they would offer England dangerous bases of operations. The name of General Weygand, who has been sent there to maintain order, does not have a very tranquilizing effect on me.[22]

By early February, Hitler had decided to lend military support to Italy. On the sixth he sent the Wehrmacht a directive to move an armored division to Libya.[23] That same day, Joachim von Ribbentrop wired Abetz a reminder of earlier instructions to keep Laval on the shelf: "I order you to take such action that Laval remain in the occupied zone and that the Laval affair be negotiated with Vichy in such a manner that no agreement be made at the moment for the entry of Laval into Vichy."[24]

Berlin would therefore stand by and allow the triumph of Darlan, who could be expected to keep French North Africa in line. Paris, however, continued to manipulate Vichy in the interest of restoring Laval at a later time.[25] Vichy's ignorance of Berlin's exclusion of Laval made it possible for Abetz to exercise influence on the formation of the Darlan government. On the same day that Abetz received his orders to exclude Laval, the cabinet debated the question of his return to power. Flandin argued that France must choose her own ministers.[26] The cabinet, however, decided to continue the negotiations.

Returning to Paris on February 7, Darlan told Abetz that Laval might now be offered a cabinet post.[27] But the German negotiated instead on the outlines of a government that would not include Laval. Abetz reported to Berlin that Darlan would become Chief of the Government and the Marshal's eventual successor. He would retain his post as Minister of Marine and also take Foreign Affairs, Interior, and Information. Flandin would be dismissed, and Peyrouton would become Ambassador to Argentina. Bouthillier would be demoted. Abetz reported further that Darlan had agreed to Laval's return at a later time, to take the posts occupied by the Admiral, who would stand in line to become Chief of State.[28] But Darlan's account was less specific on that point, stating only that the Admiral would settle later the terms of Laval's return.[29]

FORMATION OF THE DARLAN GOVERNMENT

During the remainder of February, Darlan and the Marshal reorganized the government partly along the lines discussed in Paris. On the 9th Pétain appointed Darlan Vice-President of the Council and named him to succeed Flandin as foreign minister. He retained the Ministry of Marine. Two days later, in accordance with Constitutional Act Number Four, he was named the Marshal's eventual successor. On the 17th he took the Ministry of Interior, replacing Peyrouton. The reorganization of the government was completed after Darlan visited again with Abetz on the 20th to confirm his intention to form a strong government with himself at the apex of the administrative hierarchy.[30]

Abetz continued to think in terms of an interim Darlan government. But the Admiral stood his ground. Laval would eventually be recalled, he promised, but not as Chief of the Government, nor as Minister of Interior. The Marshal and he would resign, he threatened, rather than accept that solution.[31] Darlan pointed out that he had already taken steps toward collaboration by removing Flandin and Peyrouton. He went on to say that the Marshal had given him full authority and that it seemed impossible to move much further in that direction.[32] In sum, Darlan insisted that control of the government was now his, and that he would not settle for keeping the key ministries warm for Laval.

By February 24 the Admiral had streamlined the structure to his own taste, reducing the cabinet to four posts plus himself, to include Huntziger (War), Bouthillier (Finance), Pierre Caziot (Agriculture), and Joseph Barthelemy (Justice). In addition, there were ten secretaries of state subordinated to the ministries.[33] Darlan reported only to Pétain. As Vice-President of the Council, head of three key ministries, and as heir-designate to the Marshal, Darlan enjoyed broad powers. His powers, however, were not absolute, as the Marshal's own entourage enjoyed considerable influence, and Weygand reported directly to Pétain.

Influenced by his Radical Socialist heritage, Darlan envisioned a government committed to social progress and based upon the support of the urban and rural masses. He expected to recruit men of all opinions, as long as they were patriotic reformers.[34] But as it turned out, his government was leaned heavily to the right.

It contained a rich mixture of strong personalities whose agendas often clashed. Some of them reflected the traditional attitudes of the Marshal. Others were technicians. Some were traditional intellectuals and others were doctrinaire Germanophiles. Some had been imposed Pétain, a few by Abetz.

The intellectuals, for example, included Jérôme Carcopino (Education), former Chair of Roman History at the Sorbonne and Rector of the University of Paris. Lucien Romier, historian and journalist, was charged with drafting a new constitution. Joseph Barthelemy (Justice), was a former law professor.[35] Some of the Germanophiles were also intellectuals, but their agenda focused narrowly on drawing France closer to Germany.

Typical of the Germanophiles was Jacques Benoist-Méchin. Son of a family with traditional German connections, he spoke fluent German and had a special interest in German intellectual and military affairs. Released from a prisoner of war camp in 1940, Benoist-Méchin served as Darlan's Secretary of State for Franco-German relations.[36] A zealous Germanophile, he brought to Franco-German negotiations a sincerity that Darlan could only pretend.

Among the technicians was Yves Bouthillier, whom Darlan retained in his government despite German objections to him. Another, Maurice Couve de Murville, who had a promising postwar career ahead of him despite his Vichy connection, served as acting head of the Mouvement Général des Fonds in Paris. Reporting to Vichy every two weeks, he made discreet visits to the American embassy. He provided valuable information to the Americans, who trusted him.[37] An important figure in the foreign office was Charles Rochat, who reported directly to Darlan. American embassy officials trusted Rochat and considered him to be entirely on the side of the Allies. But Rochat was an obedient bureaucrat, serving Laval in 1942 as well as he served Darlan in 1941. Darlan used Rochat to influence the Americans, who tended to exaggerate the distinction between collaborators and Frenchmen "on our side." An embassy report of late 1941 containing information on thirty-six French foreign office officials listed Rochat and thirteen others as being "on our side."[38]

Darlan relied heavily upon the loyalty of key military and naval officers in the empire, where it was important to head off secessionism and to oppose any Anglo-Gaullist aggression. French colonial administrators had taken a personal oath of loyalty to the Marshal, and for the most part they remained loyal to him. Among the military leaders was General Auguste Noguès, Resident General of French Morocco. Darlan knew Noguès well, having worked with him at the time of the Spanish Civil War.[39] General Maxime Weygand was a different case. As the Marshal's Delegate General for French Africa, Weygand remained steadfastly loyal. But Darlan mistrusted him. German police records labeled Weygand "the leader of the opposition to a policy of collaboration with Germany."[40]

The Admiral could count on the loyalty of his naval officers. His old friend, Admiral Jean Pierre Esteva, remained Resident General of Tunisia. Darlan's closest confidant, Henri Moysset, had been a friend since childhood. Though not a naval officer, Moysset had served at the Rue Royale with Georges Leygues. Darlan brought Moysset into the government as Secretary of State to the Vice-President.[41]

Several of Darlan's administrators were former businessmen connected with the Banque Worms, a financial-industrial establishment that before the war had subsidized right-wing movements. Rumors held that these men and their German friends had formed in the 1930s a mysterious fascist organization, the synarchy, to advance their capitalist interests. The rumors of a synarchist conspiracy were, however, exaggerated. Among the leaders of the Worms clique were Jacques Barnaud, Delegate General for Franco-German Economic Relations, and Pierre Pucheu, Secretary of State for Industrial Production and later Minister of Interior.[42]

Darlan's view of government reflected the tensions in his political and military background. He wanted, on the one hand, a broadly based government conforming to his republican heritage, and on the other, an authoritarian administration in the tradition of his naval experience. The latter was the dominant influence. His secular republicanism, moreover, was overshadowed by the royalism and clericalism of the Marshal. In any case, Darlan would have found it difficult to form a government that balanced perfectly the clashing traditions that had shaped his perspective.

Darlan's power base at Vichy was broad and deep. But Darlan was never secure in his position. The Germans might at any time insist upon the restoration of Laval. If the Admiral expected to remain in power and to address France's pressing needs, he would have to maintain workable relations with the Reich. If he expected to gain economic benefits from abroad, he would have to cultivate relations with the Americans. In 1941, French interests demanded a balanced policy to keep open a range of options. That was no easy task, but Darlan was more qualified for it than was Laval.

NOTES

1. See FRUS, 1940, II, 490-493.

2. Paul Baudouin, *The Private Diaries of Paul Baudouin* (London: Eyre and Spottiswoode, 1948), 291-292; Otto Abetz, *Pétain et les Allemands* (Paris: Éditions Gaucher, 1948), 147; Hervé Coutau-Bégarie and Claude Huan, *Darlan* (Paris: Fayard, 1989), 353.

3. Abetz, *Pétain et les Allemands*, 48, 50.

4. Ibid., 50. See also Baudouin, *The Private Diaries*, 292-294.

5. See Baudouin, *The Private Diaries*, 293-294; Coutau-Bégarie and Huan, *Darlan*, 354; DGFP, Series D, XI, 893-896.

6. DGFP, Series D, XI, 898.

7. Ibid., 891.

8. Ibid., 918.

9. Ibid., 951. See also Alain Darlan, *L'Amiral Darlan parle* (Paris: Amiot-Dumont, 1952), 263.

10. DGFP, Series D, XI, 951-952.

11. Paul Schmidt, *Hitler's Interpreter* (London: Macmillan, 1951), 207.

12. DGFP, Series D, XI, 952.

13. Ibid., 953.

14. Ibid., 954-955.

15. For Darlan's account of the interview, see Darlan, *Darlan parle*, 262-267.

16. Schmidt, *Hitler's Interpreter*, 207.

17. USNA, State Department Records, 740.0011 European War 1939/7300.

18. Abetz, *Pétain et les Allemands*, 68-69.

19. See DGFP, Series D, XI, 1134-1137.

20. Darlan, *L'Amiral Darlan parle*, 104-105, 268-270, 278, 280.

21. Franz Halder, "The Private War Journal of Generaloberst Franz Halder," 10 volumes (Chapel Hill: University of North Carolina Bowman Gray Collection, n.d.), V, 98.

22. DGFP, Series D, XI, 790-791.

23. Ibid., XII, 26-30.

24. Abetz, *Pétain et les Allemands*, 79.

25. On February 11 the American naval attaché in Paris reported that the Paris press "intimates that Admiral Darlan will hold the job until a more suitable candidate (Laval) is ready to take over." USNA, RG 38, ONI, C-10-J, Box 526, "Political Conditions in France."

26. Yves Bouthillier, *Le Drame de Vichy*, two volumes (Paris: Plon, 1950), I, 280-281.

27. Darlan, *L'Amiral Darlan parle*, 281-286. See also Coutau-Bégarie and Huan, *Darlan*, 785, n. 36.

28. DGFP, Series D, XII, 53-54.

29. Darlan, *L'Amiral Darlan parle*, 285.

30. Ibid., 289; Coutau-Bégarie and Huan, *Darlan*, 379-380.

31. Coutau-Bégarie and Huan, *Darlan*, 379.

32. Ibid., 379-380. Darlan's notes on which this paragraph is based is prior memorandum outlining what Darlan intended to say.

33. Darlan, *L'Amiral Darlan parle*, 289.

34. Ibid., 140-141.

35. Henri du Moulin de Labarthète, *Le Temps des illusions* (Genève: Cheval Ailé, 1946), 151, 153. See also Microfilmed German Documents, T175, Reel 483, frames 9342978-979, 9343019. These are German police records on oppositional political currents at Vichy.

36. See MGD, T175, Reel 483, frames 9342963-964.

37. Unpublished Diary of Admiral William D. Leahy (Washington: Library of Congress, Manuscripts Division), Vol. 7 (hereinafter cited as Leahy Diaries).

38. Leahy Diaries, Vol. 7.

39. Interview with Captain Henri Ballande, June 1982.

40. MGD, T175, Reel 483, frame 9343027.

41. See Henri du Moulin, *Le Temps des illusions*, 142-144; and MGD, T175, Reel 483, frame 9342953.

42. MGD, T175, Reel 483, frames 9342954, 9343016-018.

CHAPTER 13

In the Shadow of the Third Reich

Living in the shadow of the Third Reich created problems for Darlan that Americans viewed only from a safe distance. It was easy for neutrals beyond the Reich's reach to judge sternly any measures he might take to protect France from Nazi brutality.

Darlan established good relations with Admiral William D. Leahy, new American Ambassador, who opened negotiations for food shipments to France. And the Murphy-Weygand Agreement of February 26 provided economic aid to North Africa and for the entry of American economic advisers.[1] Washington soon came to regard North Africa as an area of special American influence, which helped shield it from the British. London was less likely to launch military adventures in a region Washington had staked out for itself.

ECONOMIC COLLABORATION

But Berlin held economic powers over Vichy that Washington could not match. By tightening the demarcation line, the Reich could choke off commerce and impose oppressive hardships on Frenchmen in both zones. And occupation costs of 20 million reichsmarks per day plus an unfair currency exchange rate amounted to a monstrous exploitation of the French economy. Germany plundered France so outrageously that Darlan could not ignore public demands for negotiations to ease the burdens of the occupation.

In mid-January Wiesbaden promised that French deliveries of fuel and supplies to General Erwin Rommel's Afrika Korps could lead to the solution of problems important to France. With the bait dangling before him, Darlan agreed in early February to deliver 5,000 tons of fuel oil and an equal amount of gasoline from French stocks in Tunisia. On the 7th he agreed to deliveries from

France of 8,000 trucks and 5,000 vans. And in late April he caved in to German demands to purchase four hundred trucks parked in North Africa.[2] The situation reports of the German occupation authority in Paris praised the Admiral, stating that he had "replaced sentimental collaboration with a practical one."[3] But Germany made no concessions to France.

Darlan's frequent visits to Paris inched him ever closer toward military collaboration. Abetz, wishing to drag Vichy back into the war, pushed Darlan in that direction. Although Darlan had no British war on his agenda, Abetz wired Berlin on April 25 that the Admiral was prepared to provoke an Anglo-French naval war during the coming summer.[4] Two days later Berlin decided to lend military support to an anti-British rebellion in Iraq.[5] But that support would hinge upon Darlan's permitting German aircraft en route to Iraq to refuel in Syria. When Abetz asked toward the end of April if Darlan would permit transit of the aircraft, the Admiral replied firmly "I will not let them pass unless we obtain in exchange some very important and essential things for France."[6]

When Darlan returned to Paris on May 3, Abetz indicated that France might expect a reduction in occupation costs, liberation of some prisoners, and a relaxation of the demarcation line. The application of the concessions, he cautioned, would have to await the decision of Hitler, who would receive Darlan within a few days. But France would have to prove her good faith by granting the right of transit across Syria. Darlan replied that he personally favored the proposals. But his government might not approve, he warned, because Germany had not yet granted France a single important concession. Abetz then hinted that Germany might allow some naval rearmament.[7]

Back in Paris on May 5, Darlan and Benoist-Méchin demanded the release of 83,000 war prisoners, a relaxation of the demarcation line, a 25 percent reduction in the occupation costs, a guarantee of French sovereignty over Syria, and a public declaration by the German government guaranteeing the integrity of the French empire. Abetz replied that Germany was willing to grant every demand except the last, which would require the attention of Hitler.[8] At the same time, General Oskar Vogl requested German use of French airfields and other facilities in Syria, as well as the sale of military supplies and equipment there. In return, France would be permitted to rearm seven torpedo boats, to replace the armaments sent from Syria to Iraq, and to strengthen French defenses in Syria with armaments from France. The demarcation line would be relaxed and occupation costs would be reduced from 20 to 15 million reichsmarks per day.[9]

Late in the afternoon Darlan accepted the German offer. Technical details would be settled in negotiations to begin in Paris the next day. But the Germans proceeded with the reduction of occupation costs on the basis of guidelines that would neutralize the reduction and tighten Berlin's grip on the French economy.[10] The technical negotiations bogged down with France not receiving the clear reduction the Germans had promised.[11] Darlan made up his mind to enter into the next round of negotiations with more caution.

After Britain had suppressed the Iraqi rebellion, the German planes were withdrawn. Now Berlin shifted its attention to Libya. British naval and air forces operating out of Malta and Alexandria had cut sharply into Axis shipments to

Tripoli, so that General Rommel suffered shortages of fuel and supplies. The time had come for Berlin to demand use of Bizerte, to establish an alternate supply route that by-passed Malta and was more distant from the British squadron at Alexandria.

ANOTHER INTERVIEW WITH HITLER

Darlan, however, would have to grant access to the port, which is why Hitler had invited him to Berchtesgaden. Arriving on May 11, Darlan conferred first with Ribbentrop. "One thing was absolutely certain," the German said. "Today Germany had won the war, that is, the war in general. It was essential that this fact be grasped once and for all by the French leadership."[12] He promised Darlan that French assistance in defeating Britain could lead to a generous peace settlement, so that France would emerge from the war with her empire largely undisturbed. Meeting afterward with Hitler, Darlan declared himself in favor of collaboration. He expressed the hope that "the Führer would light up the dark road along which France was moving, so that the French nation could get a clearer picture of the future."[13] Irritated, Hitler explained that the Axis were fighting for Europe, that concessions would weaken the war effort, and that he would have to ask compensation for any concessions granted France.

Darlan answered that France had recently delivered trucks to the Afrika Korps and had made airfields available to the Luftwaffe in Syria, which risked provoking British attacks on the French empire. Refusing to retreat, Darlan insisted that Frenchmen in Africa and Syria "were constantly asking him why they should defend a territory which will after all be taken away from them later on."[14] Holding his ground, Darlan complained about the treatment France had received under the armistice. "Among the French at home," he observed,

the question was raised time and again how one could cooperate with a Germany which had divided France into two parts, had imposed high occupation costs, and prevented the French Government from governing the two parts uniformly. Every gesture which would ameliorate these difficulties in this respect and reduce the occupation costs would evoke a favorable reaction among the French people.[15]

Darlan complained about food shortages in France, and he suggested that the release of even some of the prisoners would make a good impression among Frenchmen.

Hitler answered that he had already assured Pétain that Germany did not plan to dismantle the French empire. As for conditions in France, he remarked that it was necessary to keep German armies on French soil to guard against any British incursion by way of Spain or Portugal. Hitler finally came to the main point:

The Führer then asked Darlan whether the French Government would consent to letting the trucks purchased by Germany in Tunisia proceed to Tripoli with a load; since the unloading facilities of the harbors of Tripoli were being used to capacity, additional quantities of German equipment, which would be unloaded in French harbors and then transported to Tripoli with the help of these trucks, would in this manner be placed at German disposal in North Africa.[16]

The German account indicates that Darlan answered in the affirmative. But Darlan's own summary of the interview gives no indication that he agreed to concede use of the port.[17]

Next day Darlan again met with Ribbentrop. The German record concluded with the observation that Darlan had agreed to enter the war against England in the near future.[18] But Darlan's record of the interview makes no mention of France's entering the Anglo-German war. It speaks instead of giving aid to Germany in the war against England.[19] Returning to Vichy in his private coach, Darlan told Benoist-Méchin that he had agreed only "in principle" to permit German use of Bizerte.[20]

The German record of the interview, which highlights the roles of Hitler and Ribbentrop at the expense of Darlan's, glosses over the formula which would govern the exchange of concessions in the negotiations to follow. A summary written by Benoist-Méchin indicates that Hitler promised to match important French concessions with important German concessions, with the same principle governing minor concessions. Darlan saw it as a precise "give and take" arrangement, as opposed to haggling for an equal match.[21]

Darlan had moved closer to the German orbit, a shift that coincided with spectacular German victories in Libya and the Balkans. The war appeared to be approaching an end. Leahy reported in mid-May that Frenchmen "have now largely become so discouraged as to hope only for an early peace and for the liberation of the million and a half prisoners."[22] And in Africa, Murphy reported that French officials avoided him. One of them "advised vigorously that I not waste my time talking about a British victory," that "nobody is interested any more...in the British effort."[23]

DEFENDING COLLABORATION

Such was the mood among Frenchmen when Darlan reported to the cabinet on May 14. He commented that Germany would win the war, and that France would receive a generous domestic and colonial settlement if she would help the Reich during the final stages. The cabinet approved his recommendation for collaboration without war on England.[24]

On the next day, Darlan heard the first of several stern warnings from Washington. But he took little note. His message of May 19 to the French consul in New York reveals his thoughts: "The Germans have stated that if we...go along with them...they have no intention of annexing part of our colonial empire, the obligation to defend our empire at the present time being naturally for us the counterpart of this conditional assurance."[25] But having been burned in the Syrian deal, Darlan mistrusted the Germans. He noticed that Abetz was still dragging his feet on concessions to France.[26] When the final negotiations opened in Paris, Darlan was alert to the danger of falling into another German trap.

THE PARIS PROTOCOLS

The Paris negotiations that began on May 20 lasted nine days, with Darlan attending only the opening and final sessions.[27] On the first day, General Walter

Warlimont notified the French delegation of German demands that included the sale of four hundred trucks from stocks in Africa, delivery of the trucks loaded with food supplies, the placing of a North African port at the disposal of Germany, and the chartering of French ships for delivery of goods along the coast from Tunisia to Libya.[28] Responding, Darlan insisted that the trucks be loaded with food from Italy, since French food supplies were short. He warned that there would be a British reaction against Bizerte. "That is why," he insisted, "it is necessary to modify the armistice clauses concerning naval forces, naval aviation, pursuit, and anti-aircraft units."[29] He added a long list of demands that included removal of restrictions on deliveries of arms and supplies to French armies in North Africa.[30]

Darlan made clear his position on German demands for use of the port at Dakar. Troops and equipment sent to North Africa, he explained, were only replacements for materials sent to Syria; but in the case of West Africa, France was asking for an increase in armaments. He also insisted upon their being in place prior to the entry of any German submarines.[31] Darlan left for Vichy the next day, having made clear his position on both Bizerte and Dakar.

Returning to Paris a week later, he found that the French delegation had negotiated with the Germans three protocols, one confirming the Syrian agreement, a second opening the door to Bizerte, and a third making Dakar available to German submarines by July 15. Each protocol listed the military concessions the Reich would grant in return. Darlan saw that the agreements were badly out of balance.[32]

The French account of the final sessions, recorded by Lieutenant Marty, reveals that Darlan fought back stubbornly. When the session opened late in the afternoon of the 27th, Darlan insisted that Hitler had promised an equal counterpart for each French concession. The German equivalents for the French concessions in Syria, he charged, had not been forthcoming. As for Bizerte, Darlan warned that the British would attack French ports and maritime traffic. He warned that German use of Dakar would lead to the outbreak of an Anglo-French war. Further military concessions were necessary, he insisted. Finally, he upped his demands, insisting upon new political negotiations and political concessions as a condition for the application of the military agreements.[33]

When the negotiations resumed that evening, Darlan insisted that the final accord would have to await the conclusion of a separate political agreement. Warlimont objected, demanding that France fulfill her commitments at Dakar by July 15. But Darlan remained adamant: "Nothing can be done at Dakar, as long as the defensive system is not in place and the political conditions are not fulfilled."[34] Now the talks moved so fast that Marty fell behind with his notes. After midnight he concluded with the comment that an additional protocol would be necessary to prepare the way for discussions about Dakar. Benoist-Méchin and Abetz would draft it during the night.[35] Darlan had stood his ground, insisting upon the subordination of the military protocols to a political protocol.

All four protocols were ready the next day. The first confirmed the Syrian agreement of May 6. The important second protocol opened the port of Bizerte for the deposit of supplies and foodstuffs to be shipped south by rail to Libya. A small German detachment was authorized to proceed to Bizerte to supervise the passage of 1,500 vehicles from Africa and France. In return, the Germans agreed to release about 6,000 prisoners, including General Alphonse Juin, to allow limited rearmament of the French forces in North Africa, and to permit greater freedom of naval movement in the Mediterranean.[36]

The third protocol expressed French "readiness in principle" to permit German access to Dakar.[37] During the initial phase, to begin on July 15, German submarines would be supplied from a tender in the harbor, and German merchant ships would be permitted brief visits. The second phase, to begin at an unspecified time, expanded the concessions to include German use of the harbor facilities, the entry of surface units into the port, and German access to the air base at Dakar. The agreements of the second phase were, however, subordinated to implementation of German concessions to be negotiated under the fourth protocol.[38]

The third protocol assumed British reprisals and the need for France to defend West Africa. To that end, the Germans conceded the liberation of nearly 32,000 prisoners and modest military and naval rearmament, which included nine French destroyers.[39] Darlan could see that the risks far outweighed the concessions. The fourth, or supplementary, protocol observed that German use of Bizerte and Dakar would risk an immediate war with Britain or the United States. Therefore, the French government would be granted additional military and political concessions to permit the immediate assumption of the risks attendant to the services at Bizerte. But for West Africa, reinforcements would be increased prior to execution of the protocol, and the Reich would grant additional political and economic concessions to justify in France a war with the Anglo-Saxon powers.[40] The fourth protocol was signed by Darlan and Abetz, but not by Warlimont.

THE PROTOCOLS CHALLENGED

Opposition to the protocols was led by General Weygand, who arrived from North Africa on June 2. He was soon joined by Pierre Boisson, Governor General of West Africa, and Admiral Jean-Pierre Esteva from Tunisia. On the morning of June 3, the council assembled. After the Admiral had spoken mildly in favor of the protocols, Weygand insisted that he would have to resign should Vichy open Africa to the Axis. The two men briefly debated the issue until Pétain called a halt.[41] That afternoon Weygand suggested that Vichy escape from the protocols by advancing demands so high that the Reich would have to reject them. The Marshal agreed. Darlan, offering no protest, set about drafting demands in the manner Weygand had suggested.[42]

Darlan presented them on June 6 in the presence of Weygand, Boisson, and Esteva. Among the demands were replacement of the armistice with new texts, restoration of French sovereignty over all of France except Alsace-Lorraine, full freedom of transit across the demarcation line, progressive liberation of all war prisoners, and a German declaration guaranteeing the integrity of the empire.[43] Weygand insisted that Darlan stand firmly behind the French demands, and that he permit no shipments to go through Bizerte to the Axis. Darlan nodded agreement.[44]

In the meantime, Darlan informed the French delegation at Wiesbaden of his government's position toward the military protocols. He made it clear that they were purely military agreements, one part of larger Franco-German negotiations launched at Berchtesgaden. The advantages France might expect to obtain were mainly political concessions not contained in the military agreements. The military concessions contained in the document, he explained, should not be regarded as counterparts to French concessions, but merely as reinforcements to enable France to oppose any British reaction to the execution of the protocols.[45]

THE GERMAN VIEW OF THE PROTOCOLS

Reading the note containing the French demands, a surprised Abetz commented to Benoist-Méchin: "It is insane, everything you ask here."[46] Abetz stated bluntly that the Reich recognized only the military protocols. Wiesbaden took the same position. Keitel's instructions to the armistice commission omitted the political protocol. And in orders of June 6, Keitel instructed the commission to exploit as quickly as possible the commitments Vichy had made. Concessions by Vichy were to be matched equally. Should Vichy delay execution of the terms, the commission would withhold the German counterparts. Keitel further explained that the commission "should observe for the present the basic principle that an armed conflict between France and England or the United States should not be provoked."[47]

Ribbentrop carefully explained German policy to Abetz. "Nothing worse could happen to us," he remarked on June 1, "than for France to get into a war with England."[48] He suggested that the entire world situation soon would change, and that the French question would find its own solution by the end of the year. When Abetz suggested additional concessions for France, Ribbentrop answered that he had nothing more to offer. He scolded the ambassador for placing his confidence in Darlan, whose aides, he said, sat ready to bolt to North Africa.[49]

Surprisingly, selected terms of the Bizerte protocol were being implemented during the second week of June, even after Benoist-Méchin had wired Darlan from Paris on the 6th that Abetz had no political or economic concessions for France.[50] Moreover, some of the military equivalents promised France under the second and third protocols had been authorized that week.[51] Despite Weygand's demand that the protocols be scuttled, supplies moved on to the Afrika Korps from Tunisia, after Darlan's friend Esteva had returned there.

ASSESSMENT

The question is whether Darlan intended to employ the political protocol as an escape clause, or did he merely intend it as a tool to drive a harder bargain? The answer is that he intended to escape from the agreements that imposed prohibitive risks. Darlan intended all along to escape fully from the agreement regarding West Africa. He had made it clear to Warlimont on May 27 that the Dakar agreement involved the unacceptable risk of war with Britain. But he could not employ the political protocol in a manner to escape entirely from his commitments regarding Tunisia. He could see that Berlin assigned higher priority to the second protocol, which served the urgent German need to nourish the Afrika Korps. An untimely withdrawal might tempt the Axis to seize Tunisia. Moreover, the risks involving Bizerte were less than those at Dakar. Darlan would accept some of the risks under the second protocol in the interest of restraining the Reich. He reserved the option of dragging his feet or granting concessions selectively.

Shifting patterns in the European war reinforced Darlan's decision to hedge on the military protocols. The sinking of the battleship *Bismarck* on May 28 signaled British determination to continue the struggle. And reports he received soon afterward of German plans to strike into Russia further suggested that the war would continue.[52] But he had already inserted the political protocol, in the interest of blunting both German and British threats to the security of the empire.

NOTES

1. FRUS, 1941, II, 229-231, 237-239.

2. DFCAA, IV, 74-75, 82, 338-348.

3. MGD, T501, Roll 143, frame 000734, Militärbefehlshaber Frankreich/ Kommandostab/Abteilung Ia, "Legenbericht für die Monat August 1940-Juli 1941."

4. See Otto Abetz, *Pétain et les allemands* (Paris: Éditions Gaucher, 1948), 96-98.

5. DGFP, Series D, XII, 587-588, 653.

6. Jean Louis-Aujol, editor, *Le Procès de Benoist-Méchin* (Paris: Albin Michel, 1948), 127.

7. Abetz, *Pétain et les Allemands*, 99-100.

8. *Le Procès de Benoist-Méchin*, 127.

9. DGFP, Series D, XII, 740-741.

10. Ibid., 367-368, 718-720, 740-742.

11. Yves Bouthillier, *Le Drame de Vichy*, 2 volumes (Paris: Plon, 1950), II, 71-76.

12. DGFP, Series D, XII, 758.

13. Ibid., 764.

14. Ibid.

15. Ibid., 769.

16. Ibid., 772.

17. Hervé Coutau-Bégarie and Claude Huan, *Lettres et notes de l'Amiral Darlan* (Paris: Economica, 1992), 322-324.

18. DGFP, Series D, XII, 782.

19. Coutau-Bégarie and Huan, *Lettres et notes de l'Amiral Darlan*, 324.

20. Jacques Benoist-Méchin, *De la défaite au désastre*, 2 volumes (Paris: Albin Michel, 1984), I, 100.

21. Ibid., 89.

22. FRUS, 1941, II, 168.

23. Ibid., 340.

24. Henri Ballande, *De l'Amirauté à Bikini* (Paris: Cité, 1972), 286-290.

25. USNA, RG 457, VICHY FRENCH DIPLOMATIC MESSAGES, Part XXXIX, 0011488, May 19, 1942, Vichy (Darlan) to New York, #379. Misdated, it is obviously May 19, 1941 (hereinafter cited as VFDM).

26. Coutau-Bégarie and Huan, *Darlan*, 409.

27. French National Archives, AJ41-40, Cabinet 63, Négociations de Paris du 20 au 28 Mai et suites, La Direction des Services de l'Armistice, "Procès-Verbal Analytique de la Réunion tenue le 21 Mai, à 11 H. 30 à l'Ambassade d'Allemagne à Paris."

28. Ibid.

29. Ibid.

30. Ibid.

31. Ibid.

32. Ibid., sessions of 22, 23, 24, 25, and 26 May.

33. Ibid., session of 27 May.

34. Ibid.

35. Ibid.

36. DGFP, Series D, XII, 894-896.

37. Ibid., 897.

38. Ibid.

39. Ibid., 897-900.

40. Ibid.

41. Maxime Weygand, *Mémoires* (Paris: Flammarion, 1950), III, 429-431.

42. See Ibid., 432-433.

43. For full listing of the demands, see Bouthillier, *Le Drame de Vichy*, II, 78-79.

44. Weygand, *Mémoires*, III, 435.

45. French National Archives, AJ41-40, Cabinet 63, DSA, "Military Negotiations between Vichy and the Axis powers from May 41 until July 42."

46. *Le Procès de Benoist-Méchin*, 236.

47. MGD, T77, Reel 850, frames 5594751-761, Records of Headquarters, German Armed Forces High Command (Oberkommando der Wehrmacht/OKW), WiRu Amt, German Armistice Commission, Paris Office.

48. MGD, T501, Reel 122, frame 000162, Records of German Field Commands: Rear Areas, Occupied Territories, and others, Deutsche Waffenstillstandkommission für Wirtschaft.

49. Ibid., frames 000162-167.

50. Benoist-Méchin, *De la défaite au désastre*, I, 142-143.

51. DFCAA, IV, 484, 513-514.

52. Moysset, aware of German plans to attack Russia, advised Darlan to withdraw from the protocols. See Coutau-Bégarie and Huan, *Darlan*, 420.

CHAPTER 14

The Syrian War

Admiral Darlan once commented that the war in Syria enabled France to pursue a workable policy toward Germany.[1] There is much truth in the remark, for the Anglo-Gaullist attack on the French colony demonstrated the risks of permitting a German military presence in the French empire. Although Darlan had no desire for a war in Syria, the loss of the colony helped him to justify before the Germans a policy of restraint in executing the agreements he had concluded with them.

DECISION TO DEFEND SYRIA

Darlan knew that German aircraft in Syria might provoke British reprisals against the colony and perhaps elsewhere. On May 13 he requested of Wiesbaden reinforcements for both Syria and North Africa.[2] He realized that Syria could not be reinforced by sea. Isolated by British naval power, the small Syrian army under General Henri Fernand Dentz could not sustain a long struggle. Darlan remarked in June to Admiral Leahy that he had no hopes of staging a successful defense of Syria.[3]

Nevertheless, the Admiral chose to defend Syria. In mid-May he ordered Dentz to resist any Anglo-Gaullist attack.[4] Two days before the attack, he stated publicly that there were no German troops in Syria and that France would use her own troops to defend the colony against any aggression.[5] When the attack finally came on June 8, Darlan remarked to Pétain that "if we do not defend ourselves the Germans will take North Africa."[6]

Darlan had overestimated German capabilities. On June 15, Keitel wrote Ribbentrop that use of military force against Bizerte and Dakar was out of the question, and that using force against metropolitan France would provoke secessionism in North Africa. The only course left, he admitted, was negotiations.[7]

Keitel realized that the use of force against France or Tunisia was not worth the risks of upsetting the status quo in French Africa on the eve of the invasion of Russia, scheduled for June 22.

MANAGING THE WAR

Darlan worked from the beginning to localize the conflict. On June 8 he informed London through the American embassy at Vichy that France "recognized the dangers inherent in the situation and will undertake all measures to prevent the spread or prolongation of the war."[8] Next day, Under Secretary of State Sumner Welles informed Lord Halifax in Washington of the American desire that the Syrian conflict not spread to North or West Africa.[9] That was a gentle warning to London to take no reprisals against what had become an area of special American influence. The British reply expressed satisfaction that France wished to localize the conflict.[10]

The Admiral did indeed wish to localize the conflict, but the question of Axis intervention in Syria burdened his efforts. When the Italian control commission in Beirut suggested the use of Italian aircraft against British forces in the area, Dentz replied that the Italians were free to attack the British anywhere on condition that their aircraft keep away from Syrian airfields.[11] But the Germans gained the false impression that Dentz, and perhaps also Darlan, had requested German aerial intervention.[12] A German offer to use aircraft based on Crete to attack the Allies in Syria created more problems for him. German aerial intervention would risk provoking British attacks elsewhere, especially should German aircraft land on Syrian airfields.

Darlan did not reject the German offer outright; instead, he laid down conditions intended to keep Axis planes away from the battlefield. Huntziger's wire to General Paul Doyen at Wiesbaden on June 11 insisted that intervention should preclude German flights over Syria, and that British ships operating along the coast and Allied airfields in rear areas would be suitable targets. German air attacks in the combat area could take place only upon the orders of Dentz, who is such case would file his request with the Italian control commission.[13]

Then, in a long telegram to Dentz on the night of June 11-12, Darlan expressed Vichy's desire to evade the German offer, but he added that Axis intervention could take place only upon Dentz's request.[14] Clearly, Darlan intended Dentz to refuse Axis aid of his own accord. The General, however, failed to take the hint, and next day he asked Vichy to request Axis aircraft. Meantime, Darlan rushed off another telegram to Dentz informing him that French aircraft were enroute and that German aid should be refused unless it could be "not only rapid and continuous, but above all, massive."[15] Dentz therefore on the 13th withdrew his request. Later that day Darlan sent Dentz another message ordering him to hold out as long as possible to demonstrate French determination to resist Allied aggression.[16] Darlan then sent General Jean Bergeret to Beirut, to tell Dentz in confidence that German intervention was not wanted.[17] Afterward, the Admiral sidetracked German proposals to use Syrian airfields. He clearly intended to restrict German intervention to areas where the Luftwaffe required no French approval.

Darlan had more interest in localizing the war than shutting it down. Throughout June, Dentz maintained a stubborn defense, but the French position grew steadily worse. Without instructions from Darlan, Dentz on June 20 asked the American consul general in Beirut to inquire of the British about the possibilities of ending the war.[18] But Darlan, worried that a premature armistice might provoke German reprisals, refused to give up the struggle. When Huntziger wired Dentz that French resistance should continue, the General replied that Frenchmen in Syria did not understand the reasons for the heavy sacrifices their government was asking of them. Huntziger answered that Vichy had to consider both military and political circumstances in any decision to end the war.[19]

Darlan attempted to send reinforcements. Loaded trains moved to the Turkish frontier. On June 23, Benoist-Méchin departed for Ankara to make the French case for letting them pass. Further, Hitler authorized the release of the *Strasbourg* to escort reinforcements to the front. And on July 1 Darlan requested through Wiesbaden massive German aerial attacks upon British installations in Palestine and Jordan. He made it clear, however, that Syrian airfields remained off limits. In early July all of these initiatives collapsed.[20]

Darlan's only option now was to accept defeat. On the 6th, with the Anglo-Gaullist armies poised to take Beirut, Dentz wired for instructions in the event that all French resistance should collapse.[21] Knowing that further resistance was pointless, and having made a political point in fighting to the bitter end, Darlan on the 7th authorized Dentz to open negotiations with the local British commander. A week later, on July 14, the Treaty of Saint Jean d'Acre ended the Syrian war.[22]

DRAGGING HIS FEET ON THE PROTOCOLS

In June Darlan faced the troubling question of whether to apply the terms of the Paris protocols. On the third he created a negotiating commission to address the problem with German authorities. Headed by Benoist-Méchin, it was connected to the French delegation at Wiesbaden through Admiral Paul Marzin. It was anchored in the Admiral's office at Vichy under the direction of Captain Paul Fontaine.[23] Darlan therefore personally controlled the negotiations, which opened in Paris just after the outbreak of the Syrian war.

Darlan began to drag his feet on the protocols. On June 9 he instructed Benoist-Méchin to avoid technical discussions and any discussion of the protocol concerning West Africa. Accordingly, Benoist-Méchin told Abetz and Vogl that Darlan's government considered Africa too weak to defend against any British attack that might be provoked through application of the protocols. He relayed a request from Darlan for a meeting with Ribbentrop to discuss problems growing out of the military situation in Syria.[24]

Vogl, who had come to Paris to negotiate the application of the Bizerte agreement, threatened to impose sanctions should France not immediately implement its terms. But the Frenchman stood firm: "It is out of the question," he insisted. "French blood is spilled in Syria. We will not do anything which will cause us to run the same risk in North Africa."[25] Assuring Vogl that Vichy would later implement the protocol, Benoist-Méchin conceded that technical discussions might begin on condition that application of the accord await the approval of his government.[26]

Technical discussions at Wiesbaden focused on the question of using Bizerte for deliveries of trucks and supplies to Libya. On July 4, Darlan instructed Marzin to make no commitment on the execution of that part of the protocol without Vichy's approval.[27] With the Syrian war grinding to a disastrous end, and with Berlin's attention now turned toward Russia, Darlan saw an opportunity to back away from the Bizerte accord with less risk of provoking German reprisals.

WITHDRAWAL FROM THE PARIS PROTOCOLS

When Darlan met with Abetz and Vogl in Paris on July 7 and 8, he insisted that shipments through Bizerte would provoke British attacks upon Dakar, and he warned that his government could not defend before public opinion another disaster like that in Syria unless it received additional military and moral concessions. Darlan renewed his request for a meeting with Ribbentrop to discuss Franco-German relations, including the question of a peace settlement between France and Germany. In a note to Abetz, he wrote that his government had not changed its position and that his insistence upon new political discussions arose from his conviction that they were "indispensable for the French Government so that it can proceed along the path it has traced for itself."[28]

Returning to Vichy, Darlan assembled in the presence of Pétain his military chiefs--Huntziger, Bergeret, and Weygand--who had been summoned from Algiers. There was general agreement that Vichy should stand firm in refusing to cooperate in the Bizerte project.[29] Next day, July 10, the cabinet formally adopted that position, and that same evening Darlan notified Abetz of the decision.[30]

On July 14, Darlan sent Abetz a long note explaining Vichy's reasons for abandoning the Bizerte project. He noted specifically the British attack upon Syria, the growing hostility of Britain and the United States toward France, and the deadlock in Franco-German negotiations framing the three military protocols. Stressing the dangers of a British attack against Dakar, the Admiral insisted that France could not expose herself to a Anglo-French war without substantial rearmament, without the dismantling of the armistice regime, and without the return of France to the status of a great power. He requested the opening of negotiations with both Berlin and Rome with the view of arranging a broad political settlement based on the restoration of French sovereignty and a loyal cooperation between France and the Axis powers. Further, he asked for specific assurances regarding the integrity of the French empire and the French continental frontiers, less Alsace-Lorraine, in return for Vichy's entering the war against Britain, the United States, and the Soviet Union. Attached to the note were declarations for a provisional peace treaty between France and the Axis powers, for French membership in the Tripartite Pact, and for a revision of the 1940 armistice convention.[31]

Darlan obviously intended to scuttle the protocols. Had he intended to negotiate seriously, he would have presented realistic demands. But he instead advanced prohibitive demands. Further, Darlan could easily have scuttled the Bizerte project without calling Weygand to Vichy. His summoning Weygand in advance of his visit to Paris suggests he had already decided to withdraw from the protocols and to shift the blame to the General. Had he honestly intended to negotiate a settlement with the Reich, he would not have called Weygand to Vichy. And the careful timing of the delivery of prohibitive demands to coincide with the loss of Syria on July 14 suggests that he was more interested in preventing the loss of another colony than in haggling further with the Germans.

THE GERMAN RESPONSE

With their military power turned against Russia, the Reich's chiefs had fewer powers over Vichy. When he learned of Darlan's stiffening attitude, and before the French note of the 14th had been received in Berlin, Ribbentrop instructed Abetz on July 15 to see to it that the shipments through Bizerte begin as soon as possible. He reminded Abetz that he could not make any additional concessions to France, that he could not negotiate a political settlement with Darlan, and that a meeting with Darlan was not desirable at the moment.[32] Abetz, realizing that he could not persuade Darlan to concede access to Bizerte, rushed off to Berlin for conference with the foreign minister.

Next day, when the French note of the 14th arrived in Berlin by teletype, Ribbentrop commented angrily that "it is necessary to put an end once and for all to these naive French attempts at blackmail."[33] Refusing to accept the French note, he instructed Abetz to return it to Vichy "with the oral comment that the communication indicated a complete misconception of France's position as a nation defeated by Germany."[34]

At Wiesbaden the German response to Darlan's change of heart was stern and threatening. On July 24, when Vogl met with Admiral Michelier, the German stated bluntly that Darlan's note of the 14th had produced in the German military an impression of amazement. The German high command, he added, had never accepted the French position of linking the military protocols to political discussions, and he demanded that France honor its commitment to deliver supplies to the Afrika Korps. Whether the Germans would grant further concessions, he insisted, would depend upon the French attitude toward the Tunisian question.[35]

Responding on the 28th, Michelier handed Vogl a note prepared by Darlan. It cited the text of the protocols as evidence of the Reich's agreement to link the military and political discussions. Observing that the political discussions had begun at Berchtesgaden prior to the opening of the military negotiations, the note insisted that the German military command had no right to deny the connection between the two. It concluded with the observation that the French government was therefore acting entirely within its rights under the protocols. But Colonel Franz Böhme, sitting in for Vogl, refused to budge.[36]

Darlan stood his ground. Late in July he instructed Benoist-Méchin to appease Abetz with assurances of Vichy's good intentions, to dismiss the question of the Admiral's sincerity, to explain that his attitude is determined by the loss of Syria and by French public opinion, to advance the usual arguments, and to make no concessions on the basic question. "On this point," he concluded, "the desires of the Admiral are unyielding."[37]

When he met Abetz in Paris on the 30th, Benoist-Méchin followed his instructions. Abetz did likewise, informing the Frenchman of Berlin's refusal to accept the note of the 14th. After Abetz had administered a sharp scolding, Benoist-Méchin promised to press his government to permit the shipments through Bizerte. He added that Darlan would find this easier if the Reich would promise political discussions after Vichy had made the military concessions. Abetz answered that he had no instructions on that point.[38]

But in face of mounting German pressure at Wiesbaden, Darlan softened his position. After a round of conferences at Vichy, he decided in early August to hold firm on the basic point of not opening Bizerte generally to deliveries for the Afrika Korps. On the other hand, he conceded the one-time delivery of four hundred trucks he had agreed to sell to the Germans on May 21. In addition, supplies already purchased in Tunisia by the Germans were allowed to go forward to Libya. In the course of these negotiations, Darlan reported that Weygand had been persuaded to cooperate, implying that the General had been responsible for the French refusal to honor fully its commitments.[39]

SHIFTING THE BLAME TO WEYGAND

Darlan sent the same message to Paris, suggesting that Weygand had been the problem all along. Fernand de Brinon, who returned to Paris after a round of conferences with the Admiral and other French officials on August 1-2, reported to Abetz that the crisis in Franco-German relations stemmed from Weygand's opposition to the Bizerte program. He reported that Weygand had hinted before the council on June 6 of the possible defection of North Africa and that he would have to resign if France adopted Darlan's program. The council, he reported, adopted instead the program of Weygand, who since that time had become even more of a problem. Darlan, he said "had now resolved not to work with Weygand any longer and was working to get rid of him."[40] Brinon went on to report that Darlan was determined to honor his commitments and that the delivery of the four hundred trucks to the Afrika Korps had been approved by the cabinet on August 2 as an interim solution to be negotiated personally by Darlan in Paris.[41]

But Ribbentrop, suspicious of Darlan, would not receive the Admiral. In a telegram of August 13, he informed Abetz of the Reich's intention to avoid a breakdown in communications with France without becoming involved in specific discussions at the moment. He instructed Abetz to inform Darlan that Berlin was preoccupied with the Russian war, that conversations with the French government were not possible at the moment, and that the Admiral would be notified when it became possible to resume discussions.[42]

Perhaps to assure himself that the negotiations would indeed not be resumed, Ribbentrop instructed Abetz to return to Berlin after he had reported to Darlan. When the Admiral arrived in Paris on the 18th, Abetz informed him of Ribbentrop's decision. Darlan replied that that he would welcome an opportunity to see Ribbentrop again, that nothing had changed since their meeting of May 11, and that both he and Pétain wished to dismiss Weygand at the first opportunity.[43]

The Reich's leaders had long been suspicious of Weygand, so he was an easy target for the Admiral. The truth is that Darlan had harbored misgivings from the beginning about the Bizerte project. He had expressed doubts about it even before the signing of the Paris protocols, and before Weygand had been summoned to France in early June to help Vichy withdraw from them. And it was Darlan, not Weygand, who had insisted upon inserting the escape clause into the protocols. It was therefore the Admiral, rather than the General, who had taken the lead to withdraw Vichy from the protocols. But Darlan shifted the blame to Weygand.

THE SYRIAN CRISIS: AN ASSESSMENT

As a military campaign, the Syrian war was clearly a sideshow, overshadowed by the larger Russo-German conflict. But it was an important episode in Franco-German wartime relations, revealing German intentions toward France and defining more sharply the limits of Berlin's coercive powers over Vichy. The war justified Darlan's withdrawal from the most dangerous terms of the Paris protocols. He was therefore able to limit German exploitation of Bizerte and to escape altogether from his commitments at Dakar. By prolonging the war he strengthened his case with the Germans and avoided concessions that would risk provoking a war with Britain.

When Darlan finally withdrew from the Bizerte agreement, the Germans had already implemented under the second and third protocols a portion of the military reinforcements scheduled for North and West Africa, and they had released General Juin. In addition, 80,000 French war prisoners had been released in connection with the negotiations attendant to the Syrian protocol. Further, on June 11, Vichy unilaterally began payment of occupation costs at the reduced rate of 15,000,000 reichsmarks per day.[44] In August, Ribbentrop approved the reduced level.[45]

The restrained German response signaled a new posture toward France. Now Berlin's highest priority was stability in the west, which meant that the basic relationship between Vichy and the Reich had shifted more in the French favor. With German armies overextended in Russia and in Libya, Berlin could not afford to provoke separatism in Africa and a possible two-front war there. On the other hand, the outbreak of the Russo-German war meant that France could not soon expect a general diplomatic settlement with Berlin. The Reich could ill afford to permit a restoration of French military power in the midst of a two-front war with Russia and Britain. Germany would therefore continue to plunder the French economy and to reap the benefits of the occupation.

Darlan did not grasp at once the full significance of the Russian war for Franco-German relations, as we shall see, but he learned from the Syrian war and the Paris protocols that Berlin would not match French concessions with equivalents sufficient to justify French risks under the accords. His withdrawal from the protocols underscores the point that he would not gamble away the security of French Africa in military negotiations with the Reich. After he lost Syria, he took the empire off the bargaining table.

NOTES

1. Alain Darlan, *L'Amiral Darlan parle* (Paris: Amiot-Dumont, 1952), 112.

2. DFCAA, IV, 431.

3. Unpublished Diary of Admiral William D. Leahy (Washington, DC: Library of Congress, Manuscripts Division), Vol. 6.

4. Haute Cour de Justice, *Le Procès du Maréchal Pétain*, 2 volumes (Paris: Albin Michel, 1945), II, 942.

5. *Journal de Genève*, June 7, 1941.

6. Henri Du Moulin de Labarthète, *Le Temps des illusions. Souvenirs (juillet 1940-avril 1942* (Genève: Les Éditions du Cheval Ailé, 1946), 225.

7. DGFP, Series D, XII, 1034.

8. *Journal de Genève*, June 15, 1941; Hervé Coutau-Bégarie and Claude Huan, *Lettres et notes de l'Amiral Darlan* (Paris: Economica, 1992), 356-357.

9. FRUS, 1941, II, 375.

10. *Journal de Genève*, June 15, 1941. See also Du Moulin, *Le Temps des illusions*, 225-226.

11. DFCAA, IV, 540-541.

12. Ibid., 541.

13. Ibid.

14. André Laffargue, *Le Général Dentz* (Paris: Les Iles d'Or, n.d.), 118.

15. Ibid., 126.

16. Ibid., 126-128.

17. Coutau-Bégarie and Huan, *Lettres et notes de l'Amiral Darlan*, 360-361.

18. Laffargue, *Le General Dentz*, 142.

19. Ibid., 144-148.

20. See DGFP, Series D, XIII, 82, 34 note 3; DFCAA, IV, 546-547; and Jacques Benoist-Méchin, *De la défaite au désastre*, 2 volumes (Paris: Albin Michel, 1984), I, 196-224.

21. Laffargue, *Le Général Dentz*, 161.

22. For the text of the treaty, see DFCAA, IV, 627-630. It contained provisions for French prisoners to choose between repatriation and joining de Gaulle. The overwhelming majority chose repatriation.

23. DFCAA, IV, 561-562.

24. DGFP, XII, 1010.

25. Jean Louis-Aujol, editor, *Le Procès de Benoist-Méchin* (Paris: Albin Michel, 1948), 267-268.

26. Ibid, 268-269. See also Benoist-Méchin, *De la défaite au désastre*, I, 164-169.

27. DFCAA, IV, 576.

28. DGFP, Series D, XII, 99-101, and note 4.

29. Maxime Weygand, *Mémoires: Rappelé au service* (Paris: Flammarion, 1950), 440-441.

30. Ibid., 127.

31. DGFP, Series D, XIII, 142-149.

32. Ibid., 139.

33. Ibid., 143.

34. Ibid., 142.

35. French National Archives, Cabinet 63, AJ41-40, "Military Negotiations between Vichy and the Axis powers from May 41 until July 42," DSA Documentation.

36. Ibid.

37. *Le Procès de Benoist-Méchin*, 275-276.

38. DGFP, Series D, XIII, 231-233.

39. DFCAA, V, 45-56.

40. DGFP, Series D, XIII, 293.

41. Ibid., 294. Abetz was absent from Paris in early August, so Darlan approved the deliveries through Wiesbaden.

42. DGFP, Series D, XIII, 312.

43. Ibid., 326.

44. Ibid., 345.

45. Ibid., 345-348.

François Darlan, 1891. (Courtesy Francine Hezez and Hélène Bordes)

François Darlan, 1898. (Courtesy Francine Hezez and Hélène Bordes)

Naval Disarmament Negotiations. From left to right: Robert Craigie, Lord Alexander, Charles Dumont, Vice-Admiral Darlan. February 26, 1931. (Associated Press Photo, United States National Archives)

Vice-Admiral Darlan aboard the cruiser *Duguay-Trouin*. October 5, 1934. (Associated Press Photo, United States National Archives)

The Marriage of Alain Darlan to Mlle. Annie Hamon, at Biarritz. January 24, 1937.
(Associated Press Photo, United States National Archives)

Darlan promotes Captain Dignac, Deputy, to the Legion of Honor. March 3, 1937. (Associated Press Photo, United States National Archives)

The Nyon Naval Conference. Darlan reports to the press. September 1937. (Associated Press Photo, United States National Archives)

Military Maneuvers. From left to right: Pierre Cot, Admiral Darlan, General Féquant, General Gamelin. Autumn 1937. (Associated Press Photo, United States National Archives)

Admiral Darlan. July 15, 1938. (Associated Press Photo, United States National Archives)

Admiral Darlan decorating General Haarbleicher. January 10, 1939. (Associated Press Photo, United States National Archives)

The Arrival of Lord Gort at Le Bourget Airfield. From left to right: Lord Gort, General Gamelin, General Buret, Admiral Darlan, General Vuillemin. March 28, 1939. (Associated Press Photo, United States National Archives)

French Battlecruiser *Dunkerque*. (Assoiciated Press Photo, United States National Archives)

Alain Darlan at Warm Springs, Georgia. March 19, 1946. (*New York Times* Photo, United States National Archives)

Admiral Darlan and Berthe Morgan Darlan at their Villa in Algiers. December 1942. (Courtesy AP/Wide World Photos)

CHAPTER 15

Troubled Interim

During the troubled interim between the outbreak of the Russo-German war and the attack at Pearl Harbor, French affairs were thrust into the background. But France remained in Hitler's grip. The Russo-German war created new problems at home and renewed old ones abroad.

THE RISING SUN IN SOUTHERN INDOCHINA

With the Soviets no longer a threat to Manchuria, Tokyo exploited the moment to round out its strategic position in southern Indochina. Tokyo's note to Berlin of July 19 described the Indochina project as "the first step for our advance to the South."[1] Governor General Decoux had warned the Admiral of Tokyo's intentions.[2] So Darlan was not surprised when a Japanese ultimatum arrived in Vichy on July 13. Darlan instructed Benoist-Méchin to seek a solution maintaining the territorial integrity of Indochina and preserving French rights there.[3]

Darlan complained to Leahy on August 1 that the Americans had offered no help. "It is always the same story," he charged, "the United States is too late."[4] The Admiral had already signed an agreement for the joint defense of Indochina. The Japanese promised to respect French sovereignty over the colony, and Darlan agreed to conclude no agreement with any third party to oppose Japan. Darlan had lost another French colony, the second within a month.

ILLUSIONS OF PEACE

In 1941 Darlan viewed the Americans as potential peacemakers, rather than as liberators. On June 4, when Leahy expressed American determination to bring about the defeat of Germany, Darlan inquired contemptuously as to when and how the Americans expected to invade the continent. He remarked that "even Germany would have to take heed if you would use your influence for a compromise peace."[5] On August 1, he again spoke to Leahy of drawing the war to a close:

Turning once more to the United States and complaining that we were quite ready with criticism but slow in action, Darlan said: "When you have 3000 tanks, 6000 planes and 500,000 men to bring to Marseilles, let me know. Then we shall welcome you. But neither side can win the war and Europe will be exhausted. It is your interest, as well as ours, that there be an early peace."[6]

The statement, often misinterpreted as a invitation for Franco-American military cooperation, expressed the opposite. Darlan's point was that neither the United States and Britain nor Germany could defeat the other, and that all parties would benefit from an early peace.

Darlan was alarmed at the steady drift of the United States toward intervention. On November 11 he and the Marshal took steps to keep open the door for talks between Washington and Berlin. The occasion was a farewell luncheon for H. Freeman Matthews, recently reassigned to London. Matthews listened as Pétain offered his services to intervene with Berlin. The Marshal suggested that America "should delay entry into the war as long as possible and you may not have to come in at all."[7] Darlan sent the same message. But the Admiral, complaining about the unfriendly American press, was more abrupt with the American diplomat.[8] He concluded with a plea for peace:

Why do you want the war to go on? You can never beat the Germans militarily and to think that they threaten your security is laughable. The war could go on for ten years, to the destruction and starvation of Europe but I think you could find me useful as an intermediary between yourselves and the Germans and I think there will be a chance for peace negotiations in a short time.[9]

Washington made no reply.

SHIFTING POSTURE TOWARD WASHINGTON

With the United States still neutral, Darlan would not let the Americans call the signals in his relations with the Axis. He refused to give Washington full assurances on the question of German use of French facilities in North Africa. Worried that the Marshal and Darlan might cave in to Berlin, the State Department sent a personal message from Roosevelt to Pétain intended to restrain Vichy. When Leahy delivered the letter on September 12, Darlan affirmed his intention to keep French bases out of Axis hands. But he stated bluntly that minor concessions such as limited deliveries of foodstuffs through Bizerte would have to be made in order to save the port itself and to keep the Germans out of Africa.[10]

American suspicions of Vichy's intentions were matched by Darlan's anxieties about Washington's cozy relations with General Weygand, whose open hostility to Germany worried Berlin. Darlan protested as Matthews departed Vichy on November 11:

> You should not trouble us so in Africa. You just arouse German suspicions whereas if you would reduce your activities there they would never go into Africa. If they distrust our intentions too much they will go there however and they will beat you to it, which is neither to your advantage nor to ours.[11]

Nevertheless, the Admiral took care during the autumn to improve his image in Washington. Admiral Raymond Fenard, representing Darlan in Africa, told Murphy in early October "that Darlan's views on the outcome of the war and French foreign policy have undergone a profound change. He urges that it would be most beneficial if we encourage Darlan, who now wants to gain American favor."[12] And at Vichy, Leahy wrote in his diary on two occasions in mid-October that Darlan had been making deliberate efforts to maintain good Franco-American relations.[13]

The reports of his change of heart helped to prepare Washington for the impending recall of Weygand, whose departure would enable Darlan to gain full control of French relations with the United States. But recalling Weygand from Africa would risk provoking the Americans to break diplomatic relations with France. Darlan could see that Washington might accept the General's recall if the Admiral himself appeared to be moving in the right direction.

THE CRISIS OF THE HOSTAGES

Darlan's shifting attitude was also related to an ugly crisis in France that began to poison his German relations. After the outbreak of German-Soviet war, incidents of violence in the occupied zone increased sharply. On August 13 riots broke out near the St. Lazare station in Paris. Two days later General Otto von Stülpnagel, German military commander in France, issued a stern warning that communist activities would be punished by death. Nine Frenchmen were executed for participating in the demonstrations and distributing communist literature.[14] The violence continued. On the 22nd a German officer was assassinated at the Place de l'Opera in the center of Paris. Responding, Stülpnagel designated all political prisoners as hostages, so that any Frenchmen in custody risked being executed. On August 27 ten of them were executed for the killing at the Opera.[15] In September another German officer was assassinated, and seventeen hostages were shot.[16] On the 16th Hitler's headquarters issued guidelines authorizing the execution of 50 to 100 communist hostages for each German assassinated.[17]

In October the assassinations spread into the provinces. Early in the morning of the 20th, Colonel Karl Friedrich Holtz, German military commander at Nantes, was gunned down by two youths as he walked to his headquarters. That same afternoon Berlin ordered the shooting of fifty hostages at once and fifty additional ones if the assassins were not delivered by October 23. Darlan, now facing a major crisis, sent interior minister Pierre Pucheu to Paris bearing the Marshal's regrets and an offer to send a commission to assist with the Nantes investigation.[18]

While Pucheu rushed to Paris, German police at Nantes compiled a hostage list. Communist functionaries and intellectuals were placed at the top, followed by anarchists and other undesirables. Neither women nor war prisoners were to be placed on the list.[19] German police had difficulty finding fifty hostages fitting the guidelines, for the first list contained only fourteen names. The Nantes hostages were males, age nineteen to fifty-seven. There were four students, a pharmacist, a lawyer, and men from the working classes. Of the fourteen, one had already been ruled innocent of the charge against him, and six others had been charged with only minor offenses.[20] The list was made available to Pucheu on the 20th, but all fourteen were executed two days later.[21]

On the 21st Darlan rushed to Paris for a late afternoon conference with Stülpnagel. He argued that mass shooting of hostages aroused Frenchmen against the occupation authority and undermined his program of promoting good relations between the French and German people. That program, he said, rested upon a base of popular support he could not maintain if the Germans continued the mass executions.[22] But within an hour of the meeting, a German officer was shot down at Bordeaux.[23] The second assassination within two days shattered Darlan's efforts at moderation and pushed the crisis swiftly toward a climax.

Next morning, as tensions mounted, Stülpnagel considered his options. Phoning Berlin at noon, he asked permission to designate as hostages all French males in the occupation zone between the ages of sixteen and sixty. Hitler decided instead to order the immediate execution of fifty hostages for the Bordeaux slaying, to shoot an additional fifty should the assassins not be delivered within forty-eight hours, and to offer a reward of a million francs for information leading to the arrest of the assassins. At 7:25 that evening Berlin telephoned its decision to Stülpnagel, and five minutes later Darlan entered the General's office to deliver the Marshal's request for pardon of the second group of hostages in the Nantes slaying.[24]

When Stülpnagel indicated his intention to follow his orders, Darlan was powerless to oppose. He suggested that the assassinations had probably been inspired by the Russians or the English.[25] Speaking from the Paris radio that evening, Darlan urged Frenchmen to cooperate with the authorities and to end the violence.[26]

On the 23rd, while the Germans prepared the hostage lists for the Bordeaux slaying, Stülpnagel's office gave publicity to the impending executions, and the General himself announced the reward for information about the assassins.[27] That afternoon he inquired of Berlin whether he could pardon the second Nantes quota, as Pétain had requested. Late in the evening Benoist-Méchin handed him a message from Darlan requesting an extension of the deadline for the execution of the second lists so that French police might have more time to apprehend the assassins.[28]

At Vichy, Darlan watched as events took a dramatic turn. Early in the morning of Friday the 24th, after a sleepless night, Pétain unveiled to Du Moulin a scheme calculated to end the crisis. The Marshal himself would become the sole hostage. Should the Germans reject him, he would stand in waiting at the demarcation line.[29] Meanwhile, in the predawn hours when Pétain lay awake lamenting the executions, Berlin wired Paris of Hitler's decision to grant a forty-eight-hour delay for the execution of the second hostage quotas. The deadline would be midnight of the 27th for the second Nantes list and midnight the 29th for the second Bordeaux list. Stülpnagel relayed this news to Benoist-Méchin late in the morning October 24.[30]

When the ministers assembled that morning, they were unaware of Berlin's decision to postpone the deadlines. Darlan listened as Pétain outlined his plan to become a hostage. The Admiral opposed the plan, but it was Pucheu who argued stoutly against it, insisting that the hostage affair should be managed in a manner not to upset on-going relations with the Reich.[31]

Although the Marshal was persuaded to abandon his plan, Darlan was quick to exploit it. That same morning, as the first fifty hostages in the Bordeaux slaying were taken from their cells at Châteaubriant prison and executed, Pucheu rushed to Paris. Arriving late in the afternoon, he handed Stülpnagel the Marshal's plea for pardon of the second list, and he shared with the German Darlan's report of Pétain's plan to surrender himself as a hostage. He insisted that only the most forceful arguments by Darlan and himself had persuaded the Marshal to abandon the plan in favor of a confidential plea for pardon of the second quota. He added that a German rejection of the pardon would place Pétain in the same position he had occupied that morning.[32] The message was clear that Darlan could not restrain the Marshal if Hitler permitted the execution of the second group of fifty hostages. Stülpnagel immediately reported the conversation to Berlin.[33]

In the meantime, Berlin had decided to proceed with the execution of the second hostage group. Soon after Pucheu had departed Stülpnagel's office early in the evening of the 24th, the Wehrmacht High Command informed Stülpnagel of Hitler's rejection of the Marshal's first appeal.[34] When Berlin learned late on the 24th of Pétain's proposal to surrender himself, there was still plenty of time for the Nazi chiefs to reconsider their decision prior to the deadline for the execution of the second Nantes quota on the 27th. In the meantime, tensions continued to mount in Vichy. On the 25th, while Darlan waited impatiently for word of the fate of the hostages, President Franklin D. Roosevelt denounced the shootings, calling them "the butcheries in France."[35]

For whatever motives, Berlin reversed itself on the executions following receipt of Darlan's message about the Marshal's plan to surrender himself. During the morning of the 27th, just before the deadline for the shooting of the second Nantes list, Berlin ordered Stülpnagel to cease further condemnations. That same day Stülpnagel informed Darlan of the postponement of the executions on condition of continuing French cooperation. Two days later, at the expiration of the deadline for the Bordeaux hostages, Stülpnagel gave public notice of the conditional postponement of the executions.[36]

The crisis, however, had only subsided, for angry Frenchmen would later take additional German lives, and the occupation authority would again resort to executions. For the moment, Darlan had succeeded in keeping the hostages crisis in a category apart from the mainstream of Franco-German relations. But the mass executions had embittered him against the Germans.

THE RECALL OF WEYGAND

General Weygand, stoutly independent in North Africa, was not one of Darlan's men, and he reported directly to the Marshal. Moreover, Weygand's cozy relations with the Americans and his anti-German stance burdened Darlan's efforts to rearm Africa. And Darlan resented Weygand's conducting what amounted to a private foreign policy toward the Americans. Popular in North Africa, the General appeared to Darlan as a potential rebel. "As long as Pétain lives," he told Stülpnagel, "Weygand will be loyal to him, and therefore I pray to God every day that He might come fetch Weygand before He fetches Pétain."[37]

Darlan was correct in thinking that Weygand burdened French rearmament efforts. In September, Keitel ordered Wiesbaden to permit no reinforcements until "the military command in North Africa is reliable from the Axis point of view."[38] Meanwhile, Darlan mounted a campaign against Weygand. In a note of July 21 to Pétain, the Admiral insisted that he ought to be accorded full authority over all French personnel regardless of their rank or function.[39] In another note, he charged that the General's independent attitude encouraged separatist tendencies in North Africa.[40] On August 12, Vichy announced the appointment of Darlan as Minister of National Defense.[41] But Weygand remained at his post, reporting directly to Pétain.

Preoccupied with the Russian war, Berlin took little note of the Weygand affair. But in Paris, Abetz pressed Darlan to unseat the General. In separate negotiations at Wiesbaden, the Germans requested delivery of twenty heavy guns to the Afrika Korps and passage of light craft into the Mediterranean through the Rhone River.[42] When Abetz received Darlan on October 1, the Admiral made it clear that Vichy's granting those concessions would depend upon the German attitude toward the transfer of the repatriated Syrian army to North Africa and reinforcement of French forces already there. Abetz complained about Weygand, and Darlan promised that he would arrange the recall of the General in the coming weeks.[43]

In early October the Admiral proposed a package agreement in which France would receive concessions for recalling Weygand and for granting the other German demands. So Darlan summoned Weygand to Vichy, expecting the Marshal to dismiss him. The Admiral warned Abetz that the dismissal of Weygand would "stir up a sensation" in Vichy, and that he would be grateful if the Reich would release a contingent of African war prisoners and approve reinforcements for Africa. Darlan would then authorize passage of the light vessels into the Mediterranean.[44]

Wiesbaden, however, insisted that the transfer of artillery required no German concessions beyond those stated under the Paris protocols.[45] So when Weygand arrived in Vichy on the 16th, the armistice commission had made no commitment to link Weygand's retirement to any concessions. And at Vichy the Marshal failed to follow through on the recall of the General. Weygand therefore returned to his post.[46] Finally, under heavy pressure from Wiesbaden, Darlan agreed to the deliveries of artillery and the passage of the light vessels into the Mediterranean.[47] When Abetz received Darlan on the 22nd, the Admiral reported Pétain's readiness to recall the General should Berlin confirm its mistrust of him.[48] Two days later Ribbentrop instructed Abetz to inform Darlan "that General Weygand in no way enjoys our confidence."[49] The statement, however, was not enough. Darlan wanted concessions for Weygand's recall. He therefore informed Abetz in early November that Pétain would dismiss the General in return for concessions to appease French public opinion and to justify to the army Weygand's departure. The Marshal wished for a conference with a high-ranking German official such as Reichsmarshal Hermann Göring, and for military reinforcements along the lines Darlan had already advanced. If assurances on these questions could be received, Darlan reported, the Marshal would recall Weygand within a week.[50] Responding on November 12, Ribbentrop instructed Abetz to inform Vichy that the German government had already expressed its lack of confidence in Weygand, and that it would be an error to link the Weygand question with the concessions the Marshal had requested.[51]

Berlin, therefore, would not bargain with Darlan for the recall of Weygand. But Wiesbaden suggested to Berlin on the 13th that French demands for the reinforcement of West Africa could be exchanged for French commitments under the Paris protocols. For Weygand's recall, the armistice commission considered releasing contingents of white and native war prisoners, and of transferring about half of the Syrian army to North Africa.[52]

The funeral of General Huntziger, killed in an air crash on November 12, brought the chiefs of the Axis armistice commissions to Vichy. Darlan's breakfast on the 16th with Vogl and General Vacca-Maggiolini, head of the Italian commission, provided the occasion for informal discussions. After Vogl indicated his willingness to discuss rearmament for French Africa along with the Paris protocols, Darlan raised the question of Weygand. He promised to make another effort to dismiss him, to appoint a civilian governor general in Algiers, and to name General Dentz as military chief in North Africa.[53] This conversation set the stage for a settlement.

Weygand, summoned earlier, arrived in Vichy that same afternoon, after the foreign guests had departed. In a round of conferences over two days, Weygand heard that Hitler himself had insisted upon his retirement and that Vichy could no longer resist the German pressure. Giving up the struggle on the 18th, Weygand resigned all of his offices. In Darlan's presence the elderly General ended his career with the terse comment that "the Weygand case is settled."[54]

GERMAN CONCESSIONS

Wiesbaden's telegram of November 24 to the foreign office proposed concessions on grounds that German efforts to have Weygand recalled had met with success.[55] The concessions included the liberation of all French naval war prisoners, approximately 5,500 officers and men, and the release of an additional 10,000 prisoners, natives of North and West Africa. Further, they included the transfer of about half of the Syrian army to North Africa.[56] On November 25, the armistice commission notified the French delegation that the easing of the political situation in North Africa had permitted the granting of these concessions and that negotiations concerning rearmament of French Africa would open on the 27th.[57]

DECENTRALIZATION OF POWER

The retirement of Weygand was accompanied by the suppression of the General's offices. Darlan's friend Fenard was made Secretary General for French Africa, and Yves Châtel was promoted to Governor General of Algeria. General Juin inherited Weygand's military functions. Juin wrote later that Vichy had decentralized powers in North Africa "to guard against the risk of a secession in Africa instituted and determined by a single individual."[58]

Weygand's prestige and his anti-German stance had led Washington to view North Africa in a category different from Vichy. Now, with Weygand out of the way, Darlan could speak to Washington with a single voice aimed at protecting the integrity of France and her empire. But when German demands upon North Africa increased sharply in December, Weygand would no longer be available to take the blame for the Admiral's foot-dragging.

NOTES

1. DGFP, Series D, XIII, 178.

2. Admiral Jean Decoux, *A la barre de l'Indochine* (Paris: Plon, 1949), 150-151.

3. Jacques Benoist-Méchin, *De la défaite au désastre*, 2 volumes (Paris: Albin Michel, 1984), I, 260-263.

4. Roosevelt Library, Hyde Park, PSF, Box 2, Leahy to the Secretary of State, telegram 1 August 1941. See also Alain Darlan, *L'Amiral Darlan parle* (Paris: Amiot-Dumont, 1952), 306-307.

5. FRUS, 1941, II, 185.

6. Ibid., 189.

7. Ibid., 457.

8. He noted specifically *Time*, 26 May 1941; *The New Republic*, 8 September 1941; *Life*, 1 September 1941. USNA, RG 59, State Department, 851.00/2620.

9. FRUS, 1941, II, 457-458.

10. Ibid., 417, 430-431.

11. Ibid., 457.

12. Ibid., 440.

13. Unpublished Diary of Admiral William D. Leahy (Washington, DC: Library of Congress, Manuscripts Division), Folio VI, 121.

14. MGD, T501, Reel 143, frame 001043, Headquarters of the Military Commander-in-Chief in France, situation report for August and September 1941.

15. Ibid., frames 001085, 001087, 001090, appendix to the situation report for August and September 1941, containing the names of the hostages executed on the 27th. See also Reel 165, frame 000385, Headquarters of the German Military Commander-in-Chief in France, "Entwicklung der Geiselfrage."

16. MGD, T501 Reel 165, frame 000385, "Entwicklung der Geiselfrage."

17. DGFP, XIII, 541-543.

18. MGD, T501, Reel 165, frames 000385-386, "Entwicklung der Geiselfrage."

19. MGD, T501, Reel 196, frame 001062, Headquarters of the Military Commander in France.

20. Ibid., frames 001088-089.

21. See Ibid., 001087-089, Headquarters of the German Military Commander in France; and Paul Buttin, *Le Procès Pucheu* (Paris: Amiot-Dumont, n.d.), 322-327.

22. MGD, T501, Reel 192, frames 000712-713, armistice commission files.

23. MGD, T501, Reel 165, frame 000386, "Entwicklung der Geiselfrage."

24. Ibid., frame 000387.

25. Hervé Coutau-Bégarie and Claude Huan, *Lettres et notes de l'Amiral Darlan* (Paris: Economica, 1992), 408.

26. *The New York Times*, October 23, 1941, 1.

27. MGD, T501, Reel 143, frame 001179, appendix to the situation report for October and November 1941.

28. MGD, T501, Reel 165, frame 000387, "Entwicklung der Geiselfrage."

29. Henri Du Moulin de Labarthète, *Le Temps des illusions: Souvenirs (juillet-avril 1942* (Genève: Les Éditions du Cheval Ailé, 1946), 355.

30. MGD, T501, Reel 165, frame 000388, "Entwicklung der Geiselfiage."

31. Du Moulin, *Le Temps des illusions*, 355-357.

32. MGD, T501, Reel 196, frames 001096-098, Stülpnagel's report of October 24.

33. Ibid., and Reel 165, frame 000389, "Entwicklung der Geiselfrage."

34. MGD, T501, Reel 165, frame 000388, "Entwicklung der Geiselfrage."

35. *The New York Times*, October 26, 1941, 1.

36. MGD, T501, Reel 165, frame 000390, "Entwicklung der Geiselfrage."

37. MGD, T77, Reel 850, frame 5594812, armistice commission files.

38. Ibid., frame 5596017.

39. Hervé Coutau-Bégarie and Claude Huan, *Darlan* (Paris: Fayard, 1989), 451.

40. Ibid., 451-452.

41. See Coutau-Bégarie and Huan, *Lettres et notes de l'Amiral Darlan*, 397-398.

42. DFCAA, V, 168, 201.

43. MGD, T120, Reel 278, frames 213883-885, Foreign Ministry, Office of the State Secretary.

44. Ibid., frames 213897-899, 213907-908.

45. DFCAA, V, 205-210.

46. Maxime Weygand, *Mémoires* (Paris: Flammarion, 1950), 522-525.

47. DFCAA, V, 210-211, 312-314.

48. MGD, T120, Reel 278, frames 213932-934, Foreign Ministry, Office of the State Secretary.

49. DGFP, Series D, XIII, 676.

50. Ibid., 730-732.

51. Ibid., 770.

52. MGD, T120, Reel 278, frames 214040-042, Foreign Ministry, Office of the State Secretary.

53. Ibid., frames 214056-058.

54. Weygand, *Mémoires*, 530.

55. MGD, T120, Reel 278, frame 214095, Foreign Ministry, Office of the State Secretary.

56. Ibid.

57. French National Archives, Cabinet 63, AJ41-40, "Military Negotiations between Vichy and the Axis powers from May 41 until July 42," DSA documentation.

58. Alphonse Juin, *Mémoires* (Paris: Fayard, 1959), I, 29.

CHAPTER 16

The Winter Crisis

Even before Pearl Harbor, Darlan's attitude toward the Germans shifted, and his policy of collaboration began to break down. In December, he faced new Axis demands upon Tunisia just at the time when the American entry into the war demanded better relations with Washington. The events of late 1941 and early 1942 would cause him to reappraise his American policy.

AVOIDING A BREAK WITH WASHINGTON

Having recalled Weygand, Darlan moved promptly to prevent a breakdown in Franco-American relations. His explanation that the Marshal had dismissed the General because of heavy German pressure and for fear of an Axis occupation of North Africa hardly satisfied the Americans.[1] Although Pétain promised no change in Vichy's American policy, Leahy recommended to Washington suspension of the economic aid program to North Africa and the recall of himself and Robert Murphy for consultation.[2]

Darlan had remarked earlier to Charles Rochat that Weygand's recall would provoke no serious American reaction.[3] But Darlan took no chances. He sent Admiral Fenard back to Algiers to see Murphy, who reported to Washington that the Frenchman "pleaded with me for an hour this evening after his return from Vichy to urge the Department to take no hasty decision on its French policy."[4] More patient than Leahy, Murphy recommended that the department make no decision until more facts could be gathered.[5] Although Washington suspended the economic aid program, Murphy and Leahy remained at their posts, and the tensions arising from Weygand's recall soon subsided. The way was now clear for Darlan to take full charge of Vichy's American policy.[6]

SETBACK AT FLORENTIN

Meanwhile, Darlan looked for a breakthrough in his relations with Germany. Following Weygand's recall, Ribbentrop instructed Abetz to arrange a secret meeting between Pétain and Göring.[7] Accordingly, the Marshal and Darlan met the Reichsmarshal on December 1 at Florentin near the demarcation line. Darlan arrived with lofty expectations contained in an official note with attachments covering the whole range of Franco-German relations. He obviously expected to begin the process of settling with Berlin while the Wehrmacht swept to victory in Russia. He had already initiated secret contacts with Washington and London, inquiring as to whether Churchill would accept him at the peace conference should the war soon end.[8]

But Darlan's note to Göring was tactless, opening with a blunt reminder that Frenchmen had not fully approved collaboration, and that meaningful collaboration would require the restoration of normal relations with Germany. It proposed a full package of concessions that included the restoration of French military power. Collaboration was made contingent upon the implementation of this program.[9]

Darlan had overlooked the imperatives governing Berlin's French policy. Furious, the Reichsmarshal shouted his anger at Darlan: "I want you to know who is the conqueror and who is conquered. You speak a language that is unacceptable, which I dare not transmit to the Chancellor."[10] He added that "it was totally incomprehensible to him how Darlan could have even submitted such a document in this form."[11] Göring charged that the note attempted to deprive Germany of her victory, to weaken the Reich at the critical moment in the war against Russia, and to restore France at a time favorable to renew the war against Germany. "If Admiral Darlan would think the matter over coolly and soberly," he suggested, "then he would doubtless realize himself that it would be insane of Germany to comply with the French demands."[12] Regaining his composure, the Reichsmarshal explained that the Russian war required Germany to maintain her strength in the west. He touched upon the broad question of Franco-German collaboration, and upon specific issues such as French colonial rearmament and possible German use of the port of Bizerte. He insisted that Vichy would have to create in France a climate of opinion favorable to collaboration.

Darlan recovered quickly, answering that his proposals had been intended only as maximum concessions France hoped to receive gradually in return for services rendered to Germany. He added that the present discussions were but the first phase of political negotiations already projected in connection with the Paris protocols. Göring replied that Vichy would have to make specific commitments within a continuous policy of collaboration that should include specific plans for strengthening French colonial defenses. After lengthy discussion, Göring invited his French guests to join him for lunch.[13]

Göring's careful explanation of the Reich's continental position underscored the fact that Berlin would not grant political concessions while the war continued. Four days later, Darlan withdrew the note.[14] Nevertheless, Göring's interest in French colonial defenses hinted at Berlin's need for French services in North Africa.

TRIPARTITE NEGOTIATIONS AT WIESBADEN

Lurking in the background of the tripartite negotiations at Wiesbaden, under way since November 27, was an urgent Axis concern about a strong British offensive in Libya. With the Afrika Korps falling back for lack of fuel and supplies, the Germans were prepared to negotiate within the framework of the Paris protocols for French deliveries through Bizerte. Despite Göring's warning that Berlin would offer no political concessions, Darlan informed Michelier at Wiesbaden that Vichy's granting military concessions would hinge upon Germany's granting supplementary political concessions. But the Axis delegations offered only military equivalents to match their demands for deliveries to Rommel. In early December the three delegations haggled over details without reaching agreement.[15]

Toward mid-December, Darlan realized he soon would have to make a decision about the tripartite talks. The German delegation insisted that French colonial rearmament would be determined by the level of French support of the German war against the Allies, which now included the United States. Moreover, the Axis delegations increased their demands without offering important equivalents. As German pressure increased, Darlan finally agreed to deliveries of gasoline to the retreating Afrika Korps.[16] The negotiations were out of balance, and with Michelier scheduled to come to Vichy on the 18th, Darlan considered whether to withdraw from them.

A NEW AMERICAN POLICY

The United States entry into the war caused Darlan to take American relations more seriously. He therefore took steps to improve relations with Washington, not because he viewed the Americans as liberators, but because he saw that Pearl Harbor had unleashed American power that threatened the French empire. On December 11, Leahy warned Darlan and Pétain that Franco-American relations depended upon Vichy's resisting German pressure to enlist the French fleet and colonial ports into the service of the Axis.[17] If France would give the necessary assurances on this item, if the Murphy-Weygand agreement could be affirmed, and if France would promise not to change its policy toward the United States, then Washington stood ready to consider restoring the economic aid program for North Africa. Until these assurances were given, Leahy insisted, American relations with France would remain in suspense.[18]

Darlan answered that the time had come to devise a formula to avoid a break in Franco-American relations, and that he would write a report covering the questions Leahy had raised. When Leahy remarked that there now remained no doubt about the outcome of the war, Darlan nodded polite agreement.[19] Next day, Rochat delivered Darlan's memoranda addressing Leahy's questions and affirming that no French territory would be made available as bases for German military operations. Handing the document to Leahy, Rochat expressed the Marshal's pleasure that he "has been happy to give you complete satisfaction and assurances on all the questions which you raised."[20] And Roosevelt informed the Marshal on the 13th that the French assurances gave him "profound satisfaction."[21] Washington appears not to have noticed that Darlan had carefully phrased the memorandum in a manner to keep open the option of permitting deliveries to the Axis through Bizerte.

Darlan stepped up his efforts to persuade Washington to restore the economic aid program for North Africa. Fenard told Murphy on December 11 that Darlan was convinced there was no immediate danger of an Axis attack against French Africa. But Fenard painted a gloomy picture of the economic situation in North Africa. Murphy reported that Fenard, "who was obviously acting under Darlan's instructions, concluded with an urgent appeal that we make our influence felt in this area where he said we are most welcome by sending American goods and American ships 'before it is too late.'"[22] Washington kept the aid program in suspension but soon authorized two shipments of nonpetroleum products.[23]

MEETING WITH CIANO

Unknown to Darlan, the question of Axis intervention in Tunisia was under consideration among Axis authorities in December. British naval and air forces had cut heavily into Italian shipments to Tripoli, and Mussolini insisted with Berlin on December 1 that "if the French would not voluntarily concede the use of the harbor of Bizerte, one would have to take the harbor by force."[24] Mussolini understood that Bizerte was the key to Axis success in Libya. Moreover, with the Americans still unprepared, the Axis enjoyed a brief opportunity to seize Tunisia in the interest of heading off later Allied intervention in Algeria. Tunisia was in greater danger than Darlan had thought.

Hitler, however, worried that seizing the port might provoke British reprisals elsewhere at a time when German military assets were spread thin. But Ribbentrop had already given Italian Foreign Minister Count Galeazzo Ciano the green light to demand access to Bizerte at a meeting with Darlan scheduled for December 10. On December 7, however, Hitler asked Rome to make no demands on Darlan for use of the port until the Axis had gained control of the central Mediterranean. Hitler had already strengthened German air power in the region to restore the supply route to Tripoli.[25]

With the Bizerte issue tabled in advance, the Darlan-Ciano interview was entirely cordial. Darlan denounced the British, expressed a low opinion of American military power, and pressed Ciano to arrange a meeting between the two of them and Ribbentrop. When Darlan explained the risks of sending supplies through Bizerte, Ciano answered that he had no instructions to discuss that issue.[26] The meeting, therefore, did not solve the Bizerte problem. The Germans had removed it from the Turin agenda with the intention of addressing it at Wiesbaden.

SUSPENSION OF THE TRIPARTITE NEGOTIATIONS

On December 10, Wiesbaden notified Vichy that Göring stood ready to receive General Juin and colonial secretary Charles Platon for discussion of African defense.[27] Göring's snubbing Darlan threatened to sidetrack the Admiral's agenda, for neither Juin nor Platon was competent to discuss political questions that Darlan had linked to the military discussions. Göring's tactless effort to by-pass the political issues angered the Admiral, as did another round of hostage shootings in Paris that same week. On the 20th, with Platon on his sickbed, Juin departed for Berlin.

But the outcome of the tripartite negotiations had already been decided when Michelier reported to Darlan on December 18 that German demands for deliveries through Bizerte were out of balance with their counterparts, and that political concessions could not be expected. Accordingly, Darlan decided to break off the negotiations. Michelier returned to Wiesbaden with an oral commentary and a written statement from Darlan to be delivered in the name of the French government.[28]

Presenting Darlan's commentary on December 21, Michelier insisted that Wiesbaden's demanding implementation of the Paris protocols had raised the military discussions to a level that required separate political negotiations. He explained that the French government had always taken that position, had written it into the protocols, and had received no satisfaction at the political level. Reading the official French statement, Michelier noted that the French government still favored collaboration with the Reich, but collaboration, he said, "could not accommodate itself to a posture of perpetual and total submission to the desires of the German government."[29] With those strong words, the tripartite negotiations and the Paris protocols were finally laid to rest.

GERMAN PRESSURE RESUMED

But Darlan's rupturing the tripartite negotiations did not end the Bizerte crisis. Instead, it raced swiftly toward its climax as the British offensive in Libya gained momentum. During the third week of December, Darlan realized that he might have to make a another hard decision, either to help Rommel or to stand by as foreign armies waged war on French territory. Should Rommel retreat into Tunisia, the Reich would be tempted to seize Bizerte.

It was only by coincidence that Darlan's memorandum of December 21 had scuttled the Paris protocols at almost the same hour that Göring received Juin in Berlin. The Göring-Juin discussions focused on the defense of southern Tunisia and the question of deliveries to Rommel. Göring insisted that Vichy honor its commitments under the Paris protocols, and that the French armies fight alongside the Afrika Korps should Rommel retreat into Tunisia. Göring's demands nearly amounted to an ultimatum. Juin countered as best he could before rushing back to Vichy to report to Darlan.[30]

Now Darlan realized he would have to lend support to the Axis in Libya. He responded to Göring's demands in late December, informing Berlin of Vichy's willingness in principle to send supplies through Bizerte and to lend military support should the British offensive continue into Tunisia. But Darlan advanced high demands for execution of the agreement, which he insisted would provoke British reprisals. The demands included free movement for French forces in Africa and the western Mediterranean region, the release of all supplies and ammunition stockpiled in France and Africa, further release of war prisoners, and, among other things, French command of all French-German-Italian military operations in Tunisia. He suggested that the effectiveness of the program would be increased if Berlin would ease the burdens of the occupation.[31]

But Darlan had no intention of provoking Germany to use force against Bizerte, for he had already conceded deliveries to Libya through the Italian armistice commission at Turin. On December 22, after he had received Juin's report of the Göring interview, Darlan agreed to the transfer of five hundred tons of fuel to the Italians from stocks in North Africa. On the same day, in an arrangement known as the Delta transports, he authorized shipments of Italian foodstuffs and clothing from Marseilles to Tunisia and on to Libya. On the 31st he approved the Gamma transports for deliveries of Italian trucks to Libya at the rate of about a hundred and fifty vehicles per month.[32]

Darlan commented to Benoist-Méchin that his response was intended to protect Bizerte against an Axis attack and to prevent the spread of the war into Tunisia.[33] And to Esteva in Tunisia, he wrote in January that it would be better to let the supplies pass than to receive an ultimatum requiring the passage of German troops into Tunisia.[34] Darlan's reasons for granting concessions to Italy rather than Germany were largely political. He had abandoned the Wiesbaden negotiations before he learned of Göring's demands upon Juin. Therefore, when he became aware of the new German threat to Tunisia, further negotiations at Wiesbaden would have aborted the French memorandum of the 21st that had finally liberated him from the burdens of the tripartite negotiations and the Paris protocols. Making the concessions to Italy protected his decision to withdraw from the tripartite negotiations.

The tensions in Franco-German relations coincided with a new cordiality in Vichy's relations with the Italians, beginning on November 22 when Darlan signed with them a set of commercial agreements called the Accords of Rome.[35] It was in the pattern of better relations with Rome that he made the deliveries to the Italians, rather than the Germans. Wiesbaden, surprised at Darlan's according Italy concessions so recently denied Germany, had little choice but to support the Franco-Italian agreements.[36]

Darlan intended to exploit his Italian connections to reopen communications with Berlin. On December 30, Turin encouraged Darlan to think that Mussolini stood ready to support the political concessions France had demanded at Wiesbaden. Darlan responded in early January with a note to Mussolini, fishing again for a meeting with Ciano and Ribbentrop.[37] He also turned back to standard channels, pressing Abetz in Paris to arrange for him an interview with Ribbentrop.

The concessions Darlan had demanded for the African deliveries were not ignored in Berlin where Hitler received Abetz on January 5. According to Abetz's report, Hitler agreed in principle to a meeting with Darlan, should Ribbentrop approve. But Hitler clearly preferred to treat Darlan's demands in a dilatory manner until Rommel had a chance to secure his front without having to seek further French help.[38] In mid-January, Rommel finally launched a counterattack. So Turin informed the French delegation on the 23rd that Hitler had no desire for negotiations with France.[39] The message from Turin marked the end of Darlan's policy of collaboration with the Reich.

PROTESTING GERMAN BRUTALITIES

The Tunisian crisis was but one part of Darlan's troubled relations with Germany. In December, a new round of executions in the occupied zone poisoned his German relations even more. On November 28, as the tripartite negotiations opened at Wiesbaden, a bomb thrown into the lounge of a Paris hotel took two German lives.[40] There was other violence in Paris and in the provinces, so that on December 10 Abetz wired Ribbentrop recommending that reprisals be taken at the rate of a hundred executions for each violent act.[41] Although Vichy ordered stern measures against those thought to be guilty--foreigners, communists, and Jews--the Germans responded with renewed brutality.[42] Stülpnagel announced on December 14 that a hundred "Jews, communists, and anarchists associated with the guilty party have been shot."[43]

Darlan's attitude toward the Germans now hardened. In a note of December 14 to Stülpnagel, he protested that continuing with the mass executions would upset public opinion in a manner to make it difficult for the French government "to continue...its policy of accommodation with Germany."[44] Darlan's note made no effort to keep the hostages question in a category apart from the mainstream of Franco-German relations. It instead linked the two directly and threatened to end the policy of collaboration. Next day he tried to back away, insisting with Stülpnagel that he had no intention of changing his German policy.[45]

But Darlan had played a card he could not withdraw. On the 14th the Marshal informed Leahy of Darlan's message to the Germans "that collaboration was impossible when the occupying authorities took such action."[46] On the same day, Darlan played another strong card, releasing to the press a statement denouncing the executions. That was Vichy's first public statement criticizing any German action.[47] It did not go unnoticed among French collaborators in Paris who were already beginning to turn against Darlan.

AT THE END OF 1941

Darlan's year-end assessment of the world scene, expressed in private memoranda, reveals his despair at the continuation of the war. He worried that Germany might occupy France and North Africa, at the very least of Tunisia, and that a victorious Germany would reduce France to the status of Belgium. On the other hand, should the Germans be defeated, the Japanese and the Anglo-Americans would seize the empire. He thought that the Americans would not be ready for at least a year.[48] Far from being encouraged by the American entry into the war, Darlan deplored the new threats to France and her empire. He still had no vision of the Americans as liberators. Instead, he expected the Americans eventually to dominate the seas, and the Germans to dominate Europe.[49]

Darlan realized that the Axis might be tempted to seize North Africa before the Americans grew strong enough to intervene there. But he worried that should the Americans go there first, the Germans would occupy the free zone to protect their Mediterranean front. Darlan therefore drew closer to the Americans at the end of 1941 because he knew they soon would be capable of threatening the empire and upsetting the status-quo upon which Vichy's political life depended.

Darlan's first concern at the new year was to keep the Axis out of Tunisia. As for the Americans, there would be time to gain their confidence, to influence their plans, and perhaps to protect French interests against Allied adventures involving the empire. But he had no thought of conspiring with the Americans in any military plans to liberate France.

NOTES

1. See Hervé Coutau-Bégarie and Claude Huan, *Lettres et notes de l'Amiral Darlan* (Paris: Economica, 1992), 427.

2. FRUS, 1941, II., 465.

3. USNA, RG 59, Department of State, 851.00, telegram #1460, November 22, 1941, Leahy report of a conversation with a French official.

4. FRUS, 1941, II, 467.

5. Ibid., 468.

6. General Bergeret told Murphy that Weygand had been dismissed because he had conducted his own foreign policy toward the Americans and because he stood for an independent movement in North Africa. USNA, RG 59, Department of State, 851.00/tel. #598 from Algiers, 22 November 1941.

7. DGFP, Series D, XIII, 800.

8. Coutau-Bégarie and Huan, *Lettres et notes de l'Amiral Darlan*, 422. Darlan's inquiry, initiated through army intelligence services, was discussed by Churchill and Roosevelt on January 6, 1942, at the Arcadia Conference. See *Foreign Relations of the United States: The Conferences at Washington and Casablanca* (Washington, DC: U.S. Government Printing Office, 1968), 186.

9. DGFP, Series D, XIII., 930-934. Darlan's note and a French summary of the interview are contained in Henri Ballande, *De l'Amirauté à Bikini* (Paris: Cité, 1972), 291-313.

10. Jean Louis-Aujol, editor, *Le Procès de Benoist-Méchin* (Paris: Albin Michel, 1948), 304.

11. DGFP, Series D, XIII, 915.

12. Ibid., 916.

13. For other items discussed, see DGFP, Series D, XIII, 914-927. An account of the luncheon conversations is contained in Ballande, *De l'Amirauté à Bikini*, 309-313.

14. MGD, T120, Reel 278, frame 214118, Foreign Ministry, Office of State. DGFP, Series D, XIII, 934, note #17.

15. DFCAA, V, 329-333.

16. Ibid., 332, 375, 393-402.

17. On December 14 Colonel William J. Donovan, Coordinator of Information, wrote the President suggesting that it was only a question of time before the French fleet would be delivered to the Germans and that a surprise Anglo-American attack upon it should be considered. He wrote that "I suggest its consideration only because there will be few opportunities in the coming months for offensive action by us, and such offensive action is necessary both from a morale and strategic standpoint." Roosevelt Library, PSF, Box 163, Donovan Reports, Folder #1, December 12-17, 1941.

18. Unpublished Diary of Admiral William D. Leahy (Washington, DC: Library of Congress, Manuscripts Division), Folio VI, 168.

19. Ibid.

20. FRUS, 1941, II, 498, 200-201.

21. Ibid., 499.

22. Ibid., 497.

23. Ibid., 500-501.

24. DGFP, Series D, XIII, 935.

25. Ibid., 938-939.

26. Malcolm Muggeridge, editor, *Ciano's Diplomatic Papers*, trans. Stuart Hood (London: Odham's Press, 1948), 468-471.

27. Darlan had suggested to Abetz that Juin and Platon might be included in future talks about colonial defense. See DFCAA, V, 380; MGD, T77, Reel 851, frame 214157, German Armed Forces High Command, Armistice Commission; and T120, Reel 278, frames 214121-122, Foreign Ministry, State Secretary.

28. DFCAA, V, 400.

29. Ibid., 401.

30. Ibid., 381-385. See also Alphonse Juin, *Mémoires,* 2 volumes (Paris: Fayard, 1959), I, 40-45.

31. Jacques Benoist-Méchin, *De la défaite au désastre*, 2 volumes (Paris: Albin Michel, 1984), I, 348-350; MGD, T77, Reel 851, frames 214212-216, Armistice Commission.

32. DFCAA, V, 374-376, 402.

33. *Le Procès de Benoist-Méchin*, 338.

34. Coutau-Bégarie and Huan, *Lettres et notes de l'Amiral Darlan*, 450.

35. See DFCAA, V, 257-264, 274, 289-291, 375-376, 391.

36. Ibid., 376. The Germans pressed Rome to insist upon the inclusion of German trucks within the Italian quota. MGD, T120, Reel 278, frames 214263-264, telegram of January 18, 1942 from Wolfgang Welck to the Foreign Ministry.

37. Coutau-Bégarie and Huan, *Lettres et notes de l'Amiral Darlan*, 451-455.

38. MGD, T120, Reel 278, frames 214238-239, telegram Abetz to Ribbentrop, January 5, 1942.

39. DFCAA, V, 377-378.

40. MGD, T120, Reel 278, frame 214114, telephone report of Welck to the Foreign Ministry.

41. Ibid., frame 214133, telegram Abetz to Ribbentrop. See also T77, Reel 850, frames 5595074-075, German Armed Forces High Command, Armistice Commission.

42. See Coutau-Bégarie and Huan, *Lettres et notes de l'Amiral Darlan*, 435.

43. MGD, T120, Reel 278, frames 214160-163, telegram Welck to the Foreign Ministry, December 16, 1941.

44. Ibid. See also Coutau-Bégarie and Huan, *Lettres et notes de l'Amiral Darlan*, 438-439.

45. MGD, T120, Reel 278, frame 214163, telegram Welck to Foreign Ministry, December 16, 1941.

46. USNA, RG 59, Department of State, 851.00/ tel. #1539, December 14, 1941, Leahy to State Department.

47. Ibid., 851.00/2571, telegram Leahy to State Department, December 15, 1941.

48. Coutau-Bégarie and Huan, *Lettres et notes de l'Amiral Darlan*, 440-442.

49. Hervé Coutau-Bégarie and Claude Huan, *Darlan* (Paris: Fayard, 1989), 474.

CHAPTER 17

The End of the Darlan Era at Vichy

The mood of despair that fell over Vichy in early 1942 reflected the fact that France would find no relief from the burdens of the German occupation. And Darlan could see on the horizon new threats to the empire posed by American naval power. There was no easy solution to either of these problems, for his addressing one of them was sure to aggravate the other.

DOWNTURN IN FRANCO-GERMAN RELATIONS

Vichy's changing posture found expression in the Marshal's New Years' radio address to the nation. It denounced the collaborationist press in Paris, reminded Frenchmen of the harsh occupation, and complained about Berlin's refusal to grant concessions.[1] In Algiers, Murphy reported French opinion that the speech amounted to "a declaration that the policy of collaboration is at an end."[2]

Berlin informed Abetz on January 12 of reports linking Darlan's stiffening posture to German military setbacks in Russia and Africa, to the shooting of hostages in the occupied zone, and to the Reich's refusal to grant concessions.[3] Paris had already lost confidence in the Admiral. The arrival of Pierre Laval in Paris on January 7 reinforced rumors in the city that a rival French government would soon be established in the occupied zone, that Darlan's influence in Vichy had begun to wane, and that the government soon would be reshuffled.[4] The shadows were beginning to close in on Darlan because German needs to plunder more thoroughly the French economy required a French government more in step with German interests.

In December and January, Abetz renewed his schemes to drag France back into the war, but neither Berlin nor Vichy gave him support.[5] Darlan knew that Frenchmen would not fight alongside the Axis, that Germany wished to plunder

France rather than to treat her as an ally, and that an American war would lead to the loss of France's empire. His fruitless interview of January 28 with Admiral Erich Raeder was his last meeting with any important German. The time had come for him to settle with the Americans, who were already calling the signals on questions of French colonial security.

PROBLEMS IN THE ASIA

After Pearl Harbor, Darlan fell into a pattern of bowing to American power. With Vichy committed to Japan for the joint defense of Indochina, the Pacific war threatened to drag France into a confrontation with the United States. "I expressed to Admiral Leahy," he reported to ambassador Gaston Henry-Haye in Washington on December 9, "the wish that the United States would contribute, by its attitude, to keeping Indo-China outside the area of operations."[6] The American government, Darlan reported again in early 1942, "is the sole power able in the present grave situation to give authoritative advice of moderation to Marshal CHIANG KAI SHEK."[7]

When Chinese aircraft attacked Tonkin on January 22, Darlan instructed Henry-Haye to ask Washington to restrain China. He explained that renewal of the attacks would aggravate Asian tensions "at the very time when the French Government is trying continuously to remain in the neutral position it has had since the beginning of the conflict and wishes to maintain."[8] After Washington had intervened, Chungking expressed its willingness to respect the Indochina frontier.[9] Clearly, Darlan desired no conflict with the United States but instead looked to Washington to help keep France neutral.

Meanwhile, Darlan was thrust into an awkward position between Washington and Tokyo. A January 27 intercept of a Darlan message revealed Japanese demands for the delivery of the entire Indochinese merchant fleet. Washington could see that Darlan was negotiating to save half of the fleet for Indochinese commerce.[10] Another message from Darlan, intercepted February 2, explained to Henry-Haye that Tokyo had demanded the transfer of 80,000 tons of shipping, and had threatened to seize the remaining 20,000 tons should its demands not be met.[11] With the January 27 intercept in hand, Secretary of State Cordell Hull instructed Leahy to inform Pétain that any agreement to deliver Indochinese shipping "would be a most unfriendly act."[12]

When Leahy complained on February 2, Darlan answered that he was "only making an effort to save as much as is possible of the French merchant marine."[13] Darlan's report summarizing the details of the proposed agreement with Japan, which Leahy sent to Washington that evening, contained the same information the Americans had already intercepted.[14] Hull could see that Darlan was speaking truthfully. But Washington remained firm, insisting again that any agreement to deliver French ships would "be considered an unfriendly act."[15]

The negotiations continued with Washington refusing to budge. On April 1, Tokyo sent Vichy an ultimatum, insisting upon an agreement by the 5th. Still, Washington refused to yield, and on April 27 Darlan informed Leahy that Japan had seized 90,000 tons of Indochinese shipping.[16] In what amounted to a contest between Washington and Tokyo, the Admiral had yielded to Washington.

Meanwhile, in March, he rejected a proposal for a Franco-Japanese campaign to employ French troops from Indochina to reconquer dissident New Caledonia.[17] It was out of respect for American military potential that Darlan rejected Tokyo's proposal when Japanese power seemed invincible. He realized that in the long term Washington rather than Tokyo would call the signals on the security of France's Pacific possessions.

PROBLEMS IN THE CARIBBEAN

In a case involving French neutral rights in Vichy's Caribbean islands, Darlan clashed with Washington before finally accepting a compromise solution favoring the Americans. Under the terms of a 1940 agreement between Admirals Georges Robert and John W. Greenslade, the French naval squadron at Martinique in the West Indies had been confined to local waters.[18] Should the agreement break down, Washington would have to commit scarce naval assets to keep an eye on the French ships.

In February 1941, after a German submarine had delivered ashore at Fort-de-France an injured crewman, Washington demanded "categorical assurances" that no Axis ship or aircraft would be allowed to enter French ports or territories in the hemisphere. Darlan told Leahy on the 23rd that serving the injured sailor was legal under international law, but he promised to remain neutral and to refuse the Axis use of French naval bases and ships. Darlan did not want to mention specifically the Axis powers in any written agreement with Washington. Next day, in a written note, he promised that French bases and harbors in the hemisphere would not be made available to any belligerent power as a base for operations. Reporting to Washington, Leahy observed that Darlan's note fell short of what had been requested. Washington again demanded assurances.[19]

Darlan replied on the 27th with a proposal to deny all belligerent powers, including the United States, access to French ports in the Western Hemisphere. He asked specifically for American assurances in regard to the neutrality of the islands and respect for French sovereignty over them. Delivering the note, Rochat questioned whether Vichy should permit the American naval observer to remain at Martinique--a hint that France might abandon the Robert-Greenslade agreement if pressed too hard. Leahy wrote Washington that "this note appears definitely to propose that the United States and the Axis Powers be subjected to exactly the same restrictions in the French possessions mentioned therein."[20]

Flexing American muscles, Under Secretary Sumner Welles wired Leahy on March 2 that Darlan's note ignored the fact of American preponderance in the Western Hemisphere. "This Government," he concluded, "must continue to insist upon receiving the assurances previously requested that Axis planes and vessels shall not be permitted to enter French ports in this area."[21] A week later Welles advanced a near ultimatum, instructing Leahy to inform Vichy that American-French relations would depend largely upon receipt of satisfactory assurances about the status of the Caribbean colonies.[22] Welles informed Henry-Haye the next day "that the assurances requested constituted an absolutely imperative necessity for the United States."[23]

Darlan stood his ground, offering a solution intended to give Washington assurances at the local level without his having to name the Axis in any formal commitment. In a note to Leahy of March 12, he stated bluntly that Washington must understand that international law and "existing circumstances" required France to treat all belligerents equally. He added, significantly, that the French government was prepared to confirm to Admiral Robert earlier instructions "given with a view to the settlement from the local point of view and in the spirit of the existing agreements of the difficulties which might arise on French territories in the Western Hemisphere."[24] The note still did not give the categorical assurances Washington had demanded. Rochat explained, however, that his government wished to maintain in theory a posture of neutrality and that there was no question of withdrawing from the Caribbean agreements. He added that Washington's accepting the French note would be understood in Vichy as an American guarantee of his government's continuing sovereignty over the islands.

Moving astutely, Welles accepted the note but exploited it to Washington's advantage. His note of March 22 instructed Leahy to inform Darlan of Washington's satisfaction with the assurances. But he asserted the right to intervene if necessary in the French islands, adding that "in reserving this liberty of action the United States Government, however, declares that it has no intention to alter the basic French sovereignty of the territories in question whatever temporary measures are required by the exigencies of a developing war situation."[25]

Darlan's note of April 1 to Leahy affirmed Vichy's decision not to permit "under any circumstances and under any pretext whatsoever, military planes and warships of belligerent countries to enter the territories, ports, and territorial waters of French possessions in America."[26] Darlan expressed satisfaction at Washington's intention not to modify the sovereignty of the islands, but he gently protested American liberty of intervention, which he thought inconsistent with earlier statements by President Roosevelt.[27]

Washington's acceptance of the Robert-Greenslade agreement as local arrangements enabled Darlan to preserve the theory of treating all belligerents equally. But he had accepted the right of American intervention in the islands. On March 24 he admitted to Henry-Haye that the time had come "when we are being compelled to settle, to the satisfaction of the Washington Government, all the Franco-American problems that have come up during the recent weeks."[28]

FINAL SETTLEMENT WITH THE AMERICANS

Relations with Washington turned sharply downward when rumors of the Delta and Gamma programs reached the Americans on February 5.[29] On the 9th, when Leahy raised the issue of the shipments, the Admiral argued that it was better to permit small deliveries than to risk Axis seizure of Bizerte.[30] Leahy replied that France would do better in the long run "to lose Bizerte by armed attack than voluntarily to give assistance to our declared enemies."[31] But Darlan knew that losing Bizerte meant losing Tunisia.

In a meeting with Henry-Haye on the 10th, Welles dismissed as absurd Darlan's argument about the value of saving the port itself. That same day Roosevelt wired Pétain a sharp protest, demanding assurances that no more military aid go to the Axis. Otherwise, he threatened, Admiral Leahy would be recalled for consultation about the future of American policy toward France.[32] Taking the American threat seriously, Darlan that same day suspended the Gamma program for shipment of trucks to Libya.[33] He did not, however, withdraw the Delta program, for he believed that shipments of nonmilitary supplies to be legal under international law. In a long note of February 16 sent as the Marshal's reply to Roosevelt's letter, Darlan affirmed his intention to continue on a neutral course.[34] He did not, however, give the assurances that President Roosevelt had requested.

Refusing to back off, Roosevelt replied on the 19th to remind the Admiral that thirty-seven nations and three-quarters of the people of the globe had allied themselves to defeat the Axis. He stated that Leahy had been asked to return to the United States for consultation, but he left the door ajar for him to remain at his post should Vichy give the requested assurances. Both Vichy and Washington now moved to avoid a breakdown of relations. On the 21st Darlan informed Leahy of the cancellation of the deliveries of trucks to the Axis. Three days later, he promised to lend no military aid to any belligerent nation.[35] Roosevelt in turn informed Leahy that Allied military plans for the Mediterranean precluded any change in Washington's French policy, and that the ambassador would not be recalled.[36]

With Leahy therefore still at his post, the State Department on March 2 expressed satisfaction at Darlan's promise to discontinue deliveries of war materials but insisted that shipments of nonmilitary supplies also be discontinued.[37] Darlan was in an awkward position, for French ships operating under the Delta program were at that moment carrying supplies across the Mediterranean. Having already made concessions, Darlan grew impatient with the American demands. His impatience mounted when British aircraft bombed the Renault auto works in Paris on March 3. After personally inspecting the devastated area with its nearly 400 dead civilians, the Admiral let his anger spill over into his relations with the Americans.[38] Back in Vichy on the 8th, he sent Leahy a sharp note protesting the raid and charging that the American government appeared to be trying to pick a quarrel with France.[39]

But Darlan quickly regained his composure. On the 10th, Rochat informed Leahy that Darlan's government "will express its willingness to put an end to the future shipment of all supplies of any kind to the Axis forces in North Africa."[40] And on March 16, in a note to Leahy, Darlan expressed the assurances Washington had demanded.[41] Washington responded on the 22nd with an expression of satisfaction and a promise to resume the economic aid program for North Africa. To Darlan's satisfaction, the note reaffirmed Washington's "desire to maintain French authority throughout the French Empire."[42]

By the end of March, Darlan had settled to Washington's satisfaction every major issue in Franco-American relations. Receiving from Henry-Haye regular reports of American industrial production, he was becoming aware of the awesome military potential of the United States.[43] Darlan was beginning to think that the Allies might after all win the war. The question now was whether he could hold on much longer at Vichy.

JEWISH QUESTIONS

As he closed ranks with the Americans, Darlan grew increasingly unpopular with Paris and Berlin. In January he protested German proposals to force Jews in the unoccupied zone to wear the Star of David, and he succeeded in preventing its imposition during his term of office.[44] Darlan was also concerned to protect Jewish war veterans and Jewish families of long residence in France. In January he objected to a proposal of Xavier Vallat, commissioner for Jewish questions, to close additional commercial professions to the Jews. Following an investigation of the overzealous management of Jewish problems, Darlan dismissed Vallat in March.[45]

Darlan's term of office at Vichy coincided more with labor problems than with Jewish questions. The massive deliveries of French Jews to German concentration camps came after he had fallen from office. Although Darlan may have done more to protect foreign Jews and refugees, he clashed with doctrinaire anti-Semites like Vallat, whose strict enforcement of the law aggravated Vichy's mounting economic problems. The Admiral's foot-dragging on the enforcement of anti-Semitic laws and his opposition to new measures of oppression strengthened the hand of French collaborators who wanted to get rid of him.

GERMAN MANPOWER DEMANDS

Mounting labor shortages in 1942 forced the Reich to plunder more thoroughly Europe's manpower resources. Darlan came under increased criticism from Paris on the eve of the German springtime offensive against the Soviets and at the moment when Berlin's demands for French labor increased sharply. The services the Reich would require of France in 1942 were so urgent and so different from those of 1941 that Berlin could no longer tolerate the Admiral's foot-dragging.

The move to unseat Darlan was related to his obstructive attitude toward Nazi plans to conscript French workers in 1942. When the German labor supply failed to keep pace with wartime demands in January, Berlin reorganized the labor recruitment program in the occupied countries and in March appointed Fritz Sauckel to head the effort. Frenchmen refusing to volunteer for work in Germany were sometimes deprived of their work permits in France; others were given the painful choice of working in Germany or having a relative remain a prisoner there.[46] *Le Matin* carried articles encouraging French workers to take advantage of opportunities in Germany. At the same time, collaborationist newspapers in the occupied zone denounced Darlan and demanded cabinet changes.[47]

During the first three months of 1942, Darlan faced heavy demands for the delivery of workers in both zones. In February, Berlin submitted to the French employment commission a demand for 60,000 laborers.[48] There followed in March a demand for an additional 300,000.[49] But Darlan refused to cooperate.[50] The sharp increase in deportments after Darlan's departure suggests that urgent German manpower needs required a more compliant government at Vichy. Two weeks after Darlan's demotion in April, Laval and Sauckel signed an agreement for the deportation of 250,000 Frenchmen. Deportments during the first six months of 1942 numbered only about 12,000; however, by the end of the year the number had increased to 239,673. During the same six-month periods, the number of French specialists deported to Germany increased from roughly 4,000 to 137,000.[51] That Laval caved in to German demands for French labor is confirmed by Vichy's message to Henry-Haye in October that "refusal and hesitation are not any longer permissible."[52]

Other evidence suggests a connection between the Reich's labor needs and German pressure to replace Darlan with Laval. On April 27, American consul Earle Russell at Casablanca reported information from French sources that Laval had come to power "on the basis of a deal with the Germans for exchange of 70,000 French prisoners for 500,000 French workers."[53] Russell's report fits neatly with Berlin's linking war prisoners to labor recruitment. At the turn of the new year, the Germans redefined the Diplomatic Service for War Prisoners as the Delegation of the French Government for War Prisoners and Labor Questions.[54] And in a letter to Keitel on February 15, Stülpnagel reported that Franco-German negotiations had become preoccupied with labor recruitment problems, that Abetz aimed at increasing his influence on the French government, and that the French press had launched sharp attacks upon Darlan and Pétain.[55] The Germans clearly wanted to get rid of Darlan so they could conscript the French working masses for service in Germany.

THE END OF THE DARLAN ERA

In March the Paris faction enlisted Berlin's support to oust the Admiral. On the 20th, Göring told Laval in Paris that Berlin had no confidence in the Darlan government.[56] A week later, in a secret meeting with Pétain in the forest of Randan near Vichy, Laval insisted that the Admiral no longer enjoyed public support and that his remaining in power risked the creation of a rival government in Paris.[57] Laval indicated that he would return to office only with full powers, but he added that Darlan might remain as head of French military services.[58] Next day Darlan journeyed to Laval's estate at Châteldon. Laval made no specific demands, but he insisted that he would not return to office without full powers.[59]

In the meantime, on March 24, Du Moulin told Leahy of German pressure to restore Laval. The Germans, he said, realized that Darlan "had no intention of even attempting to carry out the promises he had so far made to the Germans."[60] Responding on March 30, Leahy handed the Marshal and Darlan a stern note from Washington threatening that should Laval be restored, "the United States Government would be obliged to discontinue its existing relations of confidence for our mutual welfare with the French Government at Vichy."[61] Leahy added "that an appointment of Laval to the Cabinet would probably cause a break in our diplomatic relations."[62]

Darlan fought back. In an April 2 interview with Roland Krug von Nidda, German representative in Vichy, the Admiral insisted that Laval's return would provoke the Americans to strike into Africa to form a front behind the German lines in Libya. He made the mistake of revealing Washington's threat to break diplomatic relations. Krug insisted that Laval would have to be recalled to restore Hitler's confidence in France. Now the Germans stepped up their efforts to restore Laval.[63] When Abetz learned of the American threat to recall its ambassador, he advanced the Laval case as a test of strength between Berlin and Washington.[64]

The crisis mounted on the 9th when Benoist-Méchin telephoned from Paris that Berlin counted on the return of Laval, and that Abetz "wishes to say that the Chancellor considers without doubt that a policy of Franco-German reconciliation seemed to him preferable to the use of force."[65] Abetz added that Hitler, hearing of American opposition to Laval, "considered that the Americans had thereby shown their hand and that if nothing was done, he would conclude that France had opted for the Anglo-Saxons."[66]

Two days later, on the 11th, Krug delivered an ultimatum requiring Vichy to assign Laval three key ministries and control of all of the nonmilitary ministries. It indicated that Germany would not compromise and that Vichy's failure to comply would destroy the Reich's confidence in France. Darlan could remain Pétain's successor and cabinet chief.[67] Darlan floated other proposals, but on the afternoon of the 12th de Brinon brought news that the Germans would accept but one solution: that of Laval's becoming vice-president with Darlan remaining military commander and the Marshal's successor.[68] On the morning of the 14th, when the Marshal received Darlan and Laval at the Hôtel du Parc, the Admiral accepted that solution. As military commander, he would report directly to the Marshal but would not be a part of the Laval government.[69]

Two days later, prior to any public announcement, Vichy notified all military commands that governmental changes would take place soon and that Darlan would remain military commander and the Marshal's successor. On the 17th the Admiral resigned his political offices.[70] That was the signal for Sauckel to launch with Laval a comprehensive program to conscript the French masses for labor in Germany.[71]

THE TURNING POINT

If Berlin hesitated to oust Darlan altogether, it was only because the Reich's leaders knew that his departure would risk separatism in Africa. They finally settled upon a solution to keep him on the Marshal's team but out of Laval's way. Darlan's remaining military commander kept North Africa in line and protected the area to the rear of the Axis front in Libya.

The Americans had defended Darlan stoutly. But unsure of what was happening, the State Department's Ray Atherton on April 15 telephoned Leahy, who reported that he had "no authentic knowledge" of the details of the impending cabinet reorganization, and that he "doubted whether the Axis Powers had delivered an actual ultimatum in Vichy."[72] Preoccupied with the illness of his wife, who had undergone surgery on the 9th, Leahy was out of touch with events. On April 18 Washington called Leahy home for consultation. Within a week he departed Vichy, carrying with him the remains of Mrs. Leahy, who had died on the 21st.

Laval's restoration marked a sharp turn that delivered France into the service of Germany. France emerged from the April crisis with what amounted to a two-headed government. Laval, as chief of the government at Vichy, would manage relations with Berlin in a manner to satisfy German manpower needs. Darlan, as commander of the armed services, held broad powers in French Africa where Laval could not be expected to keep Vichy's colonial administration in line. Darlan's fall from political office was the first step in a sequence of events that soon would leave France with two governments, one on the continent and another in Africa.

NOTES

1. *The New York Times*, January 2, 1942, p. 4.

2. USNA, RG 59, Department of State, 851.00/2594, Murphy to Secretary of State.

3. MGD, T120, Reel 1830, frame E019474, Foreign Ministry, Pol. II.

4. Ibid., Reel 2826, frames E444591-592, Foreign Ministry, Military Commander in France.

5. See MGD, T120, Reel 278., frames 214245, 214184, 214238-239, Foreign Ministry, for documents related to Abetz's efforts.

6. USNA, RG 457, SRVD-001, National Security Agency, VICHY FRENCH DIPLOMATIC MESSAGES, 38 Parts, I, 0000194-195, January 6, 1942, Darlan to Washington (hereinafter cited as VFDM).

7. Ibid., 0000196.

8. Ibid., III, 0000623.

9. Ibid., IV, 0000927.

10. Ibid., III, 0000686-687.

11. Ibid., 0000694-695.

12. FRUS, 1942, II, 671-672.

13. Ibid., 672-673.

14. See ibid., 673-674.

15. Ibid., 675.

16. Ibid., 680-681, 686.

17. Jacques Benoist-Méchin, *De la défaite au désastre,* 2 volumes (Paris: Albin Michel, 1984), I, 271-272. See also Amiral Jean Decoux, *A la barre de l'Indochine* (Paris: Plon, 1949), 190.

18. For the Robert-Greenslade agreement, see FRUS, 1940, II, 493ff.

19. FRUS, 1942, II, 611-615.

20. Ibid., 617.

21. Ibid., 617-618.

22. Ibid., 620. The note also insisted upon assurances about deliveries to the Axis in North Africa, then under discussion in Vichy.

23. Ibid.

24. Ibid., 621.

25. Ibid., 622-623.

26. Ibid, 623.

27. Ibid.

28. USNA, RG 457, VFDM, VI, 0001689.

29. FRUS 1942, II, 125-128.

30. See Hervé Coutau-Bégarie and Claude Huan, *Darlan* (Paris: Fayard, 1989), 517-518, for figures indicating that the shipments were small.

31. FRUS 1942, II, 129.

32. Ibid., 132.

33. Hervé Coutau-Bégarie and Claude Huan, *Lettres et notes de l'Amiral Darlan* (Paris: Economica, 1992), 473-474. DFCAA V, 407.

34. FRUS, 1942, II, 132-134.

35. Ibid., 135-137, 140-142.

36. Ibid., 139.

37. Ibid., 144.

38. See Benoist-Méchin, *De la défaite au désastre*, I, 389-390.

39. Unpublished Diary of Admiral William D. Leahy (Washington, DC: Library of Congress, Manuscripts Division), Folio VII.

40. FRUS, 1942, II, 147.

41. Ibid., 148-149.

42. Ibid., 152.

43. USNA, RG 457, VFDM, III, 0000776.

44. Jacques Mordal, "Qui était Darlan," *Revue de Paris*, LII, August 1945, 109.

45. See Coutau-Bégarie and Huan, *Darlan*, 506-508; and Charles R. Marrus and Robert O. Paxton, *Vichy France and the Jews* (New York: Schocken Books, 1983), 116-119.

46. République Française, *Commission Consultative des Dommages et des Réparations, subis par la France et L'Union Française du fait de la guerre et de l'occupation ennemie (1939-1945)*, 9 volumes (Paris: 1947-1951), I, 13, 71-73 (hereinafter cited as *Dommages*).

47. *Dommages*, I, 72-73.

48. Ibid., 65.

49. Jacques Evrard, *La Déportation des travailleurs française dans le IIIe Reich* (Paris: Fayard, 1972.), 34.

50. Vice-Admiral Jean Fernet, *Aux Côtes du Maréchal Pétain* (Paris: Plon, 1953), 192-193; Louis-Dominique Girard, *Montoire, Verdun diplomatique* (Paris: André Bonne, 1948), 371-374; Maurice Martin du Gard, *La Chronique de Vichy 1940-1944* (Paris: Flammarion, 1948), 265; Evrard, *La Déportation des travailleurs française dans le IIIe Reich*, 36.

51. *Dommages*, I, 85.

52. USNA, RG 457, VFDM, XXVIII, 0008344.

53. USNA, RG 59, Department of State, 851.00/2770, tel. Earle Russell to Secretary of State.

54. MGD, T120, Reel 278, frames 214106-107, 214290-291, Foreign Ministry, State Secretary to Abetz.

55. Ibid., T501, Reel 165, frame 000435, Military Commander-in-Chief in France.

56. Pierre Laval, *Laval parle* (Genève: Diffusion du Livre, 1948), 95.

57. FRUS, 1942, II, 157. See also Laval, *Laval parle*, 95; Girard, *Montoire, Verdun diplomatique*, 378; Henri Du Moulin de Labarthète, *Le Temps des illusions* (Genève: Cheval Ailé, 1946), 235, 413-416.

58. Laval, *Laval parle*, 95. See also FRUS, 1942, II, 156-157.

59. Darlan, *L'Amiral Darlan parle*, 92.

60. USNA, RG 59, Department of State, 851.00/2727, tel. March 24, 1942 Leahy to the Secretary of State.

61. FRUS, 1942, II, 160.

62. Ibid., 161.

63. Coutau-Bégarie and Huan, *Lettres et notes de l'Amiral Darlan*, 490, 499-501. See also USNA, RG 59, Department of State, 851.00/2724, tel. 15 April 1942, Leahy to the Secretary of State.

64. FRUS, 1942, II, 169.

65. Coutau-Bégarie and Huan, *Lettres et notes de l'Amiral Darlan*, 501.

66. Ibid.

67. Ibid., 505.

68. Coutau-Bégarie and Huan, *Darlan*, 540-541.

69. Darlan, *L'Amiral Darlan parle*, 297-298.

70. Coutau-Bégarie and Huan, *Lettres et notes de l'Amiral Darlan*, 516.

71. Evrard, *La Déportation des travailleurs française dans le IIIe Reich*, 37.

72. USNA, RG 59, Department of State, 851.00/2855, Box 46112838.

CHAPTER 18

The Road to Algiers

The restoration of Laval rescued Darlan from the graveyard of Franco-German relations and shifted his attention toward Africa. He knew that Allied military adventures in French Africa might upset the statusquo upon which Vichy's political life depended. He therefore cultivated his American connections in the hope of influencing Washington's war planning. But events beyond his control finally thrust him into the midst of a major military operation unfolding on the scene of a Darlan family crisis.

COMMANDER-IN-CHIEF

Darlan quickly settled into a routine that kept him mainly at Vichy during the summer of 1942. He passed most of the day at Hôtel Thermal, his military headquarters. Toward midday he strolled with a small guard across the Parc des Sources to the Hôtel du Parc where he maintained offices as designated successor to the Marshal. He would return to Thermal before retiring at the end of the day to a villa near the Allier where he and Mme. Darlan lived alone. They occasionally received visits from their son Alain.[1]

At Thermal Darlan surrounded himself with loyal officers. His Chief-of-Staff, General Georges Revers, had served with him in World War I. Revers was assisted by an under Chief-of-Staff for each service. Air General Bergeret, responsible for antiaircraft defense, was attached directly to Darlan. Admiral Robert Battet, Darlan's cabinet chief, was an old friend. Aide de camp Henri Ballande managed the Admiral's in-coming communications and accompanied him on tours of the provinces.[2]

French military organization was, however, badly flawed. Darlan reported directly to the Marshal, but he had no post in the government, where military affairs were represented by three secretaries of state: General Jean-François

Jeannekyn for Air, Admiral Paul Auphan for Navy, and General Eugene-Marie Bridoux for War. Each service in turn had its own Chief-of-Staff, so that there were six chiefs. Military organization was made all the more cumbersome by the fact that Bridoux, representing Laval, worked against Darlan.[3]

During the summer he clashed often with Laval, whose meddling in military matters aimed at undermining the Admiral's authority.[4] The struggle moved toward a climax in September when Bridoux issued an instruction to the top army command without notifying Darlan. On the 23rd Darlan struck back, insisting that Bridoux withdraw it.[5] Bridoux refused, and Pétain gave the Admiral little support. Furious, Darlan submitted his resignation on October 1, but the Marshal refused it.[6] But Darlan remained insecure in his command.

SECRET CONTACTS WITH THE AMERICANS

Darlan's discreet communications with Robert Murphy in North Africa became more important in 1942. Murphy, who knew that Vice-Admiral Fenard spoke for the Admiral, reported Fenard in April as "becoming vehemently pro-American."[7] In early 1942 Darlan strengthened the Fenard-Murphy connection, adding to it his son Alain, a naval reserve officer whose business interests afforded him reasons to travel to Africa.[8] Whenever he visited Algiers, Alain and his wife were house guests of the Fenard family at the villa Sidi-Allowi. Young Darlan's frequent visits there aroused no suspicion among Axis spies in the city, for the personal ties between the Darlan and Fenard families were well known.[9] Murphy, too, was a frequent visitor at Sidi-Allowi. Fenard therefore had no problem bringing Murphy and Alain together for dinner with business scheduled after the wives and servants had retired.

Murphy's memoirs are brief and circumspect on these conversations, and Alain Darlan made no mention of them in L'Amiral Darlan Parle. In 1966, Claude Paillat published in his book a letter from Alain containing more details, as Alain remembered them. In a conversation with the author in 1982, Alain explained that the line of communications he had established with Murphy ran directly to President Roosevelt, by-passing the State Department. That line, he said, enabled Admiral Darlan to communicate in confidence with the President.[10]

Alain wrote that the conversations with Murphy began in February when he met the diplomat at Fenard's villa. Retiring after dinner to the fireside, Alain indicated his father's friendly sentiments, and he spoke of the need to establish confidential communications with Roosevelt. Several days later they met again. According to Alain's letter, Murphy indicated that he now spoke for the President. Alain therefore reported to his father that the confidential line of communications with Roosevelt had been established.[11]

Murphy, however, makes no claim to have reported directly to Roosevelt, but only to Washington[12] And in a letter to Paillat in 1965, Murphy wrote that he had no memory of transmitting any communication from Roosevelt to Alain Darlan.[13] In his 1982 conversation with the author, Alain indicated that the records of the secret Darlan-Roosevelt communications are housed in the Roosevelt Library at Hyde Park. But the author's search of those files uncovered no such documents. It appears that there were no secret Darlan-Roosevelt communications.

Alain wrote that Darlan summoned him in early April and unfolded military plans for him to deliver to Fenard, who would hand them to Murphy. These plans, Alain continued, proposed French cooperation with American landings in southern France where French forces under General Jean de Lattre de Tassigny would delay any German counterattack. Alain wrote that his role was to tell Murphy that France preferred the Americans to strike into France, or into France and North Africa simultaneously, rather than into North Africa.[14]

Alain did indeed meet with Fenard and Murphy on Saturday, April 11. Murphy's report of April 14 contains the first mention of his meetings with Alain. According to the report, Alain indicated his father's confidence in an American victory, his desire to be on the American side, and his hope that Washington would understand that minor concessions would have to be made to the Axis in order to attain more important objectives. After Murphy had complained of a lack of frankness on the French side, Alain suggested that if a secure system could be devised so that "only the President, a few top State Department officials and Admiral Leahy would be informed of confidential matters of importance he was certain that the Marshal and his father would be much more inclined to take us into their confidence."[15]

But Murphy makes no mention of military proposals from Admiral Darlan. Moreover, General de Lattre de Tassigny, who Alain allegedly said in April would hurl French forces against the Wehrmacht, had not yet been promoted to command the armies in the region of the proposed American landings. Alain, therefore, did not deliver any military proposals to Murphy in April. He instead delivered in April a message similar to the one he claims to have delivered in February. Admiral Darlan had no need to send military proposals to Murphy in April. In September, however, when he expected an attack at Dakar, he had good reasons to inform Murphy of his willingness to cooperate with a campaign in southern France, rather than in Africa. Alain may indeed have carried specific military proposals in September, when his father sent him again to see Murphy.[16]

PLANNING THE LIBERATION

During the spring of 1942, Darlan's thinking about the war shifted importantly. Realizing that the Americans might be capable of launching a campaign on the Mediterranean coast of France in the spring of 1943, he made plans to cooperate with the landings. At the same time, he would oppose weak Allied attacks or commando raids against the empire, for his joining them would show his hand prematurely. He worried about an attack against West or North Africa, which might provoke Germany to occupy southern France. Darlan hoped to persuade the Americans to wait until they could come to Provence in force.

The Admiral made that point to Leahy in April before the ambassador departed for Washington. He amended his earlier statement to Leahy, spoken contemptuously in 1941, with a new slant reflecting his new position as Commander-in-Chief. When the Americans are able to come to France in force, he explained, "then I, François Darlan, will be ready to give the order to all French armed forces to fight on your side to liberate my country, and I will be in a position to see that the order is executed."[17] We find here no hint that Darlan would join in anything less than a major American campaign in France. He later remarked to Alain that "we will have only one chance, not two."[18]

Darlan's fears of British aggression stemmed from Laval's agreement of September 2 with Abetz to lease 200,000 tons of French and neutral shipping to the Germans.[19] Darlan knew the Americans had learned of it, and he expected the British to retaliate with another attack against Dakar.[20] In October, he ordered the evacuation of military dependents from the city, and he decided to go there himself to inspect defenses.

At the same time, he reviewed plans to resist any German invasion of the free zone. General Henri Giraud, recently escaped from German captivity but outside Vichy's chain of command, was one of several generals who drafted plans. General de Lattre de Tassigny, commander at Montpellier, also drafted a plan. Another, prepared by Revers and approved by Darlan, called for the forming of beachheads near Marseilles in harmony with an American landing in 1943.[21] In August, Darlan promoted de Lattre to command French military forces in Provence. When the Germans finally invaded the free zone, de Lattre attempted to implement the Revers plan. According to a French study in Office of Strategic Services files, the application "by General de Lattre de Tassigny of the plan of General Revers shows that this plan had been accepted."[22]

CONSPIRACY IN ALGIERS

In the meantime, Murphy cultivated his contacts with the resistance movement in Algiers, led by a small circle of professional men, businessmen, and royalists. Known as The Five, these men had varied political agendas, but they shared the common goal of swinging North Africa into the war in conjunction with an American landing. But The Five lacked a strong military leader capable of rallying the French military establishment at the moment of American intervention. Colonel A.J. Van Hecke, heading a paramilitary youth organization, was unsuitable for the top role. Jacques Lemaigre-Dubreuil, an industrialist who traveled between France and North Africa, and Henri d'Astier de la Vigerie, a wealthy royalist emerging as the leader of The Five, were civilians without influence among Vichy's military leaders.[23] Jean Rigault, a journalist, and Jacques Tarbé de Saint-Hardouin, a former diplomat, were also unsuitable.

The Five finally settled upon Giraud, now residing near Lyons. On July 3 Murphy wired Washington that Giraud was interested in cooperating with an operation in North Africa or southern France. The General's representative in Algiers, General Charles Mast, was Chief-of-Staff of the 19th Army Corps.[24] On August 1, Murphy was summoned to Washington where the decision had just been made to launch Operation TORCH, a combined Allied landing in North Africa.

Murphy arrived in Washington in September. Roosevelt, not wanting to boost any faction into power, instructed him to avoid dealing with the top rank of the French political or military leadership.[25] In mid-September, Murphy rushed to London for discussions with General Dwight D. Eisenhower and British officers.

There the question of including Darlan was discussed, but no decision was made. Back in Washington, Murphy received instructions from the President that made no mention of Darlan's participation in TORCH.[26] He therefore returned to Algiers with the intention of dealing with The Five and with local military officers.

OVERTURES TO THE AMERICANS

In mid-September Darlan finally saw the need to renew his contacts with the Americans.[27] Rumors spreading in Vichy held that both the Allies and the Axis were poised to strike into North Africa, and the Marshal told Darlan of reports from Portugal of an impending American attack there. Unsure of these reports, Darlan continued to think that the Allies would strike at Dakar.[28] Wishing to head off a confrontation there, he summoned Alain to deliver another message to Murphy.

According to a 1974 letter from Alain to Pierre Ordioni, Darlan's message cautioned against premature or weak operations. Proposing instead a joint Franco-American military operation in unoccupied France, it indicated that secret preparations were under way, and that local resistance in the Toulon region could be undertaken in anticipation of swift American intervention. Finally, Alain was instructed to inform Murphy that Admiral Darlan would come to North Africa in October on an inspection tour.[29]

While Alain waited for Murphy in Algiers, chargé d'affaires Pinkney Tuck wired Washington on September 27 a message that went straight to Roosevelt:

French Army Staff preparing plans for possible operations on continent in cooperation with Anglo American forces. Willing to cooperate in Africa but feel any action near future would produce disastrous results such as complete occupation of France preventing organized action in Metropole. Planning send mission to England and possibly Washington for discussions with military authorities: realization depends on attitude of Laval.[30]

Whether someone at Vichy deliberately leaked this information to coincide with Alain's mission is not certain. But the Tuck message fits neatly with Alain's claim of his carrying military proposals from Darlan to Murphy in September.

In the meantime, Colonel Jean Chrétien, chief of counterespionage in Algiers, had concluded that the Americans would soon strike into North Africa.[31] Accordingly, he rushed to Vichy where Revers informed him on the 26th of Darlan's plans to cooperate with American landings in France in 1943. But the Colonel insisted that a landing in North Africa was imminent. "What do you mean," Revers asked, "three or four months?" "No, much earlier," Chrétien answered, "November 15, at the latest."[32] When Chrétien offered to contact Murphy, Revers hesitated. Finally, after conferring with Darlan, Revers authorized a discreet contact. Chrétien had not seen Darlan personally, but he returned to Algiers with the Admiral's permission to see Murphy.

Murphy returned to Algiers on Sunday, October 11 with knowledge of Operation TORCH scheduled for November 8. Within hours of Murphy's arrival, Alain Darlan fell ill with polio. Rushed to Maillot Hospital, he was too sick to deliver the message that would have confirmed his father's desire to cooperate with landings in France rather than North Africa. Chrétien met Murphy on October 12, the same Monday that Alain became ill. With the question of French participation in TORCH still unsettled, Murphy listened as Chrétien unfolded what appeared to be an important overture from Darlan. What Murphy heard was not a message from Darlan, but Chrétien's report of what he had learned from men close to him.

Chrétien indicated that Axis sources had informed Vichy of American intentions to attack Dakar or Casablanca, and that Germany would occupy North Africa ahead of the Americans. Darlan's entourage, he continued, expected the Germans to intervene before November 1. There was a good chance, he said, that Darlan would come to North Africa and bring the fleet with him if the Americans would provide important military aid.[33] Afterward, Murphy wired Washington for permission to encourage Darlan, with the view of his cooperating with Giraud.[34]

Chrétien's report had overstated Darlan's willingness to join the Americans in a North African adventure. By mid-October the Admiral's fears of an Allied operation in Africa had subsided. His own intelligence services suggested that any Allied attack there would come only in the spring of 1943.[35] Darlan therefore persisted with his plans to persuade the Americans to strike instead into France.

Meanwhile, on October 13, Murphy received Major André Dorange, General Juin's cabinet chief. Murphy stressed with him the point that the United States now stood ready to send massive military aid, including troops, whenever the French summoned them to oppose Axis aggression. American intervention, he promised, would occur only upon the request of the legal French government or its representatives. Murphy insisted that he held full powers from President Roosevelt to negotiate directly with the French government to return France to the war. When Dorange asked whether Marshal Pétain might be informed of Murphy's special powers, the American replied that the information should be reported to Juin, who might share it with Darlan only. Details of military planning, he said, could be managed by American and French military experts meeting without delay.[36] When Dorange returned two days later, Murphy assured him: "You have nothing to fear on our part--we will not come unless you summon us."[37]

But Murphy still had no authority to deal with Darlan. It was only on the 17th that he received a message from Washington that assigned the question of settling the French command to representatives of Giraud.[38] The message did not encourage Murphy to bring Darlan into the circle of Frenchmen already conspiring with the Americans.

FRENCH REJECTION OF DARLAN

While Juin waited to deliver Dorange's report to Darlan, events moved swiftly toward a decision about the French leadership role in TORCH. On the day after his interview with Dorange, Murphy received Mast, who asked that Darlan be excluded and that Murphy arrange a secret meeting between American staff officers and local resistance leaders. He promised that Giraud's leadership would enable the Americans to enter North Africa "practically without firing a shot."[39] But Mast also brought a disturbing request from Giraud that the Americans "consider the possibility of including in Torch a plan of establishing a bridgehead in southern France before the Axis has the chance of organizing that area."[40]

Although Giraud was obviously out of step with the objectives of TORCH, Washington authorized Murphy on October 17 to arrange the meeting Mast had requested. General Mark W. Clark, deputy commander of TORCH, would head an American team to meet with Murphy and his French friends near Algiers on the 23rd. But on the same day that Murphy was notified to arrange the meeting, Eisenhower and Churchill in London devised a formula to enlist Giraud as French political chief and Darlan as military chief under the American command. Later that day Admiral Leahy, with Roosevelt's approval, wired Murphy to go ahead if necessary to include Darlan in TORCH.[41]

During the night of October 23 a team of American officers rowed quietly ashore from a British submarine opposite an isolated house near Cherchell to discuss invasion plans with Murphy and his French friends. When the question of French leadership was brought up, Clark suggested that both Darlan and Giraud be included. But Mast spoke against the Admiral.[42] Murphy therefore moved forward to conspire with The Five to stage a *coup d'état* in Algeria and Morocco in concert with the landings.[43]

REPORTS FROM CHRÉTIEN AND DORANGE

Meanwhile, Darlan remained preoccupied with planning his tour of West Africa, and with Alain's illness. On the weekend of October 17-18, Mme. Darlan and the family physician flew to Algiers to join Alain.[44] And on Tuesday, the 20th, the Admiral departed Vichy by air. During the following three days, while Murphy and Clark conspired with Mast at Cherchell, Darlan inspected the defenses at Dakar and then traveled back to Rabat. There he met the chief of the German armistice commission, Gustav Vogl, assuring him of French determination to defend West Africa against any Allied invasion.[45]

Arriving at Algiers on Wednesday, October 28, Darlan finally received Dorange's report and Juin's summary of Chrétien's interview with Murphy. "I know the Americans very well," he remarked to Juin and Fenard, "they are not ready; and if they bungle this thing, the German reaction will be terrible for us."[46] But he was impressed with Murphy's status as Roosevelt's spokesman, and with his promise to await an invitation from the French government. So he authorized Chrétien to undertake secret contacts with Murphy to explore Franco-American military cooperation should the Germans attack North Africa.[47]

Before he left Juin's residence late that afternoon to visit Alain, Darlan assured his officers that North Africa lay in no immediate danger of an American attack.[48] But he remained unsure about Dakar, where that same afternoon French military dependents boarded ships to depart the city. During the predawn hours of Friday, October 30, as the Admiral flew back to Vichy in a Glenn Martin bomber, a British submarine slipped through the waters below to fetch Giraud from France.

FAMILY CRISIS IN ALGIERS

Confident that North Africa lay in no immediate danger, Darlan considered plans to transfer Alain to the Pasteur Institute in Paris. The patient, however, was too weak to be moved. As Alain struggled for life in Algiers, Murphy and Giraud exchanged the final messages intended to bring the General to Gibraltar to join the invasion scheduled for Saturday night.[49] On Thursday the Admiral received messages from Fenard reporting a downturn in Alain's condition and urging him to come at once.[50] He therefore flew back to Algiers where he found his son near death. While the Admiral sat with Alain that afternoon, Giraud waited in France, having missed his rendezvous with the submarine. Only in the early morning hours of Friday, the 6th, did Giraud depart France. As Giraud's submarine crept silently toward Gibraltar, Darlan grieved at Alain's bedside, unaware that a major Allied campaign would be launched that same weekend on beaches not far from Maillot Hospital.

While he and his wife maintained their watch at the hospital, Darlan learned that a huge Allied convoy had steamed into the Mediterranean. But he knew that earlier convoys has passed that way to reinforce Malta and British armies in Libya. He appears not to have thought that the Americans might after all be capable of striking a major blow in 1942. Besides, Murphy had promised that the Americans would come only by invitation.

Heartsick at Alain's condition, and already making funeral arrangements, Darlan discounted reports that the convoy was headed for French Africa.[51] General Bergeret, flying to Algiers on Friday, rushed directly to Maillot Hospital where he insisted that a landing was imminent. Annoyed, Darlan scolded Bergeret: "Your information is wrong, I have information from the American envoy."[52] That same day Darlan received reports from Vichy pointing to North Africa as the destination of the convoy. "We have seen Murphy," he wired back, "no immediate danger."[53]

By early Saturday morning the convoy had formed into two groups, one to the northwest of Algiers and the other northwest of Oran. Later that day Vichy warned Darlan again that the convoys might be headed for North Africa. The Admiral addressed his response to Auphan: "I do not think that any deliberate action against French territory is presently envisaged by the Anglo-Saxons."[54] Finally, that same Saturday, Alain's condition improved, so it appeared that the crisis had passed. Relieved, Darlan instructed his pilot to prepare for the return flight to Vichy.[55]

Late that afternoon the first ships of the lead convoy steamed past Algiers. But after dark the two convoys swung back toward Algiers and Oran, and a third one crept undetected in the night toward Morocco. Simultaneously, The Five and General Mast made final preparations to neutralize Vichy's military forces in Algeria and Morocco. While Murphy and his friends gathered at their secret headquarters on Rue Michelet, young Frenchmen moved unnoticed toward their objectives in Algiers. Mast prepared to issue the final orders intended to prevent an armed clash between French and American troops. At Oran and Casablanca, similar preparations got under way.

Overjoyed at Alain's turn for the better, Darlan departed Maillot Hospital for dinner Saturday evening with Juin and Fenard at Sidi Allowi, the same villa where Murphy had dined with Alain. Among friends, Darlan relaxed. The dinner finished, he received a visit from Admiral Jacques Moreau, commander of the fourth naval district at Algiers. The two convoys presumed to be headed for Malta, Moreau observed, now stood in a perfect position to swing back toward Algiers and Oran, and to land their troops under cover of darkness. "No," Darlan answered, "I have assurances."[56]

In the darkness after midnight on Sunday, the 8th, three Allied armies approached selected beaches near Algiers, Oran, and Casablanca. In Algiers groups of conspirators seized strategic points in the city, but at Gibraltar General Giraud had arrived too late to accompany the invasion. When he finally met with Eisenhower and Clark deep inside the Rock, Giraud insisted upon taking full command of the Allied armies and diverting a part of them to form a beachhead in southern France. Thus, while American and British troops moved silently onto African beaches, while a vast conspiracy unfolded in North Africa to prepare for their arrival, and while the Generals quarreled at Gibraltar over who was to command the invasion force, and where it was to go, Admiral Darlan lay quietly asleep at Fenard's villa.

NOTES

1. Henri Ballande, *De l'Amirauté à Bikini* (Paris: Cité, 1972), 146-153.

2. Ibid., 147-149.

3. Hervé Coutau-Bégarie and Claude Huan, *Darlan* (Paris: Fayard, 1989), 546-547.

4. See Ballande, *De l'Amirauté à Bikini*, 165.

5. Hervé Coutau-Bégarie and Claude Huan, *Lettres et notes de l'Amiral Darlan* (Paris: Economica, 1992), 541.

6. Ibid., 542-546; Coutau-Bégarie and Huan, *Darlan*, 559-560; Ballande, *De l'Amirauté à Bikini*, 165-166.

7. FRUS, 1942, II, 293.

8. Alain Darlan, *L'Amiral Darlan parle* (Paris: Amiot-Dumont, 1952), 9.

9. Letter of Alain Darlan contained in Claude Paillat, *L'Échiquier d'Alger*, 2 volumes (Paris: Robert Laffont, 1966), I, 382.

10. Telephone conversation between the author and Alain Darlan, 21 May 1982, Paris. When asked why he had omitted these conversations from his book, Alain indicated that the State Department had asked him to omit them.

11. Paillat, *L'Échiquier d'Alger*, I, 383.

12. Robert D. Murphy, *Diplomat among Warriors* (New York: Doubleday, 1964), 115.

13. Paillat, *L'Échiquier d'Alger*, I, 385, n. 16.

14. Ibid., 383-384.

15. FRUS, 1942, II, 283-284.

16. Paillat, *L'Échiquier d'Alger*, I, 383-384.

17. Darlan, *L'Amiral Darlan parle*, 161.

18. Ibid.

19. On October 21 the American naval attaché in London reported the leasing of 22 foreign ships to be used where needed. USNA, RG 38, ONI, C-9-b, Box 429.

20. SHM, 1BB2 EMG/SE, Carton 208, Dossiers Amiral Darlan, "Aide Mémoire; Objet: Remise de tonnage."

21. See Albert Kammerer, *Du Débarquement Africaine au meurtre de Darlan* (Paris: Flammarion, 1947), 209-215.

22. USNA, RG 226, E97, OSS, Algiers File, Box 5, Folder 82, "Dossier Établi par Jacques Lemaigre-Dubreuil par R.P. Thery, d'Apres les Archives de la Résistance," Volume 5, no page number.

23. For an OSS report on the French leadership, see USNA, RG 226, E97, OSS, Algiers File, Box 5, Folder 77, Miscellaneous Intelligence Reports, "Report On The Allied Landing In North Africa," 28 January 1943.

24. FRUS, 1942, II, 331-333.

25. Murphy, *Diplomat among Warriors*, 102.

26. Ibid., 115.

27. Murphy's reports to the State Department (USNA, Decimal File 740.0011 European War 1939, and "Murphy Messages" OPD 336) contain no military proposals from Darlan.

28. Ballande, *De L'Amirauté à Bikini*, 160-161.

29. Pierre Ordioni, *Le Secret de Darlan* (Paris: Albatros, 1974), 142-143.

30. Roosevelt Library, Hyde Park, MR 300, Sec. 1, Box 83, Folder #3, Telegram No. 81, 27 September 1942, Tuck to Milid.

31. Author's interview with General Chrétien, Malbuisson, France, 25 May 1982.

32. General Jean Chrétien, "Souvenirs d'une vie militaire," unpublished memoirs of General Chrétien.

33. FRUS, 1942, II, 392-393.

34. Ibid., 393-394.

35. Ballande, *De l'Amirauté à Bikini*, 162-163.

36. Resumé of the Murphy-Dorange interview of 13 October 1942, compliments of General Dorange.

37. Summary of the Murphy-Dorange interview of 15 October 1942, compliments of General Dorange.

38. FRUS, 1942, II, 397.

39. Ibid., 396.

40. Ibid., 395.

41. Alfred D. Chandler, Jr., editor *The Papers of Dwight David Eisenhower: The War Years*, 5 volumes (Baltimore: Johns Hopkins University Press, 1970), I, 622-625, n. 7; Unpublished Diary of Admiral William D. Leahy (Washington, DC: Library of Congress, Manuscripts Division), VIII, 38.

42. Unpublished papers of General Mark W. Clark, The Citadel Museum, Charleston, South Carolina; interview of the author with General Clark, 17 October 1977, in Charleston.

43. USNA, Department of State, Murphy Messages to War Department, OPD 336, 31 October 1942, No. R.C. 30.

44. outau-Bégarie and Huan, *Darlan*, 565.

45. MGD, T77, Reel 851, frames 5595908-5595911, armistice commission.

46. Paillat, *L'Échiquier d'Alger*, I, 395.

47. Chrétien, "Souvenirs d'une vie militaire," 8.

48. Kammerer, *Du Débarquement africain au meurtre de Darlan*, 154-155.

49. FRUS, 1942, II, 412-422.

50. SHM, 1BB2 EMG/SE, Carton 208, Dossiers Amiral Darlan, "Voyage (sans retour) Amiral Darlan à Alger, Novembre 1942," telegrams No. 06 and 06545, 5 November 1942.

51. For Darlan's funeral plans for Alain, see Ballande, *De l'Amirauté à Bikini*, 169-170.

52. Kammerer, *Du Débarquement africain au meurtre de Darlan*, 221.

53. Amiral Jules Docteur, *Darlan, Amiral de la flotte* (Paris: Éditions de la Couronne, 1949), 167.

54. Ballande, *De l'Amirauté à Bikini*, 171.

55. Kammerer, *Du Débarquement africain au meurtre de Darlan*, 222-223. See also Henri Michel, "Darlan et le débarquement allié en Afrique du Nord," *Cahiers d'Histoire de la Guerre*, Vol. I, No. 1, January 1949, 11-13. Darlan's pilot was Colonel Lionel-Max Chassin, future biographer of Mao Tse-Tung.

56. Ordioni, *Le Secret de Darlan*, 193.

CHAPTER 19

Armistice in North Africa

As Allied ships cut through the darkness toward African beaches near midnight on Saturday, November 7, 1942, Robert Murphy and his French friends at 26 Rue Michelet realized that General Giraud would not reach Algiers on Sunday in time to neutralize Vichy's military defenses. Worried, they summoned Colonel Chrétien to arrange a meeting with Juin, who might call off French resistance. Juin listened as Murphy insisted that half a million American troops were landing that Sunday morning along the North African coast--not to fight Frenchmen, he said, but to help with the liberation of France. When Murphy asked for support, Juin answered that Admiral Darlan was in Algiers. "Very well," Murphy answered, "let us talk with Darlan."[1]

A MEETING WITH MURPHY

Seizing the telephone, Juin rang Fenard's villa. Within minutes Chrétien and Vice-Consul Kenneth Pendar sped off to get Darlan. Arriving twenty minutes later, Darlan did not notice an irregular guard lingering near the gate. Passing through, he entered the villa where he heard Murphy's plea for cooperation.[2] Before the American could finish, Darlan shot back in anger: "It is another one of those filthy tricks you Anglo-Saxons have abused us with for two years," he shouted. "I have orders from the Marshal! I will execute them! Since you want to pick a fight, we will fight."[3] Knowing the attack would trigger a German reaction, he asked angrily, "what would happen to France?"[4]

Darlan could not be certain that the attack was a major operation. Perhaps it contained British or Gaullist units. Whatever, an attack upon North Africa did not fit his plans. "I have given my oath to Pétain and preserved allegiance to the Marshal for two years," he explained. "I cannot revoke that now. This premature action is not at all what we have been hoping for."[5] Regaining his composure,

Darlan could see that an American war would be unpopular with his officers. Juin had already spoken in Murphy's presence of the need to avoid a firefight with the Americans.[6] But Darlan knew that Vichy, now threatened with a German occupation, would demand resistance. Should Darlan conclude a premature armistice, he risked the Marshal's dismissing him.

Finally, Darlan promised Murphy he would cooperate if the Marshal approved. He quickly drafted a message to Pétain reporting Murphy's claim that the Americans, upon the request of Giraud, had decided to occupy North Africa with the goal of defeating Germany and saving France. "I told him," he concluded, "that France had signed an armistice convention and that I am only able to follow the Marshal's orders to defend our territory."[7]

But while Darlan had paced the floor with Murphy, armed conspirators had seized control of the gate to Juin's villa. Now they refused to allow any Frenchmen to leave the premises. Grudgingly, Darlan agreed to allow Pendar to deliver the message to the nearby Admiralty building. Pendar sped away, not to the Admiralty, but to 26 Rue Michelet where he steamed open the envelope. Seeing that the message spoke of resistance, he decided not to deliver it.[8] Meanwhile, Darlan settled into a conversation with Murphy. When the diplomat admitted that Washington had promised Giraud a leadership role in the operation, Darlan moved to sidetrack the General: "Giraud is not your man," he said. "Politically he is a child. He is just a good divisional commander, nothing more."[9]

After Pendar returned around 3:30 a.m., Fenard grew suspicious that Darlan's message had not been delivered. But before Pendar could leave with another copy, Major André Dorange arrived with loyal forces to disperse the irregulars guarding the gate. Murphy and the other Americans were ushered at gunpoint into the servants' quarters, uncertain of their fate. While this comic episode unfolded at the Villa des Oliviers, French shore batteries found the range on two British destroyers landing troops at the nearby harbor. The sound of artillery in the distance alerted the Admiral that an invasion was indeed in progress. At about the same time, the first American lives were lost at Oran and Morocco.

TOKEN RESISTANCE

His freedom restored, Darlan took control. Before he and Juin departed for Fort Lempereur, the military command post on the western heights of Algiers, the Admiral already suspected that the attack was more than a commando raid. Accordingly, he wired the Marshal that a major attack was under way from Tunisia to Morocco, and that British troops were involved.[10] Darlan also ordered Admiral Moreau to carry out the Marshal's standing resistance order.[11]

Arriving at Fort Lempereur shortly before 6:00 a.m., Darlan resumed overall command of Northwest Africa, with Juin commanding the military forces. Now the picture became clearer. Local civilian and military conspirators had seized strategic points in Algiers during the night, but loyal officers were regaining control of the city. Reports indicated Allied landings on both sides of Algiers. An attack in the harbor area had been blunted by stout French resistance. Nearby Maison Blanche airport was under attack. He received reports of landings at Oran and Morocco, but there was no news from Tunisia.

Darlan knew he was in a tight spot. He had enough firepower to inflict heavy casualties among the invaders. The question was whether he should unleash that power against a potential ally whose declared goal was to liberate France. If the Germans were to invade Vichy in any event, would it not be better to avoid a bloodbath in Algiers and try to protect French sovereignty in North Africa? But he did not want the Marshal to disavow him. Juin pressed Darlan to seek a cease-fire with the Americans. The Admiral refused, but he did not countermand Juin's orders for French forces to maintain "an elastic but not aggressive contact" with the Allied armies approaching Algiers. Nor did he order a counterattack with armored units at his disposal.[12]

At 7:30 an urgent message came in from Auphan at Vichy: "OKW proposes Axis air support from bases on Sicily, Sardinia. In what form and in which place do you want this support?"[13] Darlan could see that rejecting the offer would damage Franco-German relations at a delicate moment. But he had no interest in providing facilities in Algeria for German aircraft. Nor was there any need to encourage the appearance of Frenchmen and Germans fighting together against the Americans. Knowing that the Axis needed no invitation to attack Allied ships at sea, Darlan wired his reply to Auphan: "Support on transports offshore near Algiers."[14]

Darlan had tacitly accepted Juin's decision to offer only token resistance. French coastal batteries flanking the harbor and armored units near the Admiralty had already offered stout resistance. But at Maison Blanche airfield the French defenders made no effort to exploit their advantage, as the official American history of Operation TORCH indicates:

A few French tanks, against which the attacking force had no suitable weapons, were encountered as the battalion neared the airfield, but after they had fired briefly as if in token resistance, they withdrew while American troops occupied the airfield. Negotiations for its surrender were completed by 0830.[15]

Darlan made no effort to defend Algiers aggressively. But his first situation report, sent to Pétain soon after 8:00, made no mention of token resistance or widespread lack of zeal to fight Americans.

At 7:30, the situation is as follows: landings have been carried out by American troops and British warships at Algiers and vicinity. Defenses have repulsed the attacks at several places, in particular in the port and at the Admiralty. At other places the landings took place successfully by surprise. The situation is getting worse and the coastal defenses are soon going to be overwhelmed. Information indicates massive landings in preparation.[16]

The report indicated resistance at Oran. Obviously preparing Vichy to accept a local armistice, Darlan slanted the report to emphasize overwhelming American power. Within minutes he received the Marshal's answer to the messages sent him earlier that morning:

For Admiral Darlan. I have received your messages by way of the Admiralty and am pleased that you are at the scene. You can act and keep me informed. You know that you have all my confidence. Signed Philippe Pétain.[17]

But Darlan would still have to act prudently. Pétain could withdraw his support as long as Vichy remained free. Darlan therefore refused to rush into negotiations with the Americans.

A LOCAL CEASE-FIRE

Late Sunday morning, as Allied troops moved unopposed toward Algiers, Darlan went to naval headquarters at Hôtel Saint-Georges. Just before noon he sent Pétain another situation report. The blunt opening sentence would catch the Marshal's attention: "Algiers will probably be taken this afternoon."[18] Darlan reported the city to be nearly encircled. Having already reported stout resistance in the harbor that morning, he let Vichy assume that resistance continued in the suburbs.

Darlan also reported his decision to reorganize Juin's command. Knowing that Juin's communications would soon be cut, the Admiral assigned a western region, including Oran and Morocco, to Resident General Auguste Noguès at Morocco. An eastern region, consisting of Constantine and Tunisia, was placed under General Georges Barré at Bizerte.[19] The reorganization isolated Algiers, reducing the area to be governed by any armistice that Darlan might authorize Juin to negotiate with the Americans.

That afternoon Darlan conferred with Juin, who reported the Americans moving slowly but in force. Nevertheless, Darlan refused to contact the Americans. Juin insisted that French honor had already been served and that a decision to request terms must be made soon.[20] In midafternoon, when American forces entered the suburbs, Juin recommended evacuation of the French garrison. Darlan instead authorized it to withdraw to Fort Lempereur. He also canceled an armored counterattack Juin's staff had prepared.[21]

Knowing he soon would have to act, Darlan made one last move to liberate himself from the Marshal. At 4:30 p.m. he wired the Admiralty at Vichy, asking whether the Germans had crossed the demarcation line. Auphan promptly answered: "As of now situation normal in free zone. No trouble interior, nor attack exterior."[22] With the Germans holding back their armies, the long shadow of the Marshal still hung over Algiers. Darlan would have to go ahead with a cease-fire at the risk of being disavowed.

As the French troops withdrew toward the fort, Darlan authorized Juin to negotiate a local cease-fire. The Admiral returned to Fenard's villa where he asked Murphy to contact the American commander. Passing through the American lines, Murphy found General Charles W. Ryder and brought him to Fort Lempereur. In the meantime, at 5:00, Darlan informed Vichy of his decision to negotiate a cease-fire for Algiers.[23] Shortly thereafter, Darlan and Juin received Ryder at the fort. There they concluded a suspension of arms, confining the French troops to their barracks but permitting them to keep their weapons. Darlan agreed to meet Ryder again that evening to discuss formal armistice terms.

When the negotiations resumed at Hôtel Saint-Georges, Darlan intended to protect French sovereignty in Africa. To make an armistice acceptable to the Marshal, and to sidetrack Giraud, he wanted the Americans to negotiate with him as the representative of the French government. Ryder made it clear, however, that he had no authority to discuss politics, and that an armistice decision would be made by General Clark, scheduled to arrive the next day. At Ryder's request, Darlan agreed to open the port early next morning so that American supplies might quickly come ashore. When he asked if that cooperation would be accepted in the name of the French government, Murphy replied that Clark would answer that question. "You know," Darlan replied, "that this question is essential for me."[24]

Another question, whether the discussions next day would deal with all of North Africa, would also have to await Clark's arrival. When Darlan offered coffee, the talks grew more friendly. Having opened the harbor, Darlan raised the question of an American economic contribution in support of French transportation services. Murphy answered that the Americans had a plan.[25] Darlan had begun to serve the American war effort even before an armistice had been signed.

Shortly after 10:00 p.m. Darlan reported to Pétain. He summarized the terms of the cease-fire, reported that the French administration would remain in place, and indicated that another meeting was scheduled for the next day.[26] Selective in its contents, the telegram reflects Darlan's concern to retain the Marshal's confidence until the Germans had struck into the free zone. It made no mention of his opening Algiers harbor to American ships, or of discussions with Murphy about Franco-American economic collaboration. He promised to report again and await instructions.

The decisions Darlan made that day protected the future. Only about two dozen Allied lives were lost in the Algiers area.[27] But at Oran and Casablanca, stout French resistance caused heavy casualties. There was no bloodbath in Algiers, where important Franco-American negotiations were soon to open.

HANGING IN THE BALANCE: TUNISIA

While heavy fighting continued at Oran and Morocco on Monday, November 9, Darlan moved toward the Americans. In contrast, Vichy moved toward Germany in a desperate gamble to head off an occupation of the free zone. Hanging in the balance was Tunisia. Darlan knew that the Allies intended to move there quickly, but already on his desk were telegrams from the Admiralty indicating negotiations to send German officers to Bizerte to arrange the arrival of Axis aircraft.[28] He could suspect that Laval intended to bargain away Tunisia for German guarantees involving the free zone. If so, Vichy's hand would benefit from continuing stout resistance at Oran and Morocco.

Early Monday, just before he departed for Munich upon a summons from Hitler, Laval wired Darlan over Pétain's signature a terse instruction that revealed nothing of Vichy's plans for Tunisia: "The Chief of the Government being presently absent, no negotiations should be contemplated before his return. Standing orders remain in force."[29] Darlan could guess that Laval had departed to negotiate the fate of the free zone.[30] And he could surmise that the Americans would demand exactly what Vichy had forbidden: a general cease-fire for North Africa.

Darlan's response to Vichy, sent soon after Clark had failed to arrive for the 10:00 a.m. meeting, indicated his intention to conclude a local settlement only.[31] At about 11:00, a message arrived from Auphan, intended, he said, to strengthen the lines of confidence dashed by the earlier message: "The Marshal and I wish to have your personal opinion of events."[32] Darlan hastily prepared a response intended to convince the Marshal of the need for a cease-fire for Oran and Morocco, at the exclusion of Tunisia, which had not been attacked. He pointed out that an early end of the fighting would facilitate his negotiating an American agreement to maintain North Africa under the legal French government. The danger, he insisted, was a premature cease-fire in Tunisia that would risk provoking a German occupation of the free zone. Darlan suggested that Vichy advance what amounted to prohibitive demands for any German intervention in Tunisia.[33] He clearly wanted Vichy to keep the Axis out of Tunisia.

But it turned out that Laval had already frittered away Tunisia. Early Monday morning, before he had departed for Germany, Laval caved in to a German ultimatum demanding access to airfields in Tunisia and also Constantine.[34] Barré and Esteva at Bizerte were promptly informed of the concession and ordered to receive the Germans. Laval had concealed the concession from Darlan. More astute than Laval, Hitler had already decided to occupy the free zone, but he knew that only a free French government could deliver Tunisia to him. He therefore avoided any violation of the demarcation line until Laval had arranged for German aircraft to land unopposed in Tunisia.

WAITING FOR GENERAL CLARK

With the Axis gaining a foothold in Tunisia, the need for a cease-fire at Oran and Morocco grew more urgent for the Allies. Ryder therefore went ahead in Clark's absence on Monday afternoon to offer Darlan generous armistice terms for all of North Africa. But the Admiral answered that he could only receive the proposals and send them to Pétain for approval.[35] Clark, flying into Algiers in the midst of a German air raid, arrived at Hôtel Saint-Georges just after 7:00 p.m. Uninformed of the local situation, and worried about American commitments to Giraud, he needed time to prepare for the negotiations with Darlan. So he scheduled another meeting for Tuesday morning.

Early in the evening Darlan wired Pétain a summary of the American proposal, which included a general cease-fire for all of North Africa with French sovereignty maintained throughout the region. He also sent a summary of the judgments of his senior officers, who recommended accepting the proposal. In his own assessment, Darlan admitted that accepting an armistice would risk provoking the Germans, but he added that "one might ask, however, if the occupation of the coastal provinces will not take place in any event."[36] He assured the Marshal that his orders would be carried out.

Darlan remained near the radio throughout the night. Murphy, who joined him, believed the Admiral to be awaiting a message from Pétain.[37] But Darlan also listened for news of any German violation of Vichy's free zone, which would liberate him from the Marshal. Just before 9:00 on Tuesday morning another message from Auphan arrived on the cable: "Situation interior unchanged.

Conference with the Marshal this morning. Probably no decision will be taken prior to return of the Chief, expected this afternoon. Gabriel."[38] Therefore, as Darlan entered into the meeting with Clark, he was still bound to Pétain.

NEGOTIATING AN ARMISTICE WITH CLARK

When Darlan arrived for the meeting Tuesday morning, November 10, he was weary from lack of sleep, but he took care to display his authority. Arriving at the Hôtel Saint-Georges with a colorful ceremonial guard, he was flanked by four generals and four admirals, all in formal military dress.[39] It was an impressive entry. Clark could not help but notice that it was Darlan, not Giraud, who called the signals for French North Africa. As the two delegations entered a room off the foyer, Clark had already decided to deal with the strongest French authority. He wanted a general armistice agreement so that his armies might move swiftly toward Tunisia.[40] He also needed French cooperation in maintaining order and security throughout North Africa, and for providing essential public services. All of these benefits would be assured if Darlan would sign the armistice proposal.

With Murphy serving as interpreter, Clark opened the meeting, insisting that Darlan sign the armistice immediately. The Admiral answered that he had sent a summary of the terms to Vichy and that an answer was not expected until the afternoon. He explained that he and his officers wished to end the fighting but that he could act only upon orders from Pétain.[41] "Tell him," Clark said to Colonel Julius Holmes, who spoke French, "that Pétain is nothing in our young lives.... As far as we're concerned we don't recognize any authority of Pétain in North Africa."[42] Towering over the French Admiral, he pounded the table, expressing his wrath in rich language that required no translation. He threatened to turn to Giraud for a cease-fire agreement. "I am not certain the troops will obey," Darlan answered.[43] He insisted that he could not take responsibility for a cease-fire, that it would provoke a German occupation of southern France.

Clark agreed that the Germans might invade Vichy, but for other reasons. Darlan understood that point, but he still would not back down, citing his oath of loyalty to the Marshal. "You are under domination," Clark shot back. "Here is an opportunity for all Frenchmen to rally and win the war. Here is your last chance."[44] Darlan asked permission to contact Vichy, but the General refused. When Clark again threatened to turn to Giraud, Darlan answered that Giraud had no authority in Morocco or Tunisia. Frustrated, Clark threatened to arrest Darlan and deal with local frontline officers. But Darlan stood his ground: "The army is still with me."[45]

Juin, fearing that Clark would indeed arrest Darlan and turn to Giraud, asked Darlan to request a five-minute recess. After the Americans had withdrawn, Juin pressed Darlan hard, insisting with the other Frenchmen that refusing Clark's terms would lead to civil war in Algeria.[46] Without protest, Darlan wrote out a message to Pétain announcing his acceptance of an armistice on grounds that Clark had threatened to deal with Giraud.[47]

But Clark would not settle for a message to the Marshal. "What I want," he insisted, "is orders to the troops."[48] With Clark's help, Darlan drafted a cease-fire order to all French commands throughout northwest Africa. It instructed French commanders at Oran and Morocco to arrange a suspension of arms with the local American commanders. Although Clark had not settled upon Darlan as his point man, he permitted the order to announce that Darlan had assumed authority in North Africa "in the name of the Marshal," and that the French administration would remain in place until further orders from the Admiral.[49]

Darlan had accepted only a portion of the package Clark had dangled before him. The General had spoken of rearming the French military forces and of eventual Franco-American military cooperation. But Darlan had ordered neutrality. When Clark that same morning gently pressed Darlan to rally the French fleet, the Admiral would make no commitment, commenting only that he had issued orders to assure that the fleet would not fall to the Germans.[50] The bloody clashes at Oran and Morocco had embittered many Frenchmen. And the Germans still had not invaded Vichy's free zone. The French entry into the war remained to be negotiated.

It was in Morocco, where the fighting continued into Tuesday, that Darlan's order had an impact. Even before the full text of the order arrived at Fez that afternoon, Noguès ordered Casablanca and Marrakech "to refrain from active hostilities pending the negotiation of an armistice."[51] Shortly thereafter, when the complete text arrived, Noguès arranged a meeting for the next morning with General George Patton. But before that meeting took place, Darlan and Noguès were thrust into the ultimate crisis of conscience.

A RINGING REPUDIATION

When the Marshal received Darlan's cease-fire order early Tuesday afternoon, Auphan urged him to support the Admiral. But Laval, contacted by telephone in Munich, threatened to resign should the Marshal approve Darlan's action.[52] Pétain responded with a ringing repudiation whose address section to all African commands announced the Marshal's assuming Darlan's post as military commander.

I have given the order to defend ourselves against the aggressor. I maintain that order. Philippe Pétain.[53]

Receiving the message at Fenard's villa, Darlan was visibly shaken. But he quickly regained his composure.[54] Summoning Juin, he learned that hostilities were already winding down at Oran and Morocco. He therefore made no effort to cancel the cease-fire order. He knew that once the fighting had stopped, it would not be resumed. At 3:35 p.m., Darlan wired the Marshal: "Received your message. I annul my order and make myself a prisoner."[55] But he did not revoke the order.

When Clark, accompanied by Murphy and Giraud, arrived within minutes, Darlan abruptly announced his repudiation: "A wrong turn, gentlemen! I have received a cable from Marshal Pétain which orders the renewal of combat: I am not authorized to negotiate with you."[56] He added that he would have to revoke the cease-fire order. Predictably, Clark moved firmly to forbid it: "You're not going to revoke any order."[57] Darlan answered that he must therefore consider himself a prisoner. Clark ordered soldiers to surround Fenard's villa.

Receiving Pétain's repudiation of Darlan, Noguès faced the bitter dilemma of choosing between Vichy and Algiers. Late that afternoon he received from Vichy a message clearly intended to head off Darlan's cease-fire order:

Pay no attention to anything concerning you in telegrams this morning from Military Post 4th Region neutralized by the Americans. The only valid orders emanate from the Admiralty.[58]

But Noguès had already taken steps to end the fighting. On Wednesday morning he arranged with General Patton a suspension of arms in time to prevent a naval bombardment of Casablanca.

Darlan had delivered Algiers to the Americans on the first day and had ordered a cease-fire for North Africa on the third. Had he defended Algiers and prolonged the war, any agreement for French services to the Allied war effort in Tunisia would have been delayed. Darlan ended the fighting in a manner that France might expect to retain control of North Africa. But in doing his duty, he lost the support of the Marshal and strained his relations with Clark.

NOTES

1. Robert D. Murphy, *Diplomat among Warriors* (New York: Doubleday, 1964), 128.

2. Pierre Ordioni, *Le Secret de Darlan, 1940-1942* (Paris: Albatros, 1974), 198; and General Jean Chrétien, "Souvenirs d'une vie militaire" (unpublished memoirs).

3. Ordioni, *Le Secret de Darlan*, 198. See also Claude Paillat, *L'Échiquier d'Alger*, 2 volumes (Paris: Robert Laffont, 1967), II, 40.

4. Murphy, *Diplomat among Warriors*, 129.

5. Ibid., 130.

6. Albert Kammerer, *Du Débarquement africain au meurtre de Darlan* (Paris: Flammarion, 1947), 268-270.

7. Alain Darlan, *L'Amiral Darlan parle* (Paris: Amiot-Dumont, 1952), 193-194.

8. Kenneth Pendar, *Adventures in Diplomacy* (New York: Dodd and Mead, 1945), 106-107.

9. Murphy, *Diplomat among Warriors*, 131.

10. Darlan, *L'Amiral Darlan parle*, 194.

11. Paillat, *L'Échiquier d'Alger*, II, 45; C.F. Caroff, *Les Débarquements Alliés en Afrique du Nord* (Paris: Service Historique de la Marine, 1960), 18.

12. Alphonse Juin, *Mémoires*, 2 volumes (Paris: Fayard, 1959), I, 83-85.

13. SHM, Carton TT Marine 00.3 Archives, Débarquement en AFN, tel. 0500/8/11.

14. Caroff, *Débarquements Alliés*, 75. See also SHM, Carton TT Marine 00.3 Archives, Débarquement en AFN, telegram of 1150.8.11.

15. George F. Howe, *Northwest Africa: Seizing the Initiative in the West* (Washington, D.C: U.S. Government Printing Office, 1957), 247.

16. Caroff, *Débarquements Alliés*, 79.

17. SHM, Carton TT Marine 00.3, Archives, Débarquement AFN.

18. Caroff, *Débarquements Alliés*, 80.

19. See Arthur Funk, *The Politics of Torch* (Lawrence: University Press of Kansas, 1974), 226.

20. Juin, *Mémoires*, I, 82-85.

21. See René Richard and Alain de Serigny, *L'Énigme d'Alger* (Paris: Fayard, 1947), 106-107; and Kammerer, *Débarquement africain*, 274-275.

22. SHM, Box TT Marine 00.3 Archives, Débarquement en AFN. Auphan's communications with Darlan throughout the week are contained in this carton.

23. Caroff, *Débarquements Alliés*, 80.

24. Jacques Raphaël-Leygues and François Flohic, *Darlan* (Paris: Plon, 1986), 179.

25. Richard and Serigny, *L'Énigme d'Alger*, 108, 266-268.

26. Caroff, *Débarquements Alliés*, 80.

27. Funk, *The Politics of Torch*, 224.

28. SHM, Box TT Marine 00.3 Archives, Débarquement en AFN, telegrams 1751. 8.11 and 1845, 1846, 8.11.

29. SHM, Box TT Marine 00.3 Archives, Débarquement en AFN. Auphan explains that the telegram was authored by Laval and sent with Pétain's approval. See Paul Auphan, *L'Honneur de servir* (Paris: Éditions France-Empire, 1978), 382.

30. Auphan wired Darlan at 3:00 p.m. that Laval had departed to negotiate with the Germans. SHM, Box TT Marine 00.3 Archives, Débarquement en AFN.

31. Caroff, *Débarquements Alliés*, 81.

32. SHM, Box TT Marine 00.3 Archives, Débarquement en AFN, telegram 58571. See also Auphan, *L'Honneur de servir*, 382.

33. Caroff, *Débarquements Alliés*, 81.

34. Kammerer, *Débarquement africain*, 306-307. See also Auphan, *L'Honneur de servir*, 381; and SHM, Box TT Marine 00.3 Archives, Débarquement en AFN, telegrams 1845, 1856, 1751, 8 November 1942.

35. Darlan, *L'Amiral Darlan parle*, 303-305.

36. Caroff, *Débarquements Alliés*, 92.

37. Murphy, *Diplomat among Warriors*, 137.

38. SHM, TT Marine 00.3 Archives, Débarquement en AFN. Xavier was the code name for Darlan, Gabriel for Auphan.

39. Unpublished Papers of General Mark W. Clark, Housed in The Citadel Library, Charleston, South Carolina. Folder entitled "Records of Events and Documents from the Date that Lieutenant General Mark W. Clark entered into Negotiations with Admiral Jean François Darlan until Darlan was Assassinated on Christmas Eve, 1942," pp. 3-4 (hereinafter cited as Clark Papers, Events and Documents).

40. Ibid., 3.

41. Ibid., 4.

42. Julius Holmes, "Eisenhower's African Gamble," *Collier's Magazine,* January 12, 1946, 33-34.

43. Clark Papers, Events and Documents, 6.

44. Ibid.

45. Ibid., 7-8.

46. Caroff, *Débarquements Alliés*, 83.

47. Ibid.

48. Clark Papers, Events and Documents, 8.

49. Caroff, *Débarquements Alliés*, 83-84.

50. Clark Papers, Events and Documents, 11, 13.

51. Howe, *Northwest Africa: Seizing the Initiative in the West*, 171.

52. Auphan, *L'Honneur de servir*, 384-386.

53. SHM Box TT Marine 00.3 Archives, Débarquement en AFN, telegram 7121.

54. Jacques Moreau, "Mémoires," 294, manuscript draft of Moreau's memoirs, compliments of Arthur Funk.

55. Caroff, *Débarquements Alliés*, 84.

56. Chamine (pseud. Geneviève Dumais), *Suite française*, 2 volumes (Paris: Albin Michel, 1952), II, 126.

57. Clark Papers, Events and Documents, 14.

58. SHM, Box TT Marine 00.3 Archives, Débarquement en AFN.

CHAPTER 20

A Step Toward the Liberation

Operation TORCH would prompt the Germans to occupy Vichy's free zone, but the moral authority of Marshal Pétain did not die easily. Frenchmen in Africa entered into a time of moral crisis, trapped between their loyalty to Pétain and the promise of liberation. Darlan's dragging Frenchmen back into the war on the American side was the first step to bridge the gap between Vichy and the liberation.

THE FIRST SECRET MESSAGE

Just after Pétain had rejected the cease-fire agreement on Tuesday, November 10, Auphan remembered that Darlan had left in Vichy a secret code intended for personal messages. The key was contained in a pocket dictionary carried by Admiral Battet. Having sent the repudiation in midafternoon, Auphan returned to the Marshal and persuaded him to authorize another message to Darlan. Auphan sent it in the secret code: "Please understand that this order was necessary for the negotiations in progress."[1] This was the first of four secret messages from Auphan that gave birth to a myth that helped turn France in a new direction.

The secret messages reinforced Darlan's belief that he was on the right track. Since the messages appeared to soften the Marshal's repudiations, they justified the Admiral's acting independently to defend French interests in Africa. They helped Darlan convince Frenchmen that Pétain privately supported him and had sent the denials only to protect France from German reprisals. But the wartime and postwar claims made of them seem extravagant.[2] The claim, for example, that the first secret message was a green light from the Marshal for Darlan to disregard Vichy's resistance order is invalid. The secret messages were not invitations for Darlan to chart an independent course. They were instead the echoes of minor concessions Auphan dragged out of Pétain after he had lost the major decisions to Laval.

Darlan understood the first secret message to mean that resistance should continue in the interest of protecting Vichy's negotiations with the Reich. He clearly did not view it as an invitation to ignore Pétain's resistance order, or to reopen negotiations with Clark, or to resume his command. He remained Clark's prisoner. But he found a way to send Auphan a response in the same code: "Received and well understood."[3]

PROBLEMS OF COMMAND

Darlan remained under house arrest at Fenard's villa, but Frenchmen in Algiers still recognized his authority, which did not escape the attention of General Clark. Upon taking leave of the Admiral on Tuesday afternoon, Clark tacitly recognized that authority by asking his prisoner to rally the French fleet. "It's not my fleet," Darlan answered, "I've been relieved."[4] With the African command system in disarray, Darlan realized that any orders from him to the fleet would be disregarded. Clark, however, refused to turn to Giraud, for fear that Darlan would revoke his cease-fire order. That afternoon he asked Giraud to settle his differences with Darlan.[5]

Darlan, receiving reports of impending German aggression against France, seized the initiative to outflank Giraud. He promptly sent word to Clark that he would ignore the Marshal's repudiation should Hitler invade Vichy's free zone.[6] Later that evening he dangled before Clark the bait of the French fleet. Stretching the truth, he stated that "the fleet is now outside Toulon awaiting orders," and he promised to "direct the French fleet to 'join the Allies' as soon as the Germans entered unoccupied France but not before."[7] His intention was to impress Clark at the expense of Giraud, who had nothing to offer concerning fleet.

At the end of that day the shadow of Vichy and the memory of war divided Frenchmen in Africa. While Vichy tried to prolong its life at the expense of North Africa, Darlan aimed at repairing his command and uniting the region under American protection. But despite his promises to Clark, Darlan could not be sure that his officers would support a war alongside the Allies. Noguès had stoutly resisted the Americans in Morocco where nearly a thousand Frenchmen had fallen in battle. To join sides today with yesterday's enemy would not be easy for him. Moreover, he had nothing but contempt for Giraud. In Tunisia, the French command under General Barré and Admirals Louis Derrien and Esteva remained under the influence of Vichy. If Darlan expected to restore his command and keep North Africa together, he first would have to free himself from Vichy's grip, for he was more a prisoner of Pétain than of Clark.

ANOTHER DISAVOWAL

Events took a decisive turn before dawn on Wednesday, the 11th, when German armies crossed the demarcation line in France. But the agony of those final hours brought Darlan another ugly surprise from Pétain, who had learned of Noguès' stout defense of Morocco.[8] Still unaware of the German aggression against Vichy, Darlan was unprepared for the message arriving at Fenard's villa early that morning: "I have designated General Noguès as my sole representative in North Africa. All decisions depend on him. Philippe Pétain."[9]

Sent to Vichy's African outposts, this second repudiation clearly shifted the Marshal's blessings to another French officer in Africa. Entering Fenard's villa a few minutes later, Clark found the Admiral in an ugly mood, obviously worried. He later wrote "how miserable Darlan looked that day."[10] In the brief interview that followed, Darlan abruptly refused to make contact with the Toulon squadron. He would promise nothing more than to declare himself to support the American war effort should the Germans occupy all of France.[11]

ANOTHER SECRET MESSAGE FROM AUPHAN

Having dispatched the announcement of Noguès' appointment on Wednesday morning, Auphan rushed back to the Hôtel du Parc where he found Pétain writing a protest of the German aggression against Vichy. As with the first secret message, Auphan took the initiative, insisting that Darlan deserved an explanation of his being replaced by Noguès. Auphan wrote out the message: "It is only because you are a prisoner that I have not designated you as my representative in Africa."[12] According to Auphan, Pétain nodded approval. Auphan rushed back to the Admiralty and sent the message in the secret code. Receiving it minutes later, Darlan noticed the familiar salutation "Gabriel to Xavier." He acknowledged receipt in the same secret code, signing with the familiar "Xavier."[13]

Although the second secret message did not restore his command, Darlan could interpret it as a vote of confidence from the Marshal. He did not know that Pétain had taken no initiative to send the message, or that Auphan had drafted the text and pressured the Marshal to approve it. He could not have known that Pétain, delighted at the stout defense of Morocco, may have preferred Noguès. Darlan knew nothing of the Marshal's comment that morning that "Morocco has saved French honor."[14] So Darlan could easily believe that the Marshal had dismissed him only because he was a prisoner.

TWO ANNOUNCEMENTS FROM VICHY

Within the hour Darlan received the message he had expected since Sunday. Sent from the Admiralty at Vichy, the telegram arrived in Algiers just after 11:30 a.m.:

Strictly secret. Occupation troops crossed into the free zone to occupy the territorial and maritime frontiers. German promise to respect the Marshal's Government.[15]

Shortly thereafter radio Algiers picked up the first of several announcements from Vichy of the Marshal's personal protest of the German aggression. Clearly, the occupation of the southern provinces was an act of aggression rather than a negotiated agreement. Darlan could now resume his negotiations with Clark, but he would have to restore the broken chain of command under his own authority before concluding any final agreement with him.

RESUMING NEGOTIATIONS WITH CLARK

Now Darlan summoned Clark. Together they concluded an informal agreement to restore the French chain of command. Darlan would take the top political office, and Giraud would be accepted as French military commander under the Admiral. But since Pétain had shifted authority to Noguès, Darlan thought he had no right to enter into a formal agreement. Noguès would therefore fly to Algiers Thursday afternoon to settle the legalities. Satisfied, Clark removed the guard from Fenard's villa.[16]

Clark pressed Darlan to rally Tunisia. Both Darlan and Juin phoned Bizerte Wednesday afternoon, and Clark left satisfied that General Barré would resist German armies arriving there.[17] Admiral Derrien, navy commander at Bizerte, agreed to oppose any German attempt to enter Tunisia by sea. But that same evening, after learning of the Marshal's decision to continue resistance in the west, Derrien ordered neutrality, and Barré, with Juin's approval, abandoned Bizerte for positions inland to guard the access routes to Algeria.[18] So while the Germans continued to enter Tunisia unopposed, Clark went ahead with plans to advance toward Tunisia on the assumption that Frenchmen there were resisting the Germans.

AN APPEAL TO THE FLEET

With German armies racing toward Toulon, Clark pressed Darlan to order the fleet to Algiers or Gibraltar. But Darlan instead issued at 3:47 p.m. an earnest appeal intended to influence Toulon without causing trouble in the navy. It observed that the armistice had been broken and that Frenchmen could protect French interests and still remain loyal to the captive Marshal. There followed a reminder of his own well-known view that the fleet would remain French or destroy itself. Insisting that the fleet could no longer remain in France, Darlan invited the commander to send it to West Africa, with American assurance that there would be no opposition in transit.[19]

Addressed to Admiral Jean de Laborde, aristocratic commander of the Toulon squadron, and no friend of Darlan, the appeal was sent by way of Vichy's Admiralty where Auphan too would read it. In his memoirs, Auphan questions whether Darlan in truth wished the fleet to depart Toulon, suggesting that the Admiral had sent the appeal mainly to buy time in his negotiations with Clark.[20] Darlan wired Auphan next day that he had expected to buy time.[21] But that was a routine courtesy sent after de Laborde had rejected the appeal.

Darlan had no interest in seeing the fleet fall into German hands. He could see that a successful appeal would strengthen his hand with Clark, but he would not send a presumptuous order to rally it to Algiers, or to the Allies. He therefore advanced a thoughtful argument to move the fleet to Dakar, still loyal to Vichy, or destroy it. But neither Auphan nor de Laborde took any action to move the ships. De Laborde's response to Darlan Thursday afternoon, a terse obscenity transmitted by wireless, made it clear that he had no intentions of letting his rival call the signals for the fleet. Darlan's reply, full of irony, was sent to Auphan in the secret code: "We appreciate Count John's response."[22]

CLASHING AGAIN WITH CLARK

Juin's efforts to swing Tunisia quickly into the war were equally disappointing. His order of November 11 to resist the Axis forces arriving in Tunisia clashed with the Marshal's order shifting power from Darlan to Noguès. Persuaded by his subordinates that the resistance order might cause trouble in the ranks, Juin suspended it just before midnight that same Wednesday.[23]

Clark had already sent advanced units to land at Bougie beyond Constantine, and airborne units were scheduled to be dropped on an airfield near Bône Thursday morning. He had counted on French cooperation. When Darlan and Juin entered Clark's office at Hôtel Saint-Georges early that morning, the General vented his anger: "All your deeds have been contrary to the aim you both volubly profess to have. Now I learn that the order for French troops to resist Axis moves into Tunisia has been revoked."[24] Juin answered that the order had only been suspended pending the arrival that afternoon of General Noguès. Clark insisted he could not wait until the afternoon, and he refused to recognize any authority on the part of Noguès. Juin indicated his willingness to fight the Germans. "But you haven't done that," Clark insisted, "and I'm sick and tired of the way you have been conducting yourself. I think you are weak!"[25]

More angry words were exchanged, but Darlan spoke little, considering himself outside the French chain of command. Murphy and Fenard looked on as Clark insisted that Juin's revoking his resistance order nearly amounted to treachery.[26] Darlan and Juin together turned to Murphy, repeating the same arguments. With everyone talking at once, Juin shouted again that the order had not been revoked, only suspended. The tensions mounted as Clark threatened to arrest the Frenchmen. Now Darlan intervened to restrain Clark. "Wait," he urged, "You will be absolutely clear this afternoon after the meeting. Until then I can't accept any responsibility." Juin added: "If Noguès will not come with you I will put myself at your disposal." When Clark answered that "Giraud is going to be the military commander," Juin conceded "Then I will go with him."[27]

Clark saw at once the importance of Juin's agreeing to serve under Giraud, which was the key to bringing the Frenchmen together and finding a place for Giraud. Although the shouting and insults continued, the two sides grew closer together. Darlan continued to insist upon his meeting with Noguès, and Juin suggested that Giraud be appointed military commander from Dakar to Bizerte, with himself commanding in Algeria. Clark agreed, but he insisted that Juin must first restore his resistance order.[28] Juin asked to speak privately to Darlan.

While Darlan and Juin went out of the room to telephone Tunisia, Fenard urged Clark to trust the Frenchmen, insisting that they all were behind Darlan and would fall in line with the Americans if Clark would just wait until the afternoon. A few minutes later, when Darlan and Juin returned, the General reported that Barré would resist any German landings on Tunisian airfields still in French hands. Satisfied, Clark turned to Darlan and promised to await the afternoon meeting with Noguès before making any decision on the French command. He shook hands with the Frenchmen.[29]

But Darlan and Juin appear to have made no contact with Barré that morning. It was not until Thursday evening that Juin finally made telephone contact with Barré and reissued his order to resist the Axis. Barré, however, was in no position to influence the events that had troubled Clark that morning.[30] Fortunately, the Germans made no attempt to occupy airfields at Constantine or Setif. They were instead landing their forces unopposed at the ports of Bizerte and Tunis.

The informal agreements painfully hammered out in that stormy session anticipated the final arrangements for Franco-American cooperation in North Africa. Juin's promise, with Darlan's tacit approval, to defend Tunisian airfields assumed a French war against Germany. And Juin's informal agreement with Clark to serve under Giraud anticipated the unification of the French factions in Algeria and the restoration of the chain of command under Darlan.

A MYSTERIOUS MESSAGE FROM AUPHAN

Late Thursday afternoon, November 12, as German armies approached Toulon, Auphan attempted to inform Darlan of his intention to protect the fleet within a fortified enclave that the Germans had promised not to violate. Auphan had noticed that the enclave stretched through Toulon's suburbs roughly from Darlan's private home at Sanary to his naval residence at Boudouvin. Thinking that Darlan would understand these points to mark the perimeter of a safe zone, he wired the Admiral another secret message: "From Sanary to Boudouvin I intend to make an entrenched camp without busying myself with anything else."[31]

Darlan mentioned the message to Clark, whose journal entry of November 14 indicates that Auphan had sent a mysterious message and was planning something special about the fleet.[32] The Admiral appears to have read the message to mean that the Germans were about to seize the ships and that Auphan intended either to offer resistance or to bolt with the fleet from the harbor. A wireless appeal sent out from Gibraltar that afternoon in Darlan's name, and reported next day by the Associated Press, seems counterfeit.[33] The Germans took positions beyond the enclave, and the fleet remained in the harbor.

DARLAN AND NOGUÈS

Noguès arrived in Algiers Thursday afternoon. But if Darlan expected Noguès to fall easily in line, he was to be disappointed. Noguès understood the reasons for Darlan's taking the top political post, but he was not certain that the Marshal approved it. The thought of entering North Africa into the war on the American side disturbed him, as did that of giving Giraud a military command. Stoutly loyal to Vichy, Noguès would expect any new political arrangement for North Africa to have the Marshal's approval.[34]

At 9:00 p.m. the top French officers gathered at Hôtel Saint-Georges. Giraud and Mast, ignored by the other Frenchmen, stood apart while Darlan conferred for an hour with Clark and Murphy. Clark insisted that the Frenchmen admit

Giraud to their company and cooperate to achieve common Franco-American objectives. Otherwise, he would arrest them all. When Giraud was finally called into the room, Darlan and Noguès grudgingly honored Clark's request that they shake hands with the French general.[35]

After Clark had departed, the divisions among the Frenchmen came to the surface amid insults and charges of treachery. As Noguès and Giraud shouted at each other, Darlan lashed out at Giraud: "You are acting like a child," adding that "you are nothing here, nothing but a rebel in the train of a foreign army."[36] Noguès made clear his opposition to giving Giraud a military command and allowing him to enter North Africa into the war. When the meeting finally broke up after midnight, the exhausted officers had worked out an arrangement that isolated Giraud. Darlan would take the top political post, and Juin would be military commander. North Africa would remain neutral for a time, but Giraud would be permitted to recruit from the army a small band of volunteers to fight the Axis in Tunisia.[37] Noguès, concerned to have Vichy's approval, rushed off a wire to Pétain just after 1:00 on the morning of the 13th. It reported the events of the evening and asked the Marshal to restore Darlan in the interest of sidetracking Giraud and heading off a war against the Axis.[38]

But later on the morning of Friday the 13th, when the Frenchmen again met at Hôtel Saint-Georges, they continued to argue over Giraud's assignment. Clark intervened again, threatening to arrest the Frenchmen if they did not reach a quick agreement.[39] While Clark rushed off to Maison Blanche airport to welcome General Eisenhower, the Frenchmen put together a fragile agreement that assigned Darlan the top political office. Noguès still had not agreed that Giraud would become military commander, but only that he would put himself under Darlan's orders, command in the name of the Marshal, and admit no jurisdiction of de Gaulle.[40] Nor had he agreed to a war against the Axis. But he had agreed to Darlan's restoration, which would enable the Admiral to sign an agreement with Clark and to impress the Americans with the appearance of French unity. Giraud's assignment and the French entry into the war could be addressed after Noguès had returned to Morocco.

Early in the afternoon the Admiral stood at the head of a French delegation awaiting the arrival of Eisenhower and British Admiral Sir Andrew Cunningham. Turning to Clark, Darlan remarked that he was signing the agreement "with the objective of defeating the Germans and restoring France to her former place."[41] Eisenhower spoke briefly, endorsing Darlan as Chief of State in North Africa.[42] His remarks confirmed the outlines of a Franco-American agreement whose details would be worked out during the following week. Eisenhower returned that same afternoon to Gibraltar.

The ceremonies over, Noguès issued a proclamation shifting his powers to Darlan "in the name of the Marshal and in accord with him."[43] Darlan's proclamation, which followed, explained the legalities of the transfer of power, indicated American support, and deftly smoothed over the question of war with the statement that "I have the assent of the American authorities upon whom I am depending to assure the defense of North Africa."[44] He promptly sent a copy of his proclamation to Vichy.

It was only the next day, after Noguès had returned to Morocco, that Darlan drafted his Decision No. 1 naming Giraud Commander-in-Chief of army and air forces in Africa and Juin as commander of army forces in North Africa. It also ordered the preparation of plans to coordinate French military action with that of the Allied forces.[45]

THE *ACCORD INTIME* MESSAGE

Late that Friday afternoon, just before he had broadcast his proclamation, Darlan received Auphan's final secret message, the controversial *accord intime* message: "From Gabriel to Xavier: Intimate agreement of the Marshal and the President, but before answering you, they are consulting the occupation authorities."[46] Darlan saw its value. "We have the consent of the old gentleman," he remarked.[47] Moving quickly, he leaked news of the message to Clark prior to a scheduled press conference that afternoon. Clark reported to the newsmen that Darlan would soon broadcast news of a Franco-American agreement, and he added "a few minutes ago I was informed that Marshal Pétain is giving our accord his blessing. Darlan and the rest of his men are tremendously pleased."[48]

Clark's comments to the press gave birth to the myth that came to surround the secret messages. His linking the *accord intime* message to the Franco-American accord created the impression that the Marshal had expressed secret support of Darlan's settlement with the Americans. Darlan built upon the myth. On November 27 he wrote Admiral Leahy in Washington that he had received via the Admiralty confidential messages from Vichy indicating that the Marshal "at the bottom of his heart" agreed with him during the week of the landings.[49]

But the Marshal had not approved of the Franco-American accord. Nor had he approved the *accord intime* message. The message instead expressed Auphan's slant on Vichy's reaction to Noguès' early morning telegram urging the Marshal to restore Darlan in the interest of sidetracking Giraud and heading off a Franco-German war in Tunisia. When Auphan took Noguès' telegram to the Hôtel du Parc early Friday morning, Pétain approved a message restoring Darlan, but on the condition that Laval also approve it. Laval professed to approve the message, but he insisted upon gaining German approval before sending it to Darlan. But by midafternoon Auphan had heard nothing more from Laval, so he set aside the Marshal's message and sent instead the *accord intime* message.[50]

That the *accord intime* message is a reference to Noguès' telegram is clearly revealed in the authentic version of the text contained in the papers of Admiral Moreau:

Reference Telegram 50803 from General Noguès.... Intimate agreement of Marshal and president Laval, but official decision submitted to occupation authorities.[51]

The message clearly did not speak to the Franco-American accord, which Vichy still did not know about.

The Franco-American accord gave Giraud a military command and entered Frenchmen into the war against the Axis. Noguès' telegram had addressed Vichy's main fears--dissidence in the ranks and an armed clash with German troops in Tunisia--and it indicated that the restoration of Darlan would head off both. That is why Pétain was willing Friday morning to restore the Admiral.[52] Dr. Bernard Ménétrel, the Marshal's physician, recorded Pétain's revealing comments of Friday afternoon that "the danger is in the marching of troops against Germany and Italy. We must nip the dissidence in the bud."[53] The *accord intime* message created the appearance of the Marshal's approving the very things he opposed, and of his supporting Darlan, who gave Giraud a command and entered France into the war.[54]

The Marshal's response to the Franco-American accord is contained, not in the *accord intime* message, but in a telegram of Saturday afternoon addressed to Darlan. When the Admiral's proclamation was received in Vichy late Friday, Pétain could see that Darlan had closed ranks with the Americans to defend North Africa against the Axis. His response was a clear repudiation:

Acknowledge your telegram to the Chief of the Government. You ought to defend North Africa against American aggression. The decision you have taken in violation of my orders is contrary to the mission you have received. I give the order to the African army to undertake no action under any circumstances against the Axis forces and not to add to the misfortunes of the homeland.[55]

Although this repudiation was sent at the insistence of Laval, it reflects the Marshal's fear of war between Frenchmen and Germans in Tunisia.

DARLAN AND THE SECRET MESSAGES

Darlan regarded the secret messages as authentic expressions of the Marshal's private approval of his authority in North Africa. He knew that the *accord intime* message was a response to Noguès' telegram, and that it did not endorse specifically the Franco-American agreement. But the main point of Noguès' telegram was the need to restore Darlan to power. On that key point, the *accord intime* message was consistent with the secret message of the 11th reporting that the Admiral had been dismissed only because he was thought to be a prisoner. That message arrived in Algiers during the same hour of the Marshal's protest of the German invasion of France's free zone, leaving the appearance that the German aggression had prompted Pétain to express in confidence his continuing support of Darlan.

Darlan had no clue that the secret messages spoke mainly for Auphan, or that Pétain had taken no initiative to send them. Knowing none of this, Darlan concluded that the secret messages expressed Petain's approval of his independent American policy. In his letter of November 27 to Leahy, Darlan wrote that "Pétain had often said to me, 'Darlan, we must always remain friends with the Unites States.'"[56] The Admiral stopped short of claiming that Pétain had supported specifically the Franco-American agreement; rather, he stated that

the Germans having breached the armistice by occupying the whole of France and Marshal Pétain having solemnly protested against that, I thought I was entitled again to act freely. I was all the more sure of being on the right track when, by confidential messages passed on to me in special code by someone in the French Admiralty, I was informed that the Marshal at the bottom of his heart agreed with me.[57]

Clearly, the Admiral's decision to act on his own was a function of the German aggression against Vichy and the Marshal's protest against it. The secret messages were useful to justify Darlan's actions. They protected him from the stigma of dissidence, and they helped him keep his followers in line. Afterward, they lent his government legitimacy.

AT THE END OF A TROUBLED WEEK

Given the confusion of events following the Allied attack, Darlan could not have moved more quickly that week. He managed in six days to end the Franco-American conflict, to restore the French chain of command, and to enter Frenchmen into the war against the Axis in a manner that protected their moral integrity. At the same time, he made it possible for the Americans to begin their drive toward Tunisia even before he joined the Allied cause later that week.

He had also managed to convince himself of the Marshal's continuing support. At the end of that troubled week, when he received Auphan's *accord intime* message late Friday afternoon, Darlan answered in the same secret code with a final word to his friend at the Admiralty: "Goodbye. Good luck to all."[58]

NOTES

1. Paul Auphan, *L'Honneur de servir* (Paris: Éditions France Empire, 1978), 386.

2. At the Marshal's postwar trial, defense lawyers cited the secret messages as evidence of Pétain's playing a double game with the Germans. See Haut Cour de Justice, *Le Procès du Maréchal Pétain*, 2 volumes (Paris: Albin Michel, 1945), II, 718-732 827-831, 1087.

3. Auphan, *L'Honneur de servir*, 387.

4. Unpublished Papers of General Mark W. Clark, Housed in The Citadel Library, Charleston, South Carolina. Folder entitled "Records of Events and Documents from the Date that Lieutenant General Mark W. Clark entered into Negotiations with Admiral Jean François Darlan until Darlan was Assassinated on Christmas Eve, 1942," pp. 14-15 (hereinafter cited as Clark Papers, Events and Documents).

5. Ibid., 15.

6. Ibid., 16.

7. Ibid., 18.

8. William A. Hoisington, Jr., *The Casablanca Connection* (Chapel Hill: University of North Carolina Press, 1984), 229-230.

9. Auphan, *L'Honneur de servir*, 391.

10. Mark W. Clark, *Calculated Risk* (New York: Harper, 1950), 115.

11. Clark Papers, Events and Documents, 20.

12. Auphan, *L'Honneur de servir*, 392. The notes of Dr. Bernard Ménétrel, the Marshal's personal physician, report a slightly different wording. See Louis Noguères, *Le Véritable procès du Maréchal Pétain* (Paris: Fayard, 1955), 461.

13. Auphan, *L'Honneur de servir*, 392.

14. Albert Kammerer, *Du Débarquement africain au meurtre de Darlan* (Paris: Flammarion, 1947), 429.

15. SHM, Box TT Marine 00.3, Archives, Débarquement en AFN.

16. Clark Papers, Events and Documents, 23-24, 30.

17. Clark, *Calculated Risk*, 116.

18. C.F. Caroff, *Les Débarquements Alliés en Afrique du Nord* (Paris: Service Historique de la Marine, 1960), 263-266.

19. Ibid., 85.

20. Auphan, *L'Honneur de servir*, 395.

21. See Hervé Coutau-Bégarie and Claude Huan, *Darlan* (Fayard, 1989), 642.

22. Ibid., 643.

23. Kammerer, *Débarquement africain*, 452-453; Caroff, *Débarquements Alliés*, 266.

24. Clark Papers, Events and Documents, 26.

25. Ibid., 27. In an interview with the author in October 1977, Clark admitted his error in accusing Juin of weakness.

26. Clark Papers, Events and Documents, 28.

27. The quotes in this paragraph are from Clark Papers, Events and Documents, 30-32.

28. Ibid., 33-34.

29. Ibid., 35.

30. See Caroff, *Débarquements Alliés*, 267-268.

31. Auphan, *L'Honneur de servir*, 398.

32. Clark Papers, Events and Documents, 46.

33. The Associated Press report appears in *The New York Times*, November 13, 1942, 1, but it omits the text. For the text, see Amiral Jules Docteur, *La Vérite sur les amiraux* (Paris: Éditions de la Couronne, 1949), 142.

34. See Chamine (pseud. Geneviève Dumas), *Suite française*, 2 volumes (Paris: Albin Michel, 1952), II, 139-145; and Hoisington, *The Casablanca Connection*, 235-238.

35. Clark Papers, Events and Documents, 39-40; Clark, *Calculated Risk*, 119-120.

36. Coutau-Bégarie and Huan, *Darlan*, 615.

37. Kammerer, *Débarquement africain*, 475.

38. Caroff, *Débarquements alliés*, 86-87.

39. Clark, *Calculated Risk*, 121.

40. Jacques Moreau, "Mémoires," 331, typewritten draft, compliments of Arthur Funk.

41. Clark Papers, Events and Documents, 43.

42. Ibid., 43-44.

43. Caroff, *Débarquements Alliés*, 88.

44. Ibid.

45. Ibid., 99.

46. Auphan, *L'Honneur de servir*, 407-408.

47. Moreau, "Mémoires," 334.

48. Clark Papers, Events and Documents, 44-45.

49. The Papers of Admiral William D. Leahy (Washington, D.C.: Library of Congress, Manuscripts Division), VIII, 66-67 (hereinafter cited as Leahy Papers).

50. Auphan, *L'Honneur de servir*, 407-409.

51. Moreau, "Mémoires," 334. See Coutau-Bégarie and Huan, *Darlan*, 619, for a copy of the message.

52. Noguères, *Le Véritable procès du Maréchal Pétain*, 488, 490.

53. Ibid., 490.

54. See Pierre Dhers, *Regards nouveaux sur les années quarante* (Paris: Flammarion, 1958), 156-157; and Général Gaston Schmitt, "Sur Vichy, La matinée du 11 novembre à Vichy," *Revue d'Histoire de la Deuxieme Guerre Mondaille*, October 1962; and Général Gaston Schmitt, "Le Général Juin et le débarquement en AFN," *Revue d'Histoire de la Deuxieme Guerre Mondaille*, October 1961.

55. Caroff, *Débarquements Alliés*, 88.

56. Leahy Papers, VIII, 66-67.

57. Ibid.
58. Chamine, *Suite française*, II, 160.

CHAPTER 21

The Last Forty Days of Darlan

Faced with an unwanted Allied occupation of North Africa, Darlan did his best to turn it to France's advantage. The forty days of the Darlan administration in Algiers were therefore important to France. Much depended upon Darlan, whose authority behind the lines enabled him to determine the level of French cooperation with the Allies and to enlist the services of other Frenchmen. He exchanged his cooperation for concessions to France.

Darlan controlled the essential services upon which the Allied war effort depended. The most important were security, communications, and political stability in the sprawling staging areas where supplies and reinforcements were landed and rushed to the Tunisian front. The local Allied military authority had no choice but to work with him. But Darlan had his own political agenda, which he easily disguised as benefits to the Allied war effort.

REORGANIZING THE IMPERIAL ADMINISTRATION

Washington refused to extend diplomatic recognition to its new junior partner. But Darlan, as High Commissioner for North Africa, considered his administration to be the legal government of France. In theory, the Admiral served as trustee of the captive Marshal's powers. His intentions were to keep the empire together and to rally distant French possessions to his authority.

Darlan's executive ordinance of November 16 created a standard spread of administrative offices, including that of Deputy High Commissioner, assigned to General Bergeret. Darlan appointed the top officials and made the most important decisions.[1] He also retained the military powers he had held at Vichy. The first article of his Decision No. 1 of November 14 named his offices, assigning to the Admiral the top military command.[2] Giraud settled for command of land and aviation forces, which Clark reported to Eisenhower with no special comment.[3] But Darlan rewarded Giraud by assigning important posts to members of his entourage, including the monarchists Henri d'Astier de la Vigerie and Alfred Pose.[4]

In early December 1942, Darlan created an Imperial Council, intended mainly to hold the empire together. Darlan served as President. Its members included Giraud, Governor General Pierre Boisson of West Africa (which had rallied to Darlan), Resident General Noguès of Morocco, General Juin, and Admiral Michelier. The Imperial Council officially recognized Pétain as Chief of State and Darlan as his substitute in French Africa.[5] Darlan would have preferred to call his sprawling empire the "French Imperial Federation," but Washington refused to recognize that or any label suggesting a *de jure* government.[6]

THE MARSHAL STRIKES BACK

During the week following Darlan's taking power in Algiers, Pétain repudiated the Admiral six times. In a radio broadcast of November 16, for example, he struck hard at Darlan's claim to legitimacy:

I repeated to him several times the order to defend Africa. He ignored it on the single pretext of preventing a rebellious and criminal leader, General GIRAUD, from usurping command of the troops. Today he endorses GIRAUD'S elevation to leadership. GIRAUD was chosen by a foreign power which has brought war to French soil. Admiral DARLAN has thus divorced himself from the national community. I declare him relieved of all public functions and all military command.[7]

But Darlan claimed that the captive Marshal had supported him while he had been free. Pétain's abdication of his powers to Laval on November 17 played directly into the hands of Darlan, whose broadcast of the 20th insisted that Pétain had abandoned his powers only because he was under German pressure. Darlan reminded Frenchmen of their duty to liberate France, and also the Marshal. Praising Pétain for his continuing friendship with the American people, Darlan declared himself to be the true interpreter of his thoughts.[8]

While he hammered home the theme of the captive Marshal, Darlan attempted to rally Vichy's overseas stations. On December 1, for example, the embassy at Buenos Aires informed Vichy of Darlan's request for cooperation upon his taking responsibility for the empire "until such time as he could again place this world trust in the hands of the Marshal."[9] Laval answered that "naturally no response should be made to the message from Admiral DARLAN."[10] On December 20 Murphy sent Washington a list of thirty-seven French stations and individuals from around the globe that had rallied to Darlan.[11] These aggressive raids upon Vichy's outposts attest to Darlan's intention to rebuild France and her empire around his government at Algiers. That agenda served American military interests at the expense of the State Department, which viewed North Africa as a conquered territory and Darlan as only the temporary head of a *de facto* civil administration.[12]

TEMPORARY EXPEDIENCY

The liberal press in the United States denounced what they termed the "Darlan deal," charging that American support of Darlan betrayed the lofty war aims of the Allies. The *Nation* and the *New Republic* spoke of Darlan as America's first Quisling. The most damaging report came from London on the evening of November 15, when the popular radio voice of CBS correspondent Edward R. Murrow spoke of Darlan as "Laval's henchman," as a man regarded throughout occupied Europe as "one of the greatest living traitors." Murrow asked "are we at some future time to occupy Norway and turn it over to Quisling?"[13]

With respected journalists such as Murrow lumping them all together--Laval, Vidkun Quisling, Darlan--few Americans paused to put the Admiral's case in perspective. There was no strong media voice to remind Americans that the Nazis had forced Darlan out of office to restore Laval, or that the Germans had rejected Darlan precisely because he was not a Quisling. But there were no grassroots protests of the arrangements with Darlan. The furor against him was a media campaign that Roosevelt might have defused had he not caved in to London.

In Britain, opposition to Darlan ran deeper. Following the British attack at Mers el-Kébir in 1940, Churchill had demonized Darlan and coddled de Gaulle as the symbol of French resistance. Englishmen, therefore, viewed Darlan as a traitor emerging in the Allied camp as a rival to de Gaulle. With the British press unleashing a storm of criticism of the "Darlan deal," Churchill on November 17 intervened with the President. The rich Churchillian language of the note obscures the Prime Minister's longtime mismanagement of his relations with the powerful French Admiral now helping the Allies:

> I ought to let you know that very deep currents of feeling are stirred up by the arrangements with Darlan. The more I reflect upon it the more convinced I become that it can only be a temporary expedient justified solely by the stress of battle. We must not overlook the serious political injury which may be done to our cause not only in France but throughout Europe by the feeling that we are ready to make terms with local Quislings. Darlan has an odious record. It is he who inculcated in the French navy its malignant disposition by promoting his creatures to command. It is but yesterday that French sailors were sent to their death against our line of battle off Casablanca and now for the sake of power and office Darlan plays turncoat. A permanent arrangement with Darlan or the formation of a Darlan government in French North Africa would not be understood by the great masses of ordinary people whose simple loyalties are our strength.[14]

A note from the Foreign Office, arriving the same day, added that de Gaulle "has already made it plain that he cannot work with Darlan under any circumstances."[15] Churchill's unhappy partnership with the strong-headed de Gaulle had now come home to burden the Anglo-American alliance.

With a press conference scheduled for that afternoon, Roosevelt hurriedly drafted a statement. It borrowed the key phrase from Churchill's note: "The present temporary arrangement in North and West Africa is only a temporary expedient, justified solely by the stress of battle."[16] The President went on to explain that working with Darlan had saved Allied lives by making a "mopping up" period unnecessary.[17] Following the British line, the statement lacked a distinctly

American perspective. It omitted any reminder that the United States had maintained diplomatic relations with France until the Germans had forced Darlan out of office, or that Washington had recalled its ambassador in protest. What remained in focus was the "temporary expedient" clause, which served London better than it did Washington.

EISENHOWER AND DARLAN RESPOND

The President's statement threatened to upset the delicate arrangements that Clark and Eisenhower were negotiating with Darlan. But Eisenhower fought back. In a letter of the 19th to General George C. Marshal, he explained the real reasons for working with Darlan:

As a result of the arrangements we have made we have secured an opportunity to press our concentration toward the east for battle in Tunisia without worrying about the rear. At every principal port we would be badly handicapped without the assistance cheerfully rendered us now by French military, naval, and civil groups. At Casablanca today there were 30,000 of our troops unloading. French army trucks driven by French army drivers were working incessantly to help us. French Marines are helping unload ships. The ships were docked with the help of French tugs. Everywhere the story is the same. What I am trying to point out is that even if we should only have passive resistance, our operations would be sadly slowed up and our position badly weakened.[18]

Concluding, he warned that upsetting these arrangements would have disastrous results.

Darlan, responding to Roosevelt in a letter of November 21 to Clark, made it clear that he had no intentions of stepping down: "Information coming from various parts tend to give credit to the opinion that 'I am but a lemon which the Americans will drop after it is crushed.'" He stated clearly that he intended to retire "when French sovereignty in its integrity is an accomplished fact."[19] The letter continued with a reminder that Allied military success depended upon the cooperation of a loyal team of French leaders who had led North Africa back into the war. It warned that Washington, in the interest of the military campaign, ought not lead Frenchmen to discount the authority of their chief. Washington could not miss the message that military success in North Africa depended upon working with the Darlan team, and that Darlan intended to remain at his post until the liberation of France.

THE CLARK-DARLAN AGREEMENT

The Americans went ahead to gain assurances of Darlan's services. The Clark-Darlan agreement of November 22 was a modification of Murphy's earlier commitments to Giraud and of lenient armistice terms approved by the Combined Chiefs-of-Staff in October.[20] It was in two parts: a Preamble followed by an Agreement of twenty-one articles. The Preamble, containing the provisions most important to Darlan, acknowledged him personally as High Commissioner of French North Africa. Further, it confirmed agreement between the Darlan group and the local American military authority for French armed forces to aid and support the Allied forces to liberate North Africa and France, and, important to Darlan, "to restore integrally the French Empire."[21] But Eisenhower made it clear that the Preamble merely restated Murphy's earlier promises to Giraud, and that Darlan's name in it implied no American commitment to the Admiral.[22]

The Agreement was not a commitment between governments; it was instead an agreement between the Allied Commander and the local French Commission responsible for civil and military functions in his area of operations. The twenty-one articles, drawn from the preliminary armistice terms, were revised to accommodate French co-belligerency with the Allies, which had not been expected in October.[23] Neither the Agreement nor the Preamble, however, recognized the French as allies of the Americans.

The twenty-one articles provided generous benefits to the Americans. The most important ones committed Darlan to cooperate with the American command and to put at its disposal French airfields, harbors, communications, and transportation facilities. As for concessions to the French, Article 7 provided American assistance for the rearmament of French warships. Article 19 created a Joint Economic Commission but made no specific provision for American economic assistance to the region.[24] Missing from the Agreement were American promises for massive military aid to the French army. Murphy later wrote that the Agreement implied French rearmament at American expense.[25] But in 1942 the Americans built up their own forces in Tunisia. There were few assets available for the French army.[26]

DELIVERY OF WEST AFRICA

Darlan's most important territorial gain was French West Africa, an area of great strategic importance that lay beyond the American grasp. Governor General Pierre Boisson had remained with his officers loyal to Pétain. But with Vichy now under German occupation and North Africa fighting the Axis, West Africa was isolated, a tempting target to the Gaullists. Boisson could see that an American agreement might sidetrack de Gaulle and preserve French sovereignty in West Africa under American protection. The first step was to shift alignment to Algiers without violating the moral integrity of Frenchmen at Dakar.

Darlan could see that the succession of the colony would bring under his authority an important area that the Allies had not occupied. Immediately after taking power in Algiers, he sent Bergeret to inform Boisson of the secret messages suggesting Pétain's support of the Admiral. Boisson then formed a delegation to view the messages and explore an agreement that would leave West Africa under French control, not to be occupied or treated as a conquered territory.[27] Boisson rushed the delegation off to Algiers late Sunday afternoon, the 15th.

On Wednesday the delegation wired Boisson that the *accord intime* message was authentic.[28] Next day Darlan wrote Boisson, inviting him to join in the creation of a great French African Federation capable of restoring France and keeping the empire together. Pointing to the danger of a Gaullist attack, he recommended the succession of West Africa to North Africa.[29] Accordingly, Boisson placed himself under Darlan's orders the next Monday.[30] He came to Algiers on the 29th with the intention of concluding an agreement with the Americans.

Signed on December 7, the Darlan-Boisson-Eisenhower agreement acknowledged the entry of the colony into the war. It committed American and British authorities to take no action that might cause Frenchmen to take up arms against each other, which protected West Africa from Gaullist aggression.[31] In December the first American ships entered Dakar, delivering materials to service American aircraft soon to pass through the colony.[32]

The Darlan-Boisson-Eisenhower accord was a notable achievement for the Admiral, enabling France to influence importantly the direction of the war. The *Richelieu*, three cruisers, and several lighter craft now came under Darlan's authority. But the services rendered by the colony itself were more important. Supplies and reinforcements poured through the colony, and the great naval base of Dakar helped the Allies dominate Atlantic waters throughout the war.

The West Africa agreement reflected the tensions in American policy toward Darlan. The State Department, suspicious of the Admiral's empire building, viewed the accord as a regional military agreement with a local *de facto* organization. But just as the American right hand hesitated to recognize the Admiral's power, the other out of military necessity helped him to extend his authority over a vastly larger territory. Washington's French policy clashed with the fact that Frenchmen from Dakar to Tunisia obeyed Darlan only because they accepted him as the legitimate leader of France.

BETTER RELATIONS WITH WASHINGTON

The succession of West Africa locked Washington into an enduring relationship with Darlan. Should they force him out of office, they could expect nothing but trouble all the way from Dakar to Tunisia. And since any invasion of Italy could be staged only from Africa, the Americans would have to stick with Darlan even after the Tunisian campaign. Washington had no choice but to back away quietly from Roosevelt's "temporary expediency" statement and hope that Darlan would step down voluntarily.

The Americans therefore moved toward a revised position that recognized informally Darlan's intention to prolong his service. But Washington wanted the Admiral to move out of the spotlight. On November 27 the War Department instructed Eisenhower to inform Darlan of his hope "that this splendid cooperation will continue in ways most effective to the end that our Axis enemies will be completely defeated and France restored to her proper position as a world power."[33] The message expressed Washington's desire that the French factions might cooperate with each other under leaders "in positions for which they are most suitable." It hinted gently at Darlan's serving as navy commander. The statement admitted to a longer tenure for Darlan, but an attachment intended only for Eisenhower informed him of the President's desire "that the assurances come from you without formally committing the United States Government at this time."[34]

When West Africa rallied to the Allies, Washington moved even closer to Darlan's position. A message of December 7 instructed Eisenhower and Murphy to explain to Darlan American policy of cooperating with all Frenchmen fighting the Axis, and of protecting the right of all captive peoples to choose their own leaders after the war. They told Darlan that "as long as his efforts are directed to the specific end of resistance to the Axis, we feel he has a definite role and a positive military contribution to make to our united effort consistent with the policy of the United States Government outlined above."[35] But they cautioned the Admiral about building up a political organization unrelated to the common war effort.

Having retreated further from "temporary expediency," Washington expected the Admiral to commit himself publicly to reform. Eisenhower and no doubt Murphy carefully orchestrated the affair, assisting Darlan with the preparation of a declaration to be issued in Washington shortly after the Admiral had issued a version of it in Algiers.[36] It was attached to Roosevelt's December 16 press release announcing Darlan's declaration.[37]

Issuing the declaration, Darlan conceded that Frenchmen would choose their own leaders after the war. He announced various reforms, such as new efforts toward restoring Jewish rights, and he promised continuing French support of the Allied war effort. Darlan concluded with a clear expression of his intention to retire upon the liberation of France.[38] Roosevelt's release of the declaration, with the departure from "temporary expediency" buried at the end, implied the President's approval of working with Darlan until the liberation, when he would retire. But the option remained of trying to counsel him out of office prior to that time.

ARABS AND JEWS

Darlan moved in measured steps to address the sensitive problem of Arab-Jewish relations. Vichy's anti-Semitic laws, which deprived North African Jews of their French citizenship and burdened them with economic and educational restrictions, were popular with the 25 million Moslems who overwhelmed the tiny Jewish community of 130,000. Moslem leaders opposed repealing the laws. At the same time, the presence of foreign armies in North Africa tended to undermine French authority in the eyes of the Arab masses.

The leaders of both groups solicited Darlan. An urgent communication, signed by twenty-three Arab leaders, stated bluntly that "Moslem opinion is profoundly troubled."[39] It insisted that Darlan summon at once a conference of Moslems to address Arab needs. An appeal signed by the President of the Jewish Consistory of Constantine reminded Darlan of traditional Jewish loyalties to France and asked him to restore Jewish rights. A moderate document, it acknowledged the dangers of moving too fast.[40]

The Admiral could see that the tiny Jewish minority was no great threat. In contrast, the restless Arab masses under militant Moslem leaders could do much damage to French and Allied interests in North Africa. Darlan therefore thought it prudent to move slowly to restore Jewish rights. As for the Arabs, he decided to grant them a Commission, whose work would be carried out under strict conditions intended to maintain French control over any reforms to benefit Moslems.[41]

SEARCHING FOR SOLUTIONS

Darlan's personal papers reveal his thoughts and plans for future French relations with the Moslem population of the region. One plan proposed a policy of continuing French support of Arab interests in Africa, aiming at the creation of a vast spiritual empire among the Moslem peoples--an empire so morally and spiritually stable that military occupation could be replaced by French economic and political leadership of the Arab masses. Key to the creation of this spiritual empire would be the establishment of an Arab client state in Tripolitania, adjacent to the kindred peoples of southern Tunisia, upon the liberation of western Libya from Italian domination. This new Arab state would inspire Moslems everywhere and restore French prestige among Moslems in that region.[42]

The plan aimed at partitioning Libya. The first step was to reinforce the French armies in southern Tunisia with Moslem troops imported from elsewhere in French Africa. Their role was to help defeat the Axis in the region, to rally the Arab people, and to set the stage for the eventual transfer of Tripolitania to France.[43] The plan fitted neatly into the military picture taking shape in Tunisia, as the French armies numbering about 14,000 defended the Allied flank stretching south beyond Tebessa. When Eisenhower learned in mid-December of Darlan's plan to reinforce southern Tunisia with 50,000 native troops from Dakar, he did not see the political motives behind it.[44]

But the reinforcement of southern Tunisia fell behind schedule. Eisenhower balked at Darlan's proposal to move troops from Dakar, because there was not enough equipment available for French troops already in Tunisia. Darlan, however, did not abandon the plan. At the end of the forty days he was still building up the French armies in that sector of the front, obviously looking to the time when his own armies would liberate Tripolitania from the Axis.[45]

Another document found among Darlan's papers reveals his conviction that education and arbitration were the keys to any solution to Moslem militancy. This plan called for the creation of an organization for Jewish affairs with an office of Jewish studies. Studies prepared under this office would consider the perspectives of Jews, Moslems, and Christians, with the goal of moderating Arab-Jewish passions. The plan called for the creation of a high court with representation from both ethnic groups to arbitrate problems in race relations. Frenchmen would begin at once to educate Moslems to accept both Christian and secular perspectives on race relations. After the war, France would seek permanent solutions, enlisting the influence of the Roman Catholic Church. Only in this manner, the document concluded, would Arab-Jewish differences finally be reconciled.[46]

Darlan carefully avoided any action that risked provoking unrest among the Moslem majority. Eisenhower and Clark, under pressure from Washington, had urged the Admiral to withdraw Vichy's anti-Semitic laws. But Darlan stopped short of that. His public statement of December 16 contained no commitment to set aside these laws; it indicated instead that "measures have been taken to stop immediately whatever persecution of Jews may have resulted from laws passed in France under German pressure."[47] Darlan feared that a quick repeal of Vichy's laws would stir Moslems to revolt. He appealed to Eisenhower on the basis of protecting the military campaign, insisting upon the need to move slowly. He had his way. In late November Clark wrote in his journal that "Darlan is instructed to proceed with great care so as not to disturb the racial masses."[48] Vichy's laws therefore remained on the books until the Admiral's successors withdrew them in 1943.

Nevertheless, Darlan continued to search for a way to keep racial and religious tensions under control. On December 24, at the end of the forty days, Murphy wired Washington that Darlan had held discussions with Arab leaders and that "future conferences would be held and a conscientious effort made to ameliorate the Arab situation and to effect whatever adjustments might be possible."[49] In that same telegram Murphy reported Darlan's creating a commission to address Jewish grievances. Darlan, he said, "hoped that department would realize the delicacy of finding an equilibrium which would arouse neither animosity on the part of the Arabs nor the Jews," and that "a serious program of adjustment is being attempted under conditions which are not easy."[50] That militant Moslem militancy dominates politics in Algeria half a century later is evidence that the problems facing Darlan in 1942 had no easy solution.

THE FATE OF THE FLEET

The French fleet remained insecure in the tiny Toulon enclave. Auphan and de Laborde issued orders, as Darlan had done in 1940, for the fleet to destroy itself if necessary to avoid seizure. By November 18, when Vichy received a demand to remove all French troops from Toulon, the Germans had already mined the exits from the harbor and had moved aircraft into the area. Darlan's final appeal to the fleet, sent on the 27th, arrived only after the ships had scuttled themselves in the harbor.[51] The fleet did not fall into German hands, as Darlan had promised the British many times. But its destruction, which included the *Strasbourg* and *Dunkerque* and more than ninety other warships, denied Darlan potential control of assets that would have added an offensive capability to his power base.

Of the remaining units of the fleet, the most important was Admiral René-Emile Godfroy's Force X, interned at Alexandria. It included the battleship *Lorraine*, four cruisers, and lesser craft. Darlan thought he could deliver Force X. His appeal of November 23 was a carefully reasoned argument for Godfroy to rally to Algiers.[52] But Godfroy refused to budge. In early December Darlan sent staff officers to Alexandria.[53] While these negotiations moved slowly, Washington received reports of Godfroy's hostile attitude toward Darlan.[54] And Churchill contacted Roosevelt to urge patience, suggesting that Force X would eventually come over to the Allies without the necessity of further entanglements with Darlan.[55] The Admiral therefore no longer figured in Allied plans to rally the squadron.

Washington's willingness to wait for Force X to drop into its lap, which it did in 1943, did little damage to Darlan. When the forty days finally came to an end, Frenchmen from Dakar to Tunisia still obeyed his orders to support the American war against the Axis. Until the very end, the Admiral's services were so valuable that Washington dared not dismiss him.

NOTES

1. Journal Officiel du Haut Commissariat de France en Afrique (Alger: Agence Havas, 1943), I, 1-3.

2. C.F. Caroff, *Les Débarquements Alliés en Afrique du Nord* (Paris: Service Historique de la Marine, 1960), 99; Amiral Jacques Moreau, *Les Derniers jours de l'Amiral Darlan* (Paris: Pygmalion, 1986), 219.

3. Unpublished Papers of General Mark W. Clark, Housed in The Citadel Library, Charleston, South Carolina. Folder entitled "Records of Events and Documents from the Date that Lieutenant General Mark W. Clark entered into Negotiations with Admiral Jean François Darlan until Darlan was Assassinated on Christmas Eva, 1942," p. 52 (hereinafter cited as Clark Papers, Events and Documents).

4. *Journal Officiel du Haut Commissariat de France en Afrique*, II, 14. See also René Richard and Alain de Serigny, *L'Énigme d'Alger* (Paris: Fayard, 1947), 150-155.

5. Roosevelt Library, Hyde Park, Map Room, Box 105, MR310 "Torch," Telegram #1208, 4 December 1942, Murphy to War Department.

6. FRUS, 1942, II, 471.

7. USNA, RG 457, VFDM, XXXII, 0009316.

8. Hervé Coutau-Bégarie et Claude Huan, *Lettres et notes de l'Amiral Darlan* (Paris: Economica, 1992), 555-556.

9. USNA, RG 457, VFDM, XXXII, 0009537.

10. Ibid., XXXIII, 0009607.

11. Roosevelt Library, Map Room, Box 106, MR305 "Torch," 1942, Outgoing Message No. 2537.

12. See George F. Howe, *Northwest Africa: Seizing the Initiative in the West* (Washington, D.C.: Office of the Chief of Military History, Department of the Army, 1957), 269; and FRUS, 1942, II, 461-462.

13. Roosevelt Library, Morgenthau Diary, Book 584, Folder 112-119, transcript of Edward R. Murrow's radio broadcast of 15 November 1942.

14. FRUS, 1942, II, 445-446.

15. Ibid., 446.

16. United States, *Department of State Bulletin*, 21 November 1942, 935.

17. Ibid.

18. Alfred D. Chandler, Jr., editor, *The Papers of Dwight David Eisenhower: The War Years*, 5 volumes (Baltimore: Johns Hopkins University Press, 1970), II, 738.

19. Clark Papers, Events and Documents, 82-83,

20. See Arthur Layton Funk, *The Politics of Torch* (Lawrence: University of Kansas Press, 1974), 265, for the text of the armistice; and Howe, *Northwest Africa*, 269-270.

21. FRUS, 1942, II, 453-454.

22. Ibid., 453, n. 78.

23. Funk, *The Politics of Torch*, 266.

24. FRUS, 1942, II, 453-457.

25. Robert D. Murphy, *Diplomat among Warriors* (Garden City, NY: Doubleday, 1964), 141.

26. Howe, *Northwest Africa*, 270.

27. Albert Kammerer, Du *Débarquement africain au meurtre de Darlan*, (Paris: Flammarion, 1947), 594; C.F. Caroff, *Les Débarquements Alliés en Afrique du Nord* (Paris: Service Historique de la Marine, 1960), 300.

28. Caroff, *Débarquements Alliés*, 300.

29. Coutau-Bégarie et Huan, *Lettres et Notes de l'Amiral Darlan*, 563-564.

30. Caroff, *Débarquements Alliés*, 301.

31. Coutau-Bégarie et Huan, *Lettres et notes de l'Amiral Darlan*, 612-614.

32. See FRUS, 1942, II, 489-490.

33. Roosevelt Library, Map Room, Box 105, MR 310, "Torch," Miscellaneous 8-30 November 1942, Outgoing Message No. R-3657.

34. Ibid.

35. FRUS, 1942, II, 473.

36. *The Papers of Dwight David Eisenhower*, II, 820-822.

37. FRUS, 1942, II, 482.

38. Ibid., 482-483.

39. "Message des Représentants des Musulmans Algériens aux Autoritiés Françaises," 22 December 1942, from The Papers of Admiral Darlan, compliments of Claude Huan. This collection originated in North Africa and was received by Captain Huan from members of the Darlan family.

40. "Le Président du Consistoire Israélite à Monsieur l'Amiral de la Flotte Darlan," 25 November 1942, The Papers of Admiral Darlan.

41. "Conférence Musulmane," undated, The Papers of Admiral Darlan.

42. "La Politique Française dans les Pays Musulmans de la Méditerranée (et la question Tripolitaine)," 3 December 1942, The Papers of Admiral Darlan.

43. Ibid. Darlan's marginal notations indicate his approval of this part of the plan.

44. See *The Papers of Dwight David Eisenhower*, II, 843-845.

45. See Ibid., 843, 844 note 2.

46. "Dispositions à étudier en ce que concerne le problème juif," 19 November, 1942, The Papers of Admiral Darlan.

47. FRUS, 1942, II, 482-483.

48. Clark Papers, Events and Documents, 86.

49. Roosevelt Library, Map Room, Box 106, MR 310 "Torch," Telegram #2951, 24 December 1942, Murphy to War Department.

50. Ibid.

51. Henri Noguères, *Le Suicide de la flotte française à Toulon* (Paris: Robert Laffont, 1961), 33-36, 248.

52. Clark Papers, Events and Documents, 85.

53. USNA, RG 165, Records of the War Department General and Special Staffs, ABC 336.2 CCS Minutes, 132, 5 December 1942.

54. FRUS, 1942, II, 223.

55. Warren F. Kimball, editor, *Churchill & Roosevelt: the Complete Correspondence*, 3 volumes (Princeton: Princeton University Press, 1984), II, 84.

CHAPTER 22

Assassination in Algiers

Charles de Gaulle had only a weak following in North Africa. In West Africa he was widely despised. But de Gaulle was not tainted by the stigma of collaboration. Enjoying a moral ascendancy outside of North and West Africa, he considered himself the legitimate head of the French nation. "I am FRANCE," he said in 1943 to Colonel Jean Chrétien.[1]

RIVAL FACTIONS

But Darlan's swift rise to power under the American umbrella threatened the General's future. Darlan commanded the loyalty of most Frenchmen in Africa. Intelligent and politically astute, he worked well with Allied authorities there. French soldiers under his authority engaged the Axis in Tunisia, and vast French territories behind the lines nourished the Allied war effort. Despite the moral blemish of his Vichy past, Darlan had managed to become the key to Allied military success in Africa. In contrast, the strong-headed de Gaulle worked poorly with the Allies. He made no contribution in Tunisia, and he had wretched relations with the Frenchmen who were most helpful to the Allies. With Darlan serving American military needs very well, the Free French movement entered into a great crisis.[2]

The monarchists, a tiny faction loyal to Henri, the Count of Paris, hardly figured in the struggle for power among Frenchmen. Lacking a popular following, they operated underground and on the fringes of other political groups. They had wormed their way into the Darlan administration, and they had Gaullist connections. Despite their marginal existence, they thought of themselves as a government in existence. Their aim was to restore the Count to his throne, but Darlan stood in the way.

The Americans, taking little note of the monarchists, pushed Darlan to close ranks with de Gaulle. But these efforts threatened the political stability of North Africa and the delicate connections with West Africa. That the Americans even considered bringing the two French factions together suggests that Washington did not perceive how deep was the current of mutual contempt that divided them.

UNDERMINING DARLAN

The problem of finding a place for de Gaulle burdened the Anglo-American alliance. On November 11 Churchill wired Roosevelt "that he and the President at all costs had to avoid the creation of rival French emigre governments, one backed by Great Britain and one by the United States."[3] Two days later British Foreign Secretary Anthony Eden wired British political adviser Harold Mack at Gibraltar that Roosevelt had approved the sending of a Gaullist mission to North Africa to explain their position to local Frenchmen and to Giraud.[4] But Eisenhower informed Mack that sending the mission would be premature.[5]

Under American pressure, Darlan finally agreed to send a staff officer, Major Beaufort, to meet Gaullist General Georges Catroux at Gibraltar on December 12. After Catroux refused to receive Beaufort as Darlan's representative, British Governor Mason MacFarlane finally brought them together as old friends. Catroux insisted that de Gaulle would gladly work with Giraud but not Darlan.[6] When Catroux insisted that de Gaulle come to North Africa as Darlan's replacement, Beaufort replied that internal conflict would ensue and that West Africa would cancel its agreement with the Allies.[7] Returning to Algiers, Beaufort reported that MacFarlane had spoken of a possible *putsch* against the Admiral.[8]

Prior to the Beaufort-Catroux interview, Darlan recorded in private notes his willingness to cooperate with the Gaullists provided they recognize Pétain's authority.[9] But now Darlan could see that de Gaulle would not cooperate, and that the best course would be one of parallel efforts in the war. Shaken by the threat of violence against him, he wrote in his notes that French support of the Allied war effort depended upon him, and that he was the only Frenchman able to keep order in the region.[10]

In London, de Gaulle pressed Churchill again to authorize the sending of a Free French observer to Algiers. Finally, Eisenhower approved a brief visit by General François d'Astier, brother of the monarchist Henri d'Astier.[11] Roosevelt's misgivings about it came too late. On December 18, the day the d'Astier party departed for Algiers, the President sent a brief note to Sumner Welles: "I think it would be a mistake for General de Gaulle to send a small mission to Algiers. Sometimes the best way to keep peace in the family is to keep the members of the family apart for a while."[12]

A MONARCHIST CONSPIRACY

On November 16, Henri d'Astier received a confidential letter from Marc Jacquet, administrative aide of Alfred Pose and a steward of the Count of Paris. Pose, a wealthy banker soon to become Darlan's Commissioner for Finance, was said to be a member of the "synarchy," an alleged cabal of French and German bankers formed before the war. Whether Pose was in fact a member of this shadowy organization is not certain.[13] But as the ruling hand behind the monarchist conspiracy, he stood for the union of high finance and royalty.[14]

Jacquet's letter insisted upon the necessity of removing Darlan from power and merging North Africa and the Free French movement under the authority of the Count of Paris. D'Astier's assignment was to persuade the Count to cooperate, to enlist de Gaulle into service under the Prince, and to persuade the Americans to accept the new regime. The letter instructed d'Astier to handle the Darlan problem carefully--not to put a corpse between himself and the Prince.[15] The plan, therefore, did not require the assassination of Darlan.

The Count, exiled to Spanish Morocco, had offered without success his services to both Vichy and Berlin.[16] The Allies were aware of him. On November 19, London warned Eisenhower that the Count might attempt to replace Darlan, not as king, "but as 'Head of the French station, North Africa.'"[17] Upon Pose's orders, the Prince was smuggled into Algiers on December 10, driven there by the Abbé Louis Cordier, d'Astier's private confessor and secretary.[18] He cloistered himself with the d'Astier family on rue La Fayette, remaining out of view. Now d'Astier informed de Gaulle of the plot against Darlan and invited the General to discuss political arrangements for North Africa.[19] Aware of the monarchist conspiracy prior to the departure of François d'Astier for Algiers, de Gaulle had time to instruct his emissary as to what posture he should take toward it.

The monarchists expected to exploit republican sentiment to persuade Darlan to step down in favor of a civilian government. Republican leaders in North Africa, citing largely forgotten laws, had already questioned the legality of Darlan's military government. On November 26 the Presidents of the three Departments of Algeria, led by Paul Saurin, invited the Admiral to step down, but he refused.[20]

Pushing the Admiral aside by peaceful means would not be easy, but d'Astier had the means to use violence if necessary. A free corps unit, which he had formed earlier, remained at nearby Cape Matifou. The young Frenchmen there received training under British officers, who may have issued some of them with weapons to assassinate Darlan.[21] According to various reports, four recruits at Cape Matifou drew straws to determine which one of them would kill Darlan. Fernand Eugène Bonnier de la Chapelle, son of an Algerian journalist, drew the fatal one. The other three youths were sent on to the Tunisian front, but Bonnier remained behind.[22] Serving as liaison between the unit and its founder, he visited regularly in the d'Astier apartment. There he met Cordier, who resided with the d'Astier family and held a minor post in the police department.[23]

Cordier had contacts with other young men, including Mario Faivre, friend of Jean-Bernard d'Astier, son of the monarchist. Roger Rosfelder had been a classmate of Faivre's. The priest often saw them and others at d'Astier's apartment or at nearby restaurants such as the Coq Hardi.[24] A sinister figure, Cordier was known to the OSS as "Necktie," from the tool he used to execute Axis spies after he had forgiven them their sins.[25]

Pose and d'Astier had lured the Count to Algiers on the pretext that the leading republicans in Algeria would support his heading a provisional government.[26] And the Count was assured that the three republican Presidents of the General Council (Amédée Froger of Algiers, Paul Saurin of Oran, and M. Deyron of Constantine) would cooperate with Pose to oust Darlan peacefully on or around December 18 and then proclaim a legal provisional government.[27] But the republicans had made no commitment to join any conspiracy against Darlan. Pose promised Froger that the three Presidents would be notified in advance of Darlan's voluntary withdrawal, and he suggested that they issue a proclamation supporting the new leadership. Pose made no mention of the Count as a possible successor to the Admiral.[28]

D'Astier intended to establish an interim republican system with the Count serving as the chief of the government. The Count would provide the link between Giraud and de Gaulle, and his presence would assure stability lacking in a military regime. But d'Astier had never concealed his intention to restore the monarchy.[29] So replacing Darlan with a republican government was but the first step in a conspiracy to restore the king to his throne.

THE GAULLIST D'ASTIER

The urgent need to unseat Darlan came into focus after François d'Astier arrived from London on Saturday, December 19. Meeting with the Count that same day, d'Astier would make no commitment on behalf of de Gaulle, and he indicated that the General would not come to North Africa immediately. But he agreed that "it is advisable, as soon as possible, to separate Admiral Darlan from his illegitimate power."[30] On Sunday, when François d'Astier met with President Saurin, the General assured him that de Gaulle was not a dictator, but a republican. Saurin countered that the Americans had no desire for de Gaulle. "What are you going to do about Darlan?" he asked.[31] The Gaullist answered to the effect that Darlan is going to disappear, not just politically, but physically.[32]

Francois d'Astier had no reason to meet with Darlan. He knew the Admiral would not step down under Gaullist pressure, so there was no point in asking him to resign. And since de Gaulle would not share power with Darlan, there was nothing to negotiate. Similarly, Darlan had no reason to meet the Gaullist General, who had arrived unexpectedly without French permission. But Eisenhower insisted upon Darlan's receiving him. They met Sunday evening at Fenard's villa with Giraud and Battet present. Captain Hourcade, the Admiral's naval aide, waited in an adjoining room.[33]

Entering, d'Astier spoke to Giraud, ignoring Darlan. When Darlan inquired about d'Astier's purpose, the General replied that he had come to discuss Gaullist participation in the war, and to preach calm and discipline among Gaullist in Africa. Darlan insisted that the problems were political as well as military, requiring preliminary discussions to assure Gaullist political neutrality in North Africa. D'Astier, however, had no authority to discuss politics, so Darlan suggested that he return to London for instructions. If d'Astier asked Darlan to resign his post, the Admiral's summary of the interview contains no hint of it.[34]

The two parted without the courtesy of a handshake. Hourcade wrote that "...the situation had become strained to the breaking point."[35]

Shaken, Darlan rushed off to Eisenhower's villa to demand d'Astier's immediate departure. But Eisenhower persuaded him to extend the visit one more day for technical discussions with Giraud. Accordingly, d'Astier met with Giraud on Monday, the 21st, and departed Algiers on Tuesday.[36]

FATAL DECISION

Monday was the day of the final meeting between the d'Astier brothers, and it was the Count's last day in the city before he retired to the suburbs on Tuesday, to nurse his health. Early Monday evening, François d'Astier had a final talk with his brother at the Hotel Aletti. Afterward, Henri d'Astier returned to his apartment where he found Mario Faivre. The Count, suffering an attack of malaria, rested in a bedroom. Madame d'Astier worked in the kitchen. Henri, with a worried look on his face, sat at a table. Suddenly, as the air raid alarm sounded, the lights went out. There in the darkness d'Astier spoke softly to young Faivre: "My brother François has brought from London formal instructions to eliminate Darlan."[37]

Continuing, Henri commented that "we have not thought enough about some of the things my brother spoke to me about." He went on to say that in France the resistance suffers daily from torture and executions. These people, he said, "despair when they find out what we have accepted here in Algiers during the past weeks." The non-communist resistance, he added, is going to abandon the fight to the extremists "if the present state of things continues any longer. We are the only hope left."[38] When Madame d'Astier returned, the two men parted with a handshake. Next day Cordier told Faivre that the elimination of Darlan meant his execution, and that the order came directly from de Gaulle.[39]

François d'Astier flew out of Algiers on Tuesday morning, December 22, leaving behind a Gaullist committee and \$40,000 to subsidize its propaganda work.[40] If the General left instructions to have Darlan executed, as Faivre claims, it was consistent with Gaullist policy toward the Admiral. On that same day, a Gaullist diplomat told the American ambassador in Moscow that the Free French government had condemned Darlan to death, explaining that "he or any patriotic Frenchman would not hesitate to shoot Darlan on sight."[41]

THE ROLE OF THE COUNT

On Wednesday, after the Count had retired to the suburbs, Madame d'Astier related to Faivre the events of Monday morning when she and her husband were summoned to the Count's bedroom. The Count, she said, declared Darlan a traitor standing in the way of any solution. He then issued the order to make Darlan disappear. Henri asked if he meant "by any method?" The Prince answered "Yes, that's it, make him disappear by any method."[42] The Count, however, later denied that he had issued such an order, explaining that he had withdrawn from the affair on Sunday upon learning from Murphy that the Americans would deny him a political role in any event. He then retired to the suburbs to regain his health.[43]

The Count, however, had not withdrawn from the conspiracy. The question is, why did he retire to the suburbs at that moment? He had already written a proclamation announcing his taking power, "on the appeal of the representatives of the three French departments still free, and on the wish of the army."[44]And Cordier had prepared photos and master prints announcing the new regime headed by the Count with de Gaulle as Minister of State and Giraud as Minister of War.[45] These materials indicate the preparation of a *coup d'etat*, but they do not assume the murder of Darlan. They are products of the plan to persuade Darlan to step down. It seems clear that the Count retired to the suburbs, not because he had withdrawn from the conspiracy, but because d'Astier had changed plans.

A CHANGE OF PLANS

D'Astier's new plans required the assassination of Darlan. According to Faivre, d'Astier and his wife reviewed the situation late Monday as they sat in their apartment. "We no longer have a choice," d'Astier remarked. Cordier entered, and Henri related to him the conversation he had just had with his brother. Finishing, he rose from his chair and in a weary voice spoke directly to Cordier: "Well, Abbé, its your turn now."[46]

In making the decision to murder Darlan, d'Astier was influenced by his Gaullist brother rather than the Count. D'Astier gave the green light to Cordier on Monday evening after the final conversation with his brother, rather than after the Count's alleged execution order that morning. The Count's statement that Darlan was a traitor blocking a solution added nothing new. But his brother's argument linking the Darlan problem to the morale of the resistance movement in France, and to the need to head off the communists, added a slant that changed d'Astier's thinking. Only then did he decide to kill Darlan. Now he would justify the act on grounds of protecting the moral integrity of the resistance movement in North Africa.

On Tuesday, Pose failed in a final effort to rally the republicans.[47] But that setback hardly mattered now. The Count's retirement to the suburbs that same day was more important, for it reflected a last-minute change in Henri d'Astier's plans. Other clues pointing in the same direction are found buried in a conversation of Wednesday, the 23rd, between d'Astier and Jacques Brunel, son of a prominent Algiers family. Faivre, who sat in a restaurant with the two older men, remembered d'Astier's comments that he did not want de Gaulle to come to Algiers, and "that he will more readily accept the agreement if the problem has been resolved in advance." He should come only later "to fit himself into those things we will have done, and at a time when he will no longer be able to impose himself as omnipotent"[48]

Clearly, something important had happened to cause d'Astier to modify his plans for the *coup d'état*. An agreement had failed, and de Gaulle will come to North Africa only after a problem is solved. The agreement in question is de Gaulle's alleged agreement to serve in a government headed by the Count. And the problem to be solved is the elimination of Darlan. The original plan for a monarcho-Gaullist *coup d'état* had collapsed.

The reason for the abrupt change in Henri d'Astier's plans is clear. It was because de Gaulle had sent word through François d'Astier that he would not participate in the *coup*, nor would he make any commitment to the royalists. That de Gaulle would not cooperate with the monarchists is confirmed by the report of a Gaullist informant to the OSS in Algiers: "The financial and monarchist gang could harbor no illusions. DeGAULLE would not agree to be the Prime Minister of a Prince-President. The restoration of the monarchy, a screen to hide a financial dictatorship, was going to be outstripped by the FIGHTING FRENCH."[49]

De Gaulle could see that the monarchists could give him nothing more than the elimination of Darlan. Since the monarchists could be led to brush Darlan aside, there was no need for de Gaulle to risk his reputation in a shabby monarchist *coup* or to concede to the royalists anything that would eventually fall into his lap anyway. So François d'Astier backed away from the monarchist conspiracy and insisted at the same time upon the assassination of Darlan. De Gaulle's refusal to cooperate explains why Cordier's placards and dummy prints picturing the Count and de Gaulle together were not brought out in the wake of Darlan's assassination.

But d'Astier persisted in his intention to boost the Count to power. The plan, however, would have to be changed. There could be no monarcho-Gaullist *coup d'état*. The materials prepared in advance were of no use. The Count would have to be brought to power by another method. Since Darlan would have to be assassinated, it became necessary to sanitize the Count, to protect his candidacy from any fallout from the crime. D'Astier therefore shuttled the Count to the suburbs in advance of the assassination.

The crime would have to appear as the act of an unknown individual motivated on his own to kill Darlan. Afterward, the Count would emerge from the suburbs and offer his services as the only person capable of rallying all Frenchmen. And if the proper strings were pulled, he would be offered the position of High Commissioner. The Count, then, would already be in power when de Gaulle arrived in Algiers. Henri d'Astier would be calling the signals from behind the scenes, and the banker-monarchists would hold the advantage over de Gaulle.

RECRUITING A GUNMAN

Having received the green light from d'Astier on Monday evening, Cordier hurried on Tuesday to plan the attack. Rosfelder and Faivre proposed a commando-type action on a city street to shoot down the Admiral with a sten gun. Cordier insisted that it risked the lives of innocent bystanders.[50] A plan proposed by Marc Jacquet would have soldiers occupy the Summer Palace, bring Darlan to trial before a military court, and execute him on the spot. Cordier objected. The execution, he said, must appear as the act of an isolated individual strongly motivated to perform the deed. Jacquet suggested Mario. Again the priest objected. The gunman, he said, must be unknown to the guards.[51]

Cordier shared with Faivre his own plan. The trick was for a gunman to gain access to Darlan's office on the second floor of the villa adjacent to the Summer

Palace. Cordier would provide forged papers and a document for an appointment with M. La Tour du Pin, who would be absent from his first-floor office. Pretending to await du Pin, the gunman would slip quietly to the second floor and await Darlan. As the Admiral approached his unlocked office door, the gunman would shoot him, dash into the office, and exit through the window, just a short jump to the courtyard below. He would carry a forged passport and a sum of French and American money to assist his escape to Spanish Morocco.[52]

With its requirement for anonymity, the plan caused Cordier to search beyond his immediate entourage for a gunman. He inquired of Faivre about two youths, regulars at the Coq Hardi. Faivre joined the pair at their usual table. Cordier sat nearby, listening as Faivre described the plan. Horrified, the young men would have nothing to do with it. Irritated that Faivre had made too much of the risks, Cordier departed in a huff. Faivre joined him in the street minutes later. "Don't bother yourself any longer with this matter," Cordier growled.[53]

Shortly afterward the priest stumbled upon Bonnier de la Chapelle near d'Astier's apartment. So Bonnier became the gunman. Too close to the conspirators, he was a poor choice. Should he be captured, or should he be recognized at the scene of the crime, the evidence would lead directly to d'Astier and the Count.

FINAL ARRANGEMENTS

Since the attempt had been set for Thursday, Cordier moved swiftly to rehearse the plan with Bonnier. Should the youth be captured, he was to admit to the act, make no mention of his sponsors, and await patiently his release.[54] Cordier provided him with forged papers, prepared in the police department where the priest had access to materials. In addition, he gave Bonnier Spanish currency and $2,000 taken from the sum that Henri d'Astier had received from his Gaullist brother.[55]

On Christmas eve morning, about 10:00, Cordier and Bonnier met in a deserted street where the priest heard the boy's confession. As Bonnier finished the sign of the cross, the priest thrust into his hands a map of the Summer Palace. In almost the same motion he handed him a large revolver, d'Astier's dueling pistol. When Bonnier finished confessing the crime he intended to commit, the priest pardoned him in the name of Jesus Christ.[56]

Shortly thereafter Jean-Bernard d'Astier, in a black Peugeot assigned to the local free corps unit, drove Bonnier the short distance to the gate of the Palace. The youth presented his papers, asked for du Pin and indicated he would wait for him. But through the window he observed Darlan leaving the premises. He returned to the crowded Coq Hardi where he noticed the Peugeot parked nearby.[57]

Bonnier worried that the ancient dueling pistol might not fire. Within minutes four youths--Mario Faivre, Jean-Bernard d'Astier, Roger Rosfelder, and Bonnier--sped in the Peugeot to a nearby suburb. The pistol fired poorly, so Faivre offered him his own gun, a Rubis 7.65. Back to the Peugeot, Faivre drove to the gate of the Summer Palace. Bonnier gained entry as he had that morning and slipped quietly to the second level where he waited in the shadows for Admiral Darlan.[58]

PALACE SECURITY

As Chief-of-Staff, Admiral Battet was responsible for Darlan's personal security. He had learned from Hourcade, in touch with the prefect of police, M. Muscatelli, that several groups in Algiers posed a growing danger to Darlan. Muscatelli, knowing more than he would reveal to Hourcade, insisted that he could speak freely only to the Admiral himself. But Battet, for reasons unknown, would not allow Muscatelli to see Darlan.[59]

In mid-December, Battet ordered additional security measures, but they were uninventive, designed for protection against an armed *putsch*. Armored vehicles were placed in the gardens at the Villa Arthur where Darlan and his wife resided with Hourcade and Battet. Cases of hand grenades were placed in the staircase of the villa. Hourcade observed that these measures seemed more dangerous than effective. Military units were placed on the grounds of the Summer Palace. But security within the building remained lax, and the Admiral himself was poorly guarded. Hourcade continued to talk with the police about security.[60] But the local security unit was unreliable. Battet failed to insist upon the obvious solution, a loyal navy guard that Moreau had already offered Darlan.[61] The Americans, meanwhile, had learned of a specific attempt to be directed against Darlan.[62] But the OSS appears not to have warned the French authorities.

THE TENSIONS OF DARLAN'S LAST DAYS

Darlan wished to broaden his government, but civilian political talent was scarce. Hourcade later wrote Alain Darlan that his father, "who desired to act in accordance with republican laws and principles, found this lack of political personnel to be extremely burdensome."[63] Hourcade added that Darlan had urged the Allies to import French civilian leaders, including Albert Sarraut, his old friend of the moderate left.

But broadening his government would not have appeased the men plotting to unseat him. Knowing of conspiracies against him, Darlan lived out his last days in fear for his life. It was during those last days, when François d'Astier arrived unexpectedly from London, that his fears came into focus.[64] One evening, as Hourcade dined with the Admiral at the Villa Arthur, Darlan was summoned to a mysterious meeting. He left visibly upset. Hourcade later wrote Alain Darlan that the Admiral "had an edge of tension in his voice and a strange look about him" as he instructed the young officer to remain strictly at the side of Madame Darlan until his return.[65]

Darlan remained uneasy about the presence of the Gaullist General. Late Monday evening, the 21st, he sent Hourcade to insist with Murphy that d'Astier depart immediately. Murphy replied that the Americans had had nothing to do with the arrival of the Gaullist General, that he nevertheless would be asked to leave, and that Darlan had no reason to worry.[66] Darlan knew better. The visit of the Gaullist d'Astier begged the question of whether Darlan should retire or remain in office at the risk of his life. But he did not want to retire. He discussed his future with Murphy and Clark at a luncheon held at the Villa Arthur on Wednesday, December 23, the last full day of his life.

THE LAST LUNCHEON

Graciously hosted by Admiral and Madame Darlan, the luncheon honored Allied officers, especially naval officers. In a special way it symbolized Darlan's improved relations with the Royal Navy. Among those present were Eisenhower, Clark, and Giraud. Robert Murphy attended, as did Elliott Roosevelt, who had arrived in Algiers that morning. Present also was a delegation of British naval officers headed by Admiral Sir Andrew Cunningham, commander of Allied naval forces in the region. But at the last moment Randolph Churchill, son of the Prime Minister, sent his regrets.[67]

The table conversation between Clark and Madame Darlan turned to the health of her son Alain, still recovering from polio in a nearby clinic. Clark knew of President Roosevelt's invitation to move Alain to the children's hospital at Warm Springs, Georgia, where the President had been treated for the same illness. Clark could see a graceful opening to raise the question of Darlan's retirement. Addressing Madame Darlan, the General remarked that it would "be fine if you could take your son to Warm Springs for treatment," and turning to Admiral Darlan, he added, "I think it could be arranged for the Admiral to go too if he chooses." Darlan nodded agreement: "I'd like to turn this thing over to General Giraud. He likes it here, and I don't."[68] But that was only table talk.

The luncheon continued in good spirit as American, French, and British officers shared fellowship on the eve of the holy season. It was the Admiral's last state function, concluding a controversial career marked by years of bitter-sweet relations with the Royal Navy. The dinner served, he made a final, gracious gesture toward his English guests. Raising his glass to Admiral Cunningham, he proposed a toast: to a British victory.[69]

After the luncheon Darlan invited Murphy into his study. "You know," he said, "there are four plots in existence to assassinate me.... Suppose one of these plots is successful. What will you Americans do then?"[70] They reviewed a list of possible successors, all of which, Murphy acknowledged, were unsuitable or unavailable to serve as High Commissioner.[71] Darlan obviously wanted to head off any American request for his retirement, which is why he stressed with Murphy the lack of a suitable successor.

THE LAST MEETING WITH MURPHY

Next morning, just hours before his assassination, Darlan received Murphy for discussions that included the search for a successor. Murphy's prompt report to Washington, indicating that the interview took place that Thursday morning, underscored the lack of a suitable successor and reminded Washington of the Admiral's strong service to the Allied war effort. Darlan's comments, he wrote, "demonstrated that he is not unconscious of the attacks and abuses which have been heaped upon him abroad at a time when he is making a wholehearted effort to prosecute by the side of the Allies the common war effort."[72]

Darlan's annotated list of possible successors reflects his concern to convince Murphy that there were no suitable candidates. Darlan thought that de Gaulle, because he was opposed by nearly everyone in French Africa, ought to be excluded. There were several others, but all were either unsuitable or unavailable. At the top of the list was Albert Sarraut, who remained in occupied France.[73]

Clearly, Darlan would not step down on his own initiative. The Warm Springs solution was but a graceful exit should the Americans demand his retirement. But the Americans, for fear of trouble behind the front lines, dared not demand it. Their only safe option was for Darlan to step down voluntarily and personally arrange the transition. In Washington, an OSS Planning Group considered bribing him: "The Group wonders if Darlan has a price, and considers his removal is worth a large sum."[74] Nothing came of that proposal. In the meantime, Darlan prepared his agenda for further talks with Murphy. On it was a proposal for Darlan to succeed Pétain provisionally as Chief of State, should he die, with the Admiral remaining High Commissioner until the end of the war.[75]

THE MURDER OF ADMIRAL DARLAN

Returning from lunch at about 3:30, Darlan arrived at the gate of the Summer Palace. Accompanied by Hourcade, he entered the narrow corridor leading to his office, unaware of any danger. The young officer recalled that they bantered lightly, that Darlan's laughter echoed off the walls. Suddenly, as the Admiral turned to his office, two shots rang out. Hourcade turned to see Darlan stumble into his office, struck with a shot in the jaw and another in the chest. Hourcade pursued as the gunman jumped over the fallen Admiral. They struggled as the youth attempted to shoot Darlan again. Two more shots rang out and Hourcade fell wounded into a corner. Now several guards arrived. They struck the youth repeatedly as he begged for his life.[76]

While Bonnier was dragged away to central security, Darlan was rushed to Maillot Hospital where Alain had lain at the point of death six weeks earlier. The fatal bullet had penetrated a lung and the lower part of the Admiral's heart. En route to the hospital, his attendant offered encouragement. Darlan gestured feebly that there was no hope. Minutes later he died in surgery.[77]

Roman Catholic services, attended by French and Allied officials, were held the day after Christmas. Afterward, the Admiral's bier was taken to the portal of the Church of St. Mary of Mustapha where French, American, and British military units filed by in official respect. The body was entombed on the grounds of the Admiralty in a casement facing the sea.[78] Much later, in 1964, a French warship transferred the Admiral to the naval cemetery at Mers el-Kébir where he rests among the graves of Frenchmen who had given their lives in his service.[79]

NOTES

1. Letter of General Jean Chrétien to the author, March 10, 1983.

2. After Darlan had rallied West Africa, London informed its representative in Algiers that de Gaulle was "deeply depressed." USNA, RG 331, AFHQ, Reel 224B, Box 53, Darlan File, telegram November 26, Foreign Office to Mack.

3. USNA, RG 218, U.S. Joint Chiefs of Staff, Chairman's File, Admiral Leahy 1942-1948, folder entitled General de Gaulle, "President Roosevelt's Policy Towards De Gaulle," 21 June 1945.

4. Roosevelt Library, Hyde Park, Map Room, Box 105, MR310, "Torch," telegram Eden to Mack, 13 November 1942.

5. Alfred D. Chandler, Jr., editor, *The Papers of Dwight David Eisenhower: the War Years*, 5 volumes (Baltimore: Johns Hopkins University Press, 1970), II, 711, n. 1 (hereinafter cited as *Eisenhower Papers*).

6. Ibid, II, 834, n. 3.

7. USNA, RG 331, AFHQ, Reel 224B, Darlan File, Eisenhower's report of the Beaufort-Catroux interview, 14 December 1942.

8. See Alain Darlan, *L'Amiral Darlan parle* (Paris: Amiot-Dumont, 1952), 232-233.

9. Jacques Raphaël-Leygues and François Flohic, *Darlan* (Paris: Plon, 1986), 270-271.

10. Ibid., 274-275; Darlan, *L'amiral Darlan parle*, 232-234.

11. *Eisenhower Papers*, II, 834.

12. Roosevelt Library, PSF Diplomatic, Box 29, "France: 1942," Memorandum for the Under secretary of State, 18 December 1942.

13. See Albert Jean Voituriez, *L'Affaire Darlan* (Paris: J.C. Lattès, 1980), 201. An OSS report on the synarchy does not however include Pose among the 44 leaders listed. USNA, RG 226, E97, OSS, Algiers File, Box 29, Folder 505 (hereinafter cited as OSS, Algiers file).

14. French informants called the Pose group "le clan financier et Monarchique." See OSS, Algiers File, Box 27, Intelligence Reports, Folder 475, "Note On Events Of The Night Of 29/30.11.42."

15. Pierre Ordioni, *Le Secret de Darlan* (Paris: Albatros, 1986), xii.

16. Ibid., xviii-xix. See also OSS, Algiers File, Box 24, Intelligence Reports from Casablanca, "Royalist Activities in Marrakech."

17. USNA, RG 331, Reel 224B, AFHQ, Darlan File, telegram Foreign Secretary to Mack, 19 November 1942.

18. See OSS, Algiers File, Box 5, Folder 77, "Miscellaneous Intelligence."

19. Ordioni, *Le Secret de Darlan*, xxvi. See also Elmar Krautkrämer, "Admiral Darlan, de Gaulle und das royalistischeKomplott in Algier 1942," *Vierteljahrshefte Für Zeitgeschichte*, April 1984; and Elmar Krautkrämer, *Vichy-Alger, 1940-1942* (Paris: Economica, 1992), 316-317, 385-386.

20. Alain Decaux, *Alain Decaux raconte*, 2 volumes (Paris: Perrin, 1979), II, 324.

21. Roger Rosfelder, "The Plot to Murder Admiral Darlan," *Today in France*, No. 99, January-February 1972, 6; Henri Rosencher, *Le Sel, La Cendre et la Flamme* (Paris: Private Printing, 1985), 152. See also Douglas Dodds-Parker, *Setting Europe Ablaze* (London: Springwood, 1983), 115, in which Dodds-Parker writes that he issued Bonnier de la Chapelle a .38 revolver. But in a letter of 14 October 1983 in the *Times Literary Supplement*, Dodds-Parker denied that the Special Operations Executive (SOE) had ordered Darlan's assassination.

22. Rosfelder, "The Plot to Murder Admiral Darlan," 6.

23. Voituriez, *L'Affaire Darlan*, 176-178.

24. Rosfelder, "The Plot to Murder Admiral Darlan," 6; Mario Faivre, *Nous avons tué Darlan* (Paris: La Table Ronde, 1975), 135.

25. Arnaud de Chantérac, *L'assassinat de Darlan* (Paris: Perrin, 1995), 46. See USNA, RG 226, E97, OSS, Box 3, Folder #24, "GENERAL REPORT from Boxer to BF," 22 February 1943.

26. See Henri, Compte de Paris, *Mémoires d'exil et de combats* (Paris: Marcel Jullian, 1979), 195-196.

27. Ibid., 198.

28. Voituriez, *L'Affaire Darlan*, 202.

29. OSS, Algiers File, Box 27, Folder 475, "Considération sur les Événements d'Alger données par un des Acteurs de la Tragédie."

30. Compte de Paris, *Mémoires*, 200.

31. Decaux, *Alain Decaux raconte*, II, 337.

32. Ibid.

33. Undated Letter of Captain Hourcade to Alain Darlan, from The Papers of Admiral Darlan, compliments of Claude Huan. See also Peter Tompkins, *The Murder of Admiral Darlan* (New York: Simon and Schuster, 1965), 181-182; and Decaux, *Alain Decaux raconte*, II, 336.

34. Raphaël-Leygues and Flohic, *Darlan*, 216-218.

35. Undated letter of Captain Hourcade to Alain Darlan, The Papers of Admiral Darlan.

36. Raphaël-Leygues and Flohic, *Darlan*, 217-218.

37. Faivre, *Nous avons tué Darlan*, 135.

38. Ibid., 136.

39. Ibid., 137.

40. Voituriez, *L'Affaire Darlan*, 132.

41. FRUS, 1942, II, 488.

42. Faivre, *Nous avons tué Darlan*, 146.

43. Compte de Paris, *Mémoires*, 201-206.

44. Pierre de Berard, "Exposé succinct relatif aux actions politique de S.A.R. Monseigneur le Compte de Paris," typewritten document.

45. Voituriez, *L'Affaire Darlan*, 126-127.

46. Faivre, *Nous avons tué Darlan*, 147.

47. Voituriez, *L'Affaire Darlan*, 202-203.

48. Faivre, *Nous avons tué Darlan*, 144.

49. OSS, Algiers File, Box 27, Folder 475, Intelligence Reports, "Note On Events Of The Night Of 29/30.11.42."

50. Rosfelder, "The Plot to Murder Admiral Darlan," 8.

51. Faivre, *Nous avons tué Darlan*, 137-138.

52. Ibid., 138-139.

53. Ibid., 139-140.

54. Voituriez, *L'Affaire Darlan*, 150.

55. Decaux, *Alain Decaux raconte*, II, 361.

56. Voituriez, *L'Affaire Darlan*, 153-154.

57. Ibid., 154; Decaux, *Alain Decaux raconte*, II, 363-364.

58. Faivre, *Nous avons tué Darlan*, 148-150; Voituriez, *L'Affaire Darlan*, 154; Decaux, *Alain Decaux raconte*, II, 363-365.

59. Undated letter of Captain Hourcade to Alain Darlan, The Papers of Admiral Darlan.

60. Ibid.

61. Admiral Jacques Moreau, *Les Derniers jours de Darlan* (Paris: Pygmalion, 1985), 275.

62. OSS, Algiers File, Box 5, Folder 72, "Intelligence Reports," report of 8 February 1943 to Eisenhower's headquarters. About another matter, it reveals prior OSS knowledge of the attempt.

63. Undated letter of Captain Hourcade to Alain Darlan, The Papers of Admiral Darlan.

64. D'Astier was accompanied by his aide, Captain Pompeii, who had published articles demanding Darlan's assassination. See Moreau, *Les Derniers jours de Darlan*, 292.

65. Undated letter of Captain Hourcade to Alain Darlan, The Papers of Admiral Darlan.

66. Ibid.

67. Ibid.; Robert D. Murphy, *Diplomat among Warriors* (New York: Doubleday, 1964), 142.

68. Unpublished Papers of General Mark W. Clark, Housed in The Citadel Library, Charleston, South Carolina. Folder entitled "Record of Events and Documents from the Date that Lieutenant General Mark W. Clark entered into negotiations with Admiral Jean François Darlan until Darlan was Assassinated on Christmas Eve, 1942," p. 90 (hereafter cited as Clark Papers, Events and Documents).

69. Murphy, *Diplomat among Warriors*, 142.

70. Ibid., 143.

71. Ibid.

72. Roosevelt Library, Map Room, Box 106, MR310, "Torch," telegram No. 2951, 24 December 1942, Murphy to WAR.

73. Raphaël-Leygues and Flohic, *Darlan*, 235-236.

74. See USNA, RG 226, E190, OSS, Box 587, Microcopy M1642, Roll 43, frames 0720-0724, Memo from OSS Planning Group to Donovan.

75. Hervé Coutau-Bégarie and Claude Huan, *Lettres et notes de l'Amiral Darlan* (Paris: Economica, 1992), 634-635.

76. Undated letter of Captain Hourcade to Alain Darlan, The Papers of Admiral Darlan.

77. Moreau, *Les Derniers jours de Darlan*, 276.

78. Ibid., 278-281.

79. Ordioni, *Le Secret de Darlan*, 292-293.

CHAPTER 23

The Cover Up

The murder of Darlan set the scene for his successors to discover a conspiracy and stage a cover up of the evidence. Their aim was to conceal the truth about the crime to protect the French administration from American intrusion. The cover up also protected the reputations of important Frenchmen.

EVIDENCE OF A CONSPIRACY

Bonnier de la Chapelle was interrogated by police officers Esquerré and Garidacci. Their superior, prefect of police Muscatelli, worked for Henri d'Astier. Admitting to the crime, Bonnier promptly signed a statement that he had acted alone, without assistance, out of his own patriotic convictions.[1] The policemen presented Bonnier's brief confession to a military judge on December 25 and to a military court hearing the case later in the day, but they concealed from the jurists a more detailed confession pointing to the involvement of d'Astier and Cordier. Whether they concealed evidence to protect their chief, or to blackmail him, is not clear.

Found guilty, Bonnier was executed early next morning by a French firing squad. Justice had been dispensed all too swiftly, allegedly to discourage further disorders and to impress the Americans with a display of French efficiency.[2] The swift punishment of Bonnier silenced a witness whose testimony would have damaged the careers of other Frenchman.[3] Nevertheless, Bonnier left behind a trail of evidence pointing to a conspiracy. Papers found on his person--a forged identification card and a forged passport--suggested the criminal involvement of the local police department. The faked documents had obviously originated in the security office headed by police commissioner André Achiary. A sum of $2,000 found in Bonnier's possession indicated the assistance of people with financial means.

Bonnier had talked freely with his interrogators and his guards, on condition that they take no notes. These statements, summarized later, along with the second confession, implicated Cordier and d'Astier and hinted at the involvement of the Count of Paris and Charles de Gaulle. Bonnier revealed that Cordier had given him an unreliable pistol, and that he and his young friends had tested the weapon and exchanged it, he said, for Gilbert Sabatier's personal revolver.[4] Bonnier also alluded to his being rescued in the course of a *coup d'état* to be staged by his seniors. While Bonnier freely revealed the names of Cordier and d'Astier, he said that he had been instructed not to do so.[5]

THE MONARCHISTS' BID FOR POWER

Alfred Pose had already taken steps aimed at boosting the Count of Paris to power. Moving quickly, he returned the Count to the city just hours after Darlan's assassination. Before the end of the day, Pose had arranged for the Count to meet with General Bergeret, a member of the Imperial Council responsible for appointing a successor to Darlan as High Commissioner.[6] On Christmas day Bergeret heard the Count's plea that he alone could rally the French factions. The Count came away encouraged that Bergeret would place his name before the Imperial Council.[7] Afterward, the Count met with Robert Murphy, but the American would support Giraud as his candidate to succeed Darlan.[8]

Murphy's report to Washington early Saturday, the 26th, mentioned the Count's proposal to establish a Council with the Count as President, de Gaulle as Vice-President, and Giraud as military commander. In the same message Murphy reported a conversation he had had with Bergeret: "He asked my personal opinion and I told him unequivocally that I felt that General Giraud is the only possible choice."[9] Murphy urged Washington to adopt a clear position. "We should," he recommended, "insist with General Giraud that he assume at least provisionally the responsibility of both civil and military government in this area."[10] While Murphy awaited Washington's reply, the Count conferred with Giraud Saturday morning. But Giraud made no commitment. Later that morning, Pose's deputy, Marc Jacquet, pressed Pierre Ordioni to intervene on behalf of the Count with Governor General Yves Châtel, but that effort also failed.[11]

Washington's reply came later that Saturday morning in the form of a telegram from General George C. Marshal to Eisenhower: "With the approval of the President you are authorized to appoint General Giraud provisionally in charge of both Civil and French Military Authorities in your area."[12] Murphy and Eisenhower had already influenced the Imperial Council in that direction. Therefore, when it met on Saturday afternoon it promptly elected Giraud as High Commissioner.[13] With that action, Pose's role as kingmaker came to an end.

After the election of Giraud, Bergeret allegedly received reports of an armed *coup d'état* scheduled for the evening of December 29. There were also rumors that both Giraud and Murphy would be assassinated.[14] But French informants reported to the OSS that there was no conspiracy, that Bergeret used the pretext of a plot against Murphy and Giraud to justify the arrest of Gaullist leaders in Algiers.[15] Bergeret was under pressure from the Americans to end the atmosphere of intrigue in the city, and he suspected local Gaullist involvement in the

Darlan assassination.[16] Moving swiftly, he arrested on the 29th fourteen suspects, mainly Gaullists from the local Jewish community.[17] They had no connection with either the conspiracy to murder Darlan or the alleged conspiracy to seize power in the wake of Giraud's election. Among those detained shortly thereafter were Achiary and Muscatelli, policemen who knew considerably more about the Darlan assassination than did the local Gaullists. The scene was now set for the cover up.

AN INDEPENDENT INVESTIGATION

With the statements of Achiary and Muscatelli in hand, Bergeret realized that the monarchists were the conspirators behind Darlan's murder. He then summoned an outside magistrate to inquire into the case. Colonel Larroubine, Commissioner of the Military Tribunal at Casablanca, was selected, because of his loyalty and his good record of prosecuting dissident groups in Morocco.[18] Larroubine assigned the investigation to his assistant, Albert Jean Voituriez, who arrived in Algiers on January 8. Giraud and Bergeret, worried that the Americans might take over the civil administration of North Africa because of French bungling of the Darlan case, were determined to settle the matter as soon as possible. They promised Voituriez full support but asked that the inquiry be completed quickly. They also worried that the Darlan murder might have been orchestrated from London.[19]

Bergeret could see that the evidence in hand might enable him to pass off the crime as nothing more than a local affair, as a key report found in the Darlan File of the Allied Force Headquarters reveals. Dated January 10, 1943, it summarizes a meeting between Bergeret and Colonel Julius Holmes of Eisenhower's staff. The meeting took place after the interrogation of Achiary and Muscatelli but before the results of the Voituriez inquiry had become available to Bergeret. Following are the essential sections of Holmes' report:

1. This morning General Bergeret asked for Mr. Murphy to go to see him, and as the latter is ill, I went in his place. General Bergeret announced to me that the situation in regard to Admiral Darlan's murder and recent arrests has been definitely clarified. Mr. Achiari, supported by Mr. Muscatelli, the former having been of the police and the latter his personal assistant, and both having been included in the arrests, have made a sworn statement in which they disclose the complete story of the assassination. The affair was planned by Dastier de la Virgirie [sic], a priest named Cordier, and a third person of no political consequence, who furnished not one but two pistols to the assassin. The testimony signed by Achiari, is supported by further documentary evidence and General Bergeret says there is not the shadow of a doubt that they now have a complete story.

2. A military prosecuting attorney, whose name is Colonel Laroubie [sic], has been summoned from Casablanca to take charge of the case. Colonel Laroubie is known as the man who arrested German Spies here against the desires of the Laval Government and is known to Murphy.

3. The investigation and trial will take place this week. The trial will be public and the accused will have counsel.

4. General Bergeret seemed very relieved and stated that in his opinion those guilty will
   be punished and the atmosphere will be cleared. All of the others, including Achiari
   and Muscatelli will be released during the week.

5. General Bergeret also stated that Achiari swears that at the time of the visit of General
   Dastier de la Virgirie, that he gave his brother $38,000, which he had brought with
   him from London. The boy who killed Admiral Darlan was paid a pittance of 10,000
   francs. This fact is brought out by a signed statement of the boy who did the killing
   and which was found in the possession of a police officer, who had kept it in anticipation of using it for the purpose of blackmail against Dastier [sic] at some later date.

6. I asked General Bergeret what he thought the effect of this situation would be on the
   possibility of bringing Giraud and De Gaulle together. He said that he felt perfectly
   well that De Gaulle had no part in it and in his opinion the punishment of the crime
   would be ratified by De Gaulle and 90% of his followers.[20]

Bergeret concealed the fact that he and Giraud already suspected a Gaullist
connection, and he twisted the facts concerning the money found on the gunman.
The document betrays Bergeret's intention to confirm the assassination as nothing more than a local affair. He expected the magistrate to conclude his inquiry
quickly. A public trial would be held, the assassins would be found guilty,
American suspicions would be eased, and the Darlan case would be put to rest in
a manner to protect the French administration.

But Voituriez was already filing away new evidence that would upset
Bergeret's plans. Before dawn on the morning of January 10, following his interrogation of Achiary, Voituriez staged a surprise search of Henri d'Astier's
apartment. He discovered there the materials prepared for the original *coup*
against Darlan, which included the dummy front page of a newspaper announcing the Count's taking power in Algiers. It featured a large photograph of the
Count flanked by pictures of de Gaulle and Giraud. Other documents carried the
Count's proclamation with a ministerial list that included de Gaulle as Minister
of State and Giraud as Minister of War. Henri d'Astier would take the Interior
Ministry, and Marc Jacquet that of Justice. Alfred Pose would be Minister of
Finance. The ministry included six other Gaullists.[21]

On the basis of this evidence, d'Astier was arrested, joining Cordier who had
already been detained. The evidence suggested a broad conspiracy against Darlan that may have involved Giraud, de Gaulle, and a high-ranking member of the
government. Giraud was innocent, but he would have been embarrassed to explain these materials in public. He could not allow them to be displayed at the
trial Bergeret had promised Holmes.

Voituriez continued to press the Darlan case, interrogating Pose, d'Astier,
Cordier, and the policemen Garidacci and Esquerré. He interviewed several others, including the policemen who had guarded Bonnier during his final hours.
From these interrogations Voituriez accumulated evidence that could not help
but damage Giraud. The evidence left little doubt that the guiding hand behind
the conspiracy to murder Darlan was Alfred Pose, Giraud's finance minister.[22]
Other evidence hinted that the $2,000 found on the gunman had been taken from
a sum of $40,000 that the Gaullist François d'Astier had left with his brother.[23]

Giraud had not expected the inquiry to turn out this way. Embarrassed by the evidence as he prepared to leave for the Casablanca Conference, he abruptly withdrew his cooperation. He dragged his feet on the question of filing charges against Pose and Jacquet, insisting that the inquiry be suspended until his return from Morocco. The Americans, he told Voituriez, had been convinced that the Gaullists were behind the assassination of Darlan, and he had arrested the local Gaullists and the policemen to demonstrate his own innocence. The Americans were still not satisfied, he added; and they had threatened to take over the French administration and to press Churchill to cut off de Gaulle's supplies.[24]

Giraud went on to explain to Voituriez that the Americans had now become convinced that collusion between de Gaulle and the Count of Paris was only an appearance. They now believed that the conspiracy originated in Algiers with the goal of restoring the monarchy, and that de Gaulle had only intended to profit from events he had not caused. It was important, he thought, that the results of the inquiry be kept in confidence during the next several days when he would take the first step at Casablanca to form a common French front with de Gaulle.[25]

Giraud refused to permit Voituriez to interview the Count. Those already in jail, Giraud insisted, are guilty. "Even if they are not the leaders of the conspiracy, they are enough for me," he said. "I don't want to push higher. That would lead to useless complications."[26] The Count therefore was not interrogated. Under pressure from Giraud, Voituriez permitted the Count to file with the court a statement of his innocence. Giraud then had him escorted back to Spanish Morocco, where he could do no damage.[27]

Before he departed for Casablanca on Sunday, January 17, Giraud suspended the inquiry.[28] That action, in the wake of the arrest of d'Astier and Cordier, sidetracked the public trial and completed the first phase of the cover up of the Darlan assassination.[29] With d'Astier and Cordier safely behind bars, with the inquiry suspended, with Pose not likely to cause any trouble, and with the Count out of sight, Giraud could go to Casablanca and worry later about the scandal in his government. The first phase of the cover up concealed the corruption in the government while Giraud attended the Casablanca Conference.

The next phase, aimed at suppressing entirely the evidence of a treasonous conspiracy against Darlan, began when Giraud and Bergeret received Voituriez in late January, following the Casablanca Conference. According to Voituriez's account, Giraud indicated that de Gaulle had agreed that exposing all of the treason and intrigue among Frenchmen would damage the French position with the Allies. "The inquiry has ended," he said. "The Allies are satisfied and we are pleased with you."[30] He then asked Voituriez to issue a nonsuit on behalf of the accused.

But Voituriez refused to drop the charges. When Giraud and Bergeret insisted, Voituriez resigned from the inquiry. He suggested, however, that they might drag out the proceedings until another judge would issue a nonsuit at a timely moment.[31] Voituriez returned to Casablanca, leaving with Bergeret a thick file of evidence that had to be concealed in the interest of protecting the reputations of both Giraud and de Gaulle.

Giraud and Bergeret were now free to drag out the case. In early February the Military Tribunal filed charges against the monarchists and the policemen. Pose, Jacquet, d'Astier, and Cordier were cited for conspiring against the internal security of the state. But on the 8th, Giraud himself issued a nonsuit in the cases of Pose and Jacquet, indicating that any decision in their regard would be taken only later. Pose remained at his post. D'Astier and Cordier were charged with attempted assassination of Darlan. They remained in confinement at Laghouat, distant from Algiers. Garidacci and Esquerré were charged with dereliction of duty.[32]

Giraud had succeeded in sweeping the Darlan case under the rug with no damage to himself or to de Gaulle. Except for Pose and Jacquet, those directly involved in the murder of Darlan remained safely behind bars. Giraud now had no reason to rush ahead to get a settlement in the case. The trial that Bergeret had promised Holmes was never held. The hearings in all cases were dragged out, repeatedly rescheduled during the spring and summer of 1943. Later, after de Gaulle had come to Algiers, the charges were quietly dropped, and those still in confinement were released. All of the accused were eventually rehabilitated. In 1945 a Gaullist-dominated Court annulled the judgment against Bonnier. Cordier and Henri d'Astier were decorated for wartime services.[33] After the war, Jacquet became a minister in de Gaulle's government.

The cover up concealed from the Americans a body of evidence that would have been especially damaging to de Gaulle, who had already proposed a meeting with Giraud to patch up the differences between the French factions.[34] The door remained open for de Gaulle to inherit eventually Darlan's sprawling empire.

WAS IT NECESSARY TO MURDER DARLAN?

With important evidence related to Darlan's murder carefully suppressed, de Gaulle arrived in North Africa in June 1943 to chair with Giraud the French Committee on National Liberation. Even before Giraud retired in 1944, de Gaulle had become the undisputed leader of the French resistance movement in the overseas territories. De Gaulle's ultimate triumph did not, however, depend upon the assassination of Darlan, who was fatally tainted by his Vichy connection. Even had Darlan survived Bonnier's attack, de Gaulle enjoyed a moral advantage that would have boosted him ahead of the Admiral at the end of the war. Had Darlan and de Gaulle continued to fight the war on parallel tracks, de Gaulle would have been better situated to demand a military role in the liberation of France.

For the moment, however, Darlan held the stronger hand, ruling over a vast empire that served vital Allied interests. Murphy recalled later that "we never thought of retaining him for the longer term,"[35] which meant that the Allies could in time boost de Gaulle ahead of him. There would have been good military reasons to continue with Darlan beyond the Tunisian war and into the Italian campaign, but he could easily have been denied a role in the eventual invasion and liberation of France.

De Gaulle could see that Darlan's tight grip on the vast staging area of a vital theater of military operations would make it difficult for the Americans soon to discard him. The Admiral appeared to be a permanent part of the Mediterranean war. If the Gaullists were involved in the conspiracy to murder Darlan, it was because he had emerged as a threat to the wartime image of de Gaulle as the unique symbol of French resistance to the Axis.

A GAULLIST ROLE IN THE MURDER OF DARLAN?

The timing of events leading to the assassination of Darlan is no proof that the murder was orchestrated from London by de Gaulle. But the evidence points to a sequence of events that begs the question. In November and December, de Gaulle did nothing to discourage the monarchist conspiracy to oust Darlan. Nor did he cause the monarchists to think that he would refuse to join a royalist government afterward. But at the last moment de Gaulle's agent, François d'Astier, arrived in Algiers and refused to cooperate with the *coup* the royalists had prepared. Witnesses close to the conspiracy wrote later that de Gaulle's agent insisted before his departure upon the physical elimination of Darlan, as we have seen.

There is no documentary evidence that de Gaulle sent an order to have Darlan assassinated. Either of the d'Astier brothers might have manufactured the story of de Gaulle's sending an assassination order. Or François d'Astier could have taken the initiative to flash the green light to relieve his chief of that burden. De Gaulle, moreover, would not have left any written records linking himself to the assassination.

But the royalist conspiracy had been under way for six weeks during which no attempt had been made upon Darlan's life. Then, two days after the departure of François d'Astier, the Admiral was assassinated by a youth close to Henri d'Astier. The fact that Darlan was assassinated immediately after the visit of the Gaullist d'Astier is what caused Giraud and the Americans to suspect that the murder had been orchestrated from London.

A LETTER FROM GENERAL CHRÉTIEN

Late in 1943, after he had come to Algiers, de Gaulle received in his office Colonel Jean Chrétien, Chief of Military Intelligence in Algiers at the time of Darlan's death. Chrétien's account of the interview, expressed in a letter to the author, is not proof of de Gaulle's personal responsibility for Darlan's murder. It is instead the statement of a shrewd intelligence officer who arrived independently at much the same verdict as those close to the conspiracy who claimed a personal role for de Gaulle. Chrétien's letter opens with the prudent statement that he had no proof of de Gaulle's responsibility for Darlan's assassination. But Chrétien went on to explain that in 1943 he gradually became convinced of the General's responsibility for it. The letter continues:

But my conviction was especially reinforced by the long interview that I had with DE GAULLE in 1943, soon after his arrival in Algiers. His greeting was friendly, for we had

had pleasant relations at NATIONAL DEFENSE before the war, where I shared his ideas, and he knew that I had been an ardent partisan of the war on the side of the Allies.

But with the small talk finished, he changed completely when we turned to the problems of the moment; in particular the death of DARLAN. When I said "the Admiral was assassinated by...," he interrupted me abruptly: "not assassinated: executed!" then he delivered a furious diatribe against ROOSEVELT, MURPHY, the Americans "who jumped in up to their neck with Vichy, who tried to drag me through the mud, who wanted to overthrow me."

His excitement increased, and, his arms crossed, and with a wild look in his eyes, he paced back and forth across the room proclaiming "I am FRANCE, I am FRANCE, and those who are not with me are against FRANCE."

Dumbfounded, I submitted to a long diatribe, in the course of which he vented his anger and fierce hatred against everyone who had not rallied to London, officers, administrators, and businessmen; by this time he had regained his composure, though he remained excited; but when he was pacing back and forth with his arms crossed, I thought I was dealing with a madman, and I think he was that at times.

At this moment, I think that he had DARLAN assassinated and the question he asked me was a trap to make me say that I knew it; very fortunately, I did not fall for it, otherwise I would not be in the process of writing you.[36]

If de Gaulle had indeed spoken as Chrétien remembered it, he had declared himself the author of Darlan's assassination. He had defined Darlan's death as an execution--an act of the state--and in almost the same breath he defined himself as the state. "I am FRANCE," he repeated, making clear the point. In putting it that way, de Gaulle obviously intended to make the point that Darlan had been put to death by the state that the General considered himself to embody.

In the absence of a written assassination order, any claim of de Gaulle's personal responsibility for the crime would be premature. But the evidence that the Gaullists played the decisive card is impressive. Had there been no cover up of the evidence available in 1943, and had Giraud not suppressed the open trial Bergeret had promised Holmes, the moral advantage that de Gaulle held over other Frenchmen would have been tarnished by public suspicion of a Gaullist role in the murder of Darlan. And the Americans would have had second thoughts about letting the General come to North Africa.

NOTES

1. Albert Jean Voituriez, *L'Affaire Darlan* (Paris: Lattès, 1980), 136.

2. Ibid., 88.

3. The efforts of the conspirators to save Bonnier are recorded in Chamine (pseud. Geneviève Dumais), *Suite française*, 2 volumes (Paris: Albin Michel, 1952), II, 550-554. But French informants reported to the OSS that Bonnier "was condemned and executed by those who had armed him (thus he could no more talk and the KING would not be compromised in the public opinion)." USNA, RG 226, E97, OSS, Algiers File, Box 27, Folder 495, Intelligence Reports, "Note On Events Of The Night Of 29/30.11.42" (hereinafter cited as OSS, Algiers File).

4. Bonnier appears to have confused Gilbert Sabatier with Mario Faivre. Sabatier, a young officer in the free corps, was later charged with attempted assassination of Darlan.

5. Voituriez, *L'Affaire Darlan*, 148-158.

6. Pierre de Berard, "Exposé succinct relatif aux actions politiques de S.A.R. Monseigneur le Compte de PARIS," typewritten document, compliments of Claude Huan (hereinafter cited as Berard, "Exposé succinct").

7. Henri, Compte de Paris, *Mémoires*, 206; Berard, "Exposé succinct."

8. Compte de Paris, *Mémoires*, 296-207.

9. Roosevelt Library, Map Room, Box 106, MR310, "Torch," telegram 3124, Murphy to AGWAR, 26 December 1942.

10. Ibid.

11. Berard, "Expose succinct"; Pierre Ordioni, *Le Secret de Darlan* (Paris: Éditions Albatros, 1986), xxix. Ordioni served as the official link between Darlan and Châtel.

12. Roosevelt Library, Map Room, Box 106, MR310, telegram 485, Marshall to Eisenhower, 26 December 1942.

13. Amiral Jacques Moreau, *Les Derniers jours de Darlan* (Paris: Pygmalion, 1986), 289.

14. Ibid.; Peter Tompkins, *The Murder of Admiral Darlan* (New York: Simon and Schuster, 1965), 204; *The New York Times*, December 31, 1942, 1.

15. OSS, Algiers File, Box 5, Folder 77, Miscellaneous Intelligence Reports, report of Karsenty and Morali. See also Box 27, Folder 475, "Considération Sur Les Événements d'Alger Données Par Un Des Acteurs De La Tragédie."

16. See Voituriez, *L'Affaire Darlan*, 85-91.

17. André Morali and Bernard Karsenty escaped to London where they filed their report with the OSS. OSS, Algiers File, Box 5, Folder 77, Miscellaneous Intelligence Reports, report of Karsenty and Morali.

18. Larroubine had prosecuted cases involving Gaullists at Casablanca. See OSS, Algiers File, Box 25, Folder 423, Miscellaneous Intelligence Reports, unlabeled document; Box 28, Folder 494, Miscellaneous Intelligence Reports, unlabeled report; and Box 5, Folder 77, Miscellaneous Intelligence Reports.

19. Voituriez, *L'Affaire Darlan*, 86-93, 237.

20. USNA, RG 226, AFHQ, Supreme Allied Commander's Secretarial Records, APO 794, Film No. B-226, Admiral Darlan File, "Memorandum For: Chief-of-Staff," 10 January 1943.

21. Ibid., 126-127. See also Arnaud de Chantérac, *L'assassinat de Darlan* (Paris: Perrin, 1995), 198.

22. Voituriez, *L'Affaire Darlan*, 199-203.

23. Ibid., 148, 175, 212-214, 228-230, 233, 273.

24. Ibid., 237.

25. Ibid., 237-238.

26. Ibid., 220.

27. Ibid., 220-221; and OSS, Algiers File, Box 5, Folder 77, Miscellaneous Intelligence Reports, untitled document, 29 June 1943.

28. See Voituriez, *L'Affaire Darlan*, 235-238.

29. French informants reporting to the OSS clearly regarded the arrests and the suspension of the inquiry as a cover up aimed at avoiding a public trial and silencing the conspirators. They noted that the authorities in Algiers admitted that to be the case. OSS, Algiers File, Box 5, Folder 77, Miscellaneous Intelligence, untitled document, 29 June 1943.

30. Voituriez, *L'Affaire Darlan*, 238-239.

31. Ibid., 241.

32. Chamine, *Suite française*, II, 577-578.

33. Voituriez, *L'Affaire Darlan*, 242-245.

34. For de Gaulle's letter, see Roosevelt Library, Map Room, Box 106, MR310, "Torch," telegram #5979, London USFOR to the War Department, 27 December 1942.

35. Letter of Robert Murphy to Arthur Layton Funk, 5 March 1970, compliments of Professor Funk.

36. Letter of General Jean Chrétien to the author, 10 March 1983.

CHAPTER 24

Darlan: Myth and Reality

Since 1945 Americans have not moved far from the Anglocentric view of Darlan shaped mainly by the wartime press. That narrow view judges him in terms of foreign interests, overlooks his prewar career, and lumps him with Europeans who were unlike him. Darlan was a complex French statesman who fits poorly into the simple categories Americans employed during the war to define friends and enemies. There is no need to celebrate Darlan among Americans, but it is important to discard the mythology that obscures our understanding of him as a Frenchman.

PRAGMATIC COLLABORATION

In 1941 ordinary Americans might easily have missed the point that Frenchmen in touch with the Axis were not all alike. They may not have noticed that Darlan was different from Laval and others who collaborated out of ideological conviction. Darlan brought with him no doctrinaire commitment to collaboration. He was instead a pragmatic statesman who bargained with the Reich to gain concessions for France. A skillful negotiator, he defended French interests so well that the Germans finally got rid of him.

Americans tended to view any French business with the Germans as collaboration, and they assigned it a moral stigma. But French views of the German problem did not coincide neatly with American views. With the German occupation growing more oppressive in early 1941, and with Russia and the United States still neutral, Frenchmen accepted diplomacy as a legitimate option. Armed resistance promised no solution, so Frenchmen living under the occupation had no reason to oppose diplomacy aimed at easing their burdens. Darlan's diplomatic efforts to gain concessions from the Germans matched the mainstream of French opinion.

Unlike the doctrinaire collaborators, whose ideas remained largely fixed, the pragmatic Darlan was able to shift his position. In early 1941 he took office full of zeal to improve France's position under the armistice. But he soon came to understand that Berlin would permit no important change to improve France's condition. He therefore moved toward a stern policy that everyone--Germans, Paris collaborators, and American statesmen--recognized as a sharp departure from his earlier position. His attitude toward collaboration had begun to harden even before Pearl Harbor, and his early 1942 settlement with Washington completed the cycle of change during his term of office. Laval, intellectually committed to collaboration, was incapable of shifting focus from Berlin to Washington. Ironically, Darlan was more astute in his relations with the Axis than with the Allies, who surprised him twice with armed attacks in North Africa.

DARLAN AND THE DICTATORS

Because of his Vichy connection, the postwar acclaim assigned to those who had opposed prewar appeasement of the dictators failed to rub off on Darlan. But his record of opposing fascist aggression is impressive. He was among the first to recognize the new German threat. During the critical early years of the 1930s, while London neglected the Royal Navy in a vain pursuit of disarmament, Darlan stood openly in favor of naval rearmament. He was on the right track in the early 1930s when there was still time to prepare for the great war looming on the horizon.

Darlan was among the few to understand that combined naval power in the Mediterranean was the strongest card in the Anglo-French hand. With Darlan playing a key role, the 1937 Nyon operation was the only occasion prior to the war that the democracies unleashed military force to blunt fascist aggression. But Chamberlain frittered away the opportunity to build a solid alliance upon Nyon and to use the threat of Anglo-French naval power to drive a wedge between Mussolini and Hitler.

THE QUISLING MYTH

Wartime press labels of Darlan as a quisling obscured the differences between the Admiral and the Norwegian Nazi. Unlike Vidkun Quisling, Darlan was not a Nazi, nor did he betray his country into the hands of a foreign enemy. Nor was he a puppet ruling as the appointed agent of a foreign power. He instead served a French government that controlled a large empire beyond the Axis reach.

In 1940 and 1941 ordinary Frenchmen did not regard Darlan as a quisling. Although the American press often pretended that most Frenchmen supported de Gaulle and resisted the Germans, the great majority of Frenchmen in fact supported Marshal Pétain and his diplomatic efforts to ease their burdens. Nor did the American government regard Darlan as a traitor or refer to him as a quisling. That Darlan was perceived in France as a traitor is an invention of British and American newsmen out of touch with conditions in France in 1941. It is a myth that gained acceptance in France only later in the war, when resistance finally supplanted diplomacy as the best method for dealing with the German problem.

THE MYTH OF DARLAN AS FASCIST

Similarly, press labels of Darlan as a fascist fit poorly the pattern of French fascism, dominated by doctrinaire intellectuals friendly to German institutions. But Darlan, with his Radical Socialist heritage, was comfortable in the service of the left-leaning Popular Front. Like many Frenchmen, he became stoutly anti-Communist in 1939 when Moscow and Berlin partitioned Poland to begin World War II at the expense of the democracies.

But Darlan was no fascist. Certainly the French fascists in Paris who helped push him from office in 1942 did not think of him as one of their own. His habits of mind were pragmatic and his political beliefs were largely tentative. If he adhered consistently to any political conviction, it was that of secularism, a product of the left. The wartime myth of Darlan as fascist is an invention of foreign journalists who did not know him well.

THE MYTH OF DARLAN AS OPPORTUNIST

The popular Anglo-American myth of Darlan as opportunist is largely an invention of Winston Churchill. The charge of opportunism dates back to the fall of France when Darlan accepted a political post in the Pétain government after he had declined British invitations to bolt with the fleet to England. Afterward, Churchill frequently spoke of Darlan as an opportunist. His postwar memoirs reinforced the myth, picturing Darlan as driven by an obsessive ambition for political power.

Darlan was indeed ambitious. But so was Charles de Gaulle, who somehow escaped the special charge of opportunism that Churchill reserved in his speeches for the Admiral. To apply the label of opportunism uniquely to Darlan is to overlook important differences in the wartime careers of the two Frenchmen. It was de Gaulle, not Darlan, who bolted to London at the moment of France's greatest agony in a gamble intended to advance his own career. He took that step even before the 1940 armistice and before France had collaborated in any way with Germany or Italy. His decision to abandon the homeland and to chart an independent course for himself at that early moment in the war cannot be explained as a protest against collaboration. It was instead an act of opportunism.

In contrast, Darlan refused to abandon France in her agony. To label him an opportunist is to ignore the dominant element of loyalty inherent to his character. A consistent theme running through Darlan's entire career is that of loyal service to his government. Treason was not a part of his nature. Consistently obedient to the legal French authority, Darlan was not the type to nourish his own career at the expense of his government. He was no doubt politically ambitious, but the label of opportunism fits the General better than it does the Admiral.

THE MYTH OF CHRONIC ANGLOPHOBIA

At Vichy Darlan made no effort to conceal his Anglophobia or to deny that he had always hated the English. It was therefore easy for newsmen to view his Anglophobia as a product of his youth, a chronic condition inherent in his family background. But that image of him does not fit the facts.

Nothing in Darlan's early years suggests an attitude toward the English much different from that of any other French naval officer. In the early 1930s he opposed British disarmament proposals. So did most French naval officers. But he soon came to understand that French security against the Axis hinged upon forging an Anglo-French alliance. He therefore emerged as a leading advocate of closer relations with Britain. His relations with British naval officers after 1936, when he took command of the navy, were warm and cordial.

Although his confidence in the British ally began to wane during the Battle of France, Darlan remained on good terms with his British counterparts until the Royal Navy attacked his fleet at Mers el-Kébir. The attack sparked in him a hatred so intense as to become a central feature of his public image. But Darlan had not always hated the English. His Anglophobia was not a chronic condition endemic to his family background. It was instead a product of the war, a reaction to the surprise British attack against his fleet.

THE MYTH OF THE DOUBLE-GAME THEORY

American statesmen at Vichy sometimes divided Frenchmen into two groups: collaborators on the one hand, and on the other, friendly Frenchmen who pretended to collaborate while privately awaiting American military intervention. In 1941 some American statesmen thought that Darlan played that kind of double-game, awaiting American intervention.

But in 1941 Darlan viewed the Americans as potential peacemakers, rather than as liberators. Even when the Americans entered the war in December, he did not think them capable of liberating France. Afterward, he settled differences with the Americans because he regarded them as a new threat to the empire. It was only after his fall from political office that he came to regard the Americans as potential liberators. The double-game theory was useful to postwar historians eager to justify Washington's Vichy policy, but it does not fit Darlan.

DARLAN AND THE DECLINE OF IMPERIAL FRANCE

The career of the Admiral spanned the period from the glory years of the French empire at the turn of the century until its swift decline during World War II. His basic assumptions about France and her imperial life shaped over four decades of naval service influenced importantly his World War II diplomatic performance.

Young Darlan entered into his formative years during the turn-of-the-century decades when the Great Powers fell into a love affair with navalism. Those decades gave birth to the first great fleets that nourished the new colonialism and made modern naval warfare possible. Symbols of national pride and prestige, these new fleets were the instruments whereby the Great Powers extended and protected their global interests. Darlan's career coincided almost exactly with the era of the first generation of modern ships that saw service in both World Wars.

Impressed with the new naval technologies and influenced by doctrines linking naval power to national destiny, Darlan and a new generation of future world leaders committed themselves to navalism as a way of national life. Darlan's commitment to navalism matched that of young Winston Churchill and Franklin Roosevelt. They shared a common naval heritage dating from the time when the first modern battle fleets entered service. They were all navy men who thought of their nations as sea powers.

Darlan viewed France as a vast global empire held together by the navy. To him, the empire was an essential source of nourishment for the homeland. He was convinced that the loss of the empire would reduce France to the rank of a secondary power. The link between his prewar career and his service at Vichy is obvious. Preserving French control of the empire was always his first priority at Vichy. That objective guided his policy toward both the Axis and the Allies. It was an article of faith with him that France would return to the ranks of the Great Powers if she could somehow hold on to her empire.

That Darlan, stout defender of the empire, should finally preside over its decline is not surprising. The navy was never strong enough to defend all of the empire, already overextended when Darlan entered the service at the turn of the century. It survived World War I because the great naval powers except Germany fought on the French side. Ironically, the empire's entry into troubled times coincided almost exactly with the years when Darlan commanded the navy. French imperial decline was anticipated by the 1936-1937 shift in the world naval balance. With Japan now in league with Germany and Italy, imperial defense depended upon Anglo-French naval cooperation. But that broke down in 1940, so that all of France's former allies threatened the empire. By the time of Darlan's death, foreign armies were present in every major French colony.

OTHER AMERICAN VIEWS OF DARLAN

The final assessments of Darlan by the two Americans who knew him best contrast sharply with popular views of him. Admiral William D. Leahy and Robert Murphy were closer to Darlan than were the newsmen who shaped his public image. Although Leahy had clashed often with Darlan, he defended the Admiral when the Germans pushed him out in 1942. Later, when Leahy learned of Darlan's assassination, his thoughts turned to Madame Darlan, who had been kind to him at the time of Mrs. Leahy's death at Vichy. Leahy's diary entry of the day after Darlan's death reveals his private opinion of the Admiral's service to France:

> In this sad Christmas for me, I have been unable to keep out of my thoughts its sadness for Madame Darlan who has an only son recently stricken with infantile paralysis and who has now lost her distinguished husband at the hand of an assassin. It is my opinion that if we the Allies succeed in crushing Germany, Admiral Darlan will join the centuries old galaxy of Heroes of French History.[1]

Leahy's assessment of Darlan as a French hero perhaps overshoots the mark, but he would not have assigned that status to Laval.

Murphy, close to Darlan in Algiers, wrote admiringly of his diplomatic talents:

Probably I got to know him better than any other American ever did and, strangely, I grew to like him. I was particularly impressed by how cleverly Darlan safeguarded French national interests. Although he was leading from weakness..., no negotiator could have obtained more Allied concessions for the benefit of France.[2]

Murphy is on the mark in assessing Darlan in terms of his defense of French rather than foreign interests.

IN THE SHADOW OF VICHY

Half a century later the news media routinely identify Vichy with war crimes and servile collaborationism, making no distinction between the Darlan era and the Laval era that followed. But the history of Vichy took a sharp turn when the Germans forced Darlan from office in 1942. Afterward, Laval routinely caved in to Berlin, delivering thousands of French workers to Germany. It skews the record to lump Darlan into one package with Laval and the French fascists who pushed him aside for the purpose of swinging Vichy into line with German needs.

Nevertheless, Darlan remains in the shadow of Vichy, his reputation ever burdened with the stigma of the regime that rejected him in the interest of serving the Germans. The Admiral's early image as a collaborator has survived to obscure his hardening German policy of mid-1941, his protest of Nazi executions of civilian hostages, his refusal to deliver French workers to Germany, his keeping the Axis out of Tunisia, and his settling French differences with Washington before the Germans finally got rid of him in April 1942. The record is clear that Vichy rejected Darlan, that the pro-German faction at Vichy pushed him aside in 1942 in favor of Laval, and that the Americans defended the Admiral and withdrew their ambassador in protest of Laval's restoration.

To interpret Darlan as just another Vichy politician is to miss the rich complexity of the man and his career. He is best understood as a loyal Frenchman whose defense of French interests at Vichy ruined the good reputation he had enjoyed before the war. His Vichy connection overshadowed and obscured his prewar record of opposition to appeasement, his support of an Anglo-French alliance, his cordial relations with the Royal Navy, and his key role in blunting fascist aggression in the Mediterranean in 1937.

Whatever his record at Vichy, Darlan had considerable impact on international affairs both before and during the war. He was too complex and too important over more than a decade of crisis to be judged in terms of Anglo-American wartime interests. A French Admiral of the left center who served both the Popular Front and Vichy, who defended French interests against both the Axis and Allies, and whose murder eased the way for Charles de Gaulle is more unique than common. At Vichy he served France as he saw his duty, and he paid a high price for it.

EPILOGUE

Berthe Morgan Darlan, widow of the Admiral, returned to France after the liberation. In 1946 she died at Nérac and is buried there. The Admiral's sister, Louise-Hélène, died in 1958. Madame Francine Hezez, a niece of Admiral Darlan, lives in a Paris suburb.[3] At the invitation of President Roosevelt, Alain Darlan and his mother came in 1943 to Warm Springs where he received medical treatment for polio, an illness that left him confined to a wheelchair. At Warm Springs, Alain married his second wife, Phyllis Debrick, a nurse who had assisted with the treatment of President Roosevelt for the same illness. She returned to France with Alain and remained with him until her death in 1957. Alain married again and remained at Sanary, near Toulon, where he managed his own language translation service until his death on May 10, 1983. An adopted son, Eric Darlan, survives him.

NOTES

1. The Papers of William D. Leahy (Washington, DC: Library of Congress, Manuscripts Division), VIII, 67. Madame Louis de la Monneraye provided information about Madame Darlan's kindness to Admiral Leahy at the time of Mrs. Leahy's death.

2. Robert D. Murphy, *Diplomat among Warriors* (New York: Doubleday, 1964), 140.

3. Madame Hezez and the late Henri Ballande provided information about the Darlan family.

Notes on Archival Sources

The recent appearance of numerous new materials bearing on Darlan has helped clear up some of the mystery that has surrounded his career. But Darlan was such a complex figure that the wealth of new information will no doubt generate additional controversy. There is a need for continuing research on Darlan.

French archives, which reflect upon Darlan's entire career, are the most helpful. American and German collections have added valuable information about Darlan's wartime experience. But the several sets of archives do not all tell the same story. The picture of Darlan emerging from German documents is not identical with that reflected in French documents. American sources add yet another perspective. No single archival collection tells the full story. Each contains important information that simultaneously adds to our knowledge and tests our judgment.

Rich collections of Darlan papers are housed in Paris archives. The French National Archives in downtown Paris contain materials especially useful for study of Darlan's Vichy years. Materials used as evidence at the several postwar legal proceedings against Vichy officials are housed there, as are the records of the French Delegation to the German Armistice Commission and the office at Vichy that directed armistice services. Materials contained in Series AJ41-39, Cabinet 61 and AJ41-40, Cabinet 63 are especially useful. There are other useful materials there as well, including papers of participants close to Darlan.

The richest collection is contained in the French Naval Archives at Vincennes, a nearby Paris suburb. Housed at the Château de Vincennes, and supervised by the Service Historique de la Marine (SHM), this collection is especially rich on Darlan's prewar career. It contains numerous materials on Darlan and the French navy before the war, the disarmament negotiations, the Admiral's relations with British naval and diplomatic personnel during the 1930s, the Spanish

Civil War, the Nyon Conference, naval planning and operations early in World War II, and the French response to the Allied landings in North Africa in 1942. Darlan's daily journal of events is among these records. Valuable materials are contained in SHM, Sous-Series 1BB2 EMG/SE, Cartons 191-233. Darlan's personal file, Dossiers Amiral Darlan, is found in Carton 208. Good materials from the early war years are contained in SHM Sous-Series TT and TT.T. The largest published collection of Darlan papers, gleaned mainly from French archives and personal collections, is Hervé Coutau-Bégarie and Claude Huan, *Lettres et notes de l'Amiral Darlan* (Paris: Economica, 1992).

Numerous Darlan materials are found in various American archives. The Mark W. Clark papers, containing among other things the minutes of Darlan's conversations with General Clark in Algiers, are housed at The Citadel Museum in Charleston, South Carolina. Valuable materials are contained in the Franklin D. Roosevelt Library in Hyde Park, New York. The Map Room collection there is perhaps the richest. Especially useful is Map Room, Box 105, MR310, "Torch" and Box 106, MR310 "Torch." In the PSF File, Boxes 4, 26, 41, and 163 are helpful. And from the Official File, Boxes 1, 5197, and 5199 contain good Darlan materials. The Diary of Admiral William D. Leahy, housed in the Manuscripts Division of the Library of Congress in Washington, contains in addition to the Diary itself a number of Darlan's personal papers and an assortment of materials related to him from 1941 and 1942.

The largest collection of American documents containing Darlan material is housed at the United States National Archives II at College Park, Maryland. These archives house a set of the Microfilmed German Documents, files captured by Allied armies at the end of the war. They contain political and military records that shed light on Darlan's German relations in 1941 and 1942. The Department of State records housed at Archives II contain helpful information about Darlan not contained in the published collection, *Foreign Relations of the United States*.

Useful materials about Darlan and the French navy are scattered among the records of the Military Archives Division at Archives II. Record Group 38 contains Office of Naval Intelligence files, naval attaché reports, and numerous other valuable documents about French affairs. Especially rich is Record Group 226, containing among other things OSS field files from Algiers and other North African outposts from the early war years. Materials contained in RG 226, E97, Algiers File, Boxes 5, 24, 25, 27, 28, 29 and 50 are rich with intelligence reports and other materials about the conspiracy against Darlan and his assassination. Also, RG 226, E190, contains helpful materials from the files of William F. Donovan, Director of the OSS.

Also housed at the Military Archives Division is Record Group 457, SRVD-001, National Security Agency materials entitled VICHY FRENCH DIPLO-MATIC MESSAGES. This is a collection of several thousand confidential French messages, many of them from Darlan, that were intercepted by Canadian and American intelligence services. Of special interest are early 1942 communications between Darlan and French Ambassador Henry-Haye in Washington concerning the Admiral's efforts to stabilize Franco-American relations following the American entry into the war. Record Group 457 also contains intercepts of Free French messages, but American intelligence services did not penetrate Free French codes until the summer of 1943.

The records of the Allied Force Headquarters in Algiers, Record Group 331, are also housed at Archives II. A small but useful file, APO 794, Film No. B-226, "Admiral Darlan File, November 1942, December 1942," is contained in this collection.

Index

Entente Cordiale of 1904, 7
Esteva, Admiral Jean-Pierre: in
  Darlan's government, 104; friend-
  ship with Darlan, 6–7, 47; and
  implementation of Nyon Arrange-
  ment, 38; and Mediterranean, 48; in
  North Africa, 184; opposition to
  Paris protocols, 112–113
Ethiopia, Mussolini's war against, 28
Excelsior, 58 n.7
Executions, of French hostages, 129–
  31, 141, 143

Faivre, Mario, 211–12, 228 n.4
FELIX, operation, 94
Fenard, Admiral Raymond, 129, 134,
  137, 160–61
Figaro, 39
Finland, 63–64
The Five, 162, 166
Five Power Treaty, 15
Flandin, Pierre-Étienne, 100, 101
Fontaine, Captain Paul, 119
Force H, 83–84, 90
Force X, 82–83, 203
France: armistice with Germany, 73–
  77; execution of hostages by
  Germany, 129–31; German invasion
  of, 176, 184–85; military
  organization, 159–60, 183–92
  passim; and occupation costs, 107–
  8; plans for allied invasion of, 161–
  64; public opinion on alliance with
  England, 39, 41 n.43; security of
  colonial empire, 44, 52, 108, 109,
  110, 114, 123, 234–235. *See also*
  Navy, French
French Cameroons, 91
French Raiding Force, 48, 61
French War Committee, 62

Gamelin, General Maurice, 62, 65, 71
Gamma program, 151
Gasnier-Duparc, Alphonse, 9, 27–28,
  30
Geneva, World Disarmament
  Conference at, 18–22
Genoa, Italy, 73
Gensoul, Marcel, 7, 47, 83–84

Germany: assumptions about initial
  attack, 44–45; coastal attack on, 53,
  57, 58 n.19; Darlan's assessment of,
  99, 143; and executions of French
  hostages, 129–31, 141, 143; fear of
  Anglo-French war, 113; interest in
  North Africa, 86, 173; labor
  recruitment from France, 152–53;
  and Laval's supplanting Darlan,
  153–54; and the Nyon conference,
  37, 40n. 27; and *panzerschiffe,* 17,
  25–26; rapprochement with Japan
  and Italy, 26, 31; and Syria, 108,
  118–19; and Weygand's recall, 132–
  33; and World Disarmament
  Conference at Geneva, 21–22. *See
  also* Abetz, Otto; Executions, of
  French hostages; Hitler, Adolf;
  Munich Crisis
Gibraltar: and British blockade, 90, 91;
  French aerial attacks against, 91;
  Hitler's interest in, 94; and Mers el-
  Kébir attack, 85; plans to guard
  against Italy, 55
Giraud, General Henri: and allied
  invasion of France, 162, 164–66,
  167; and assassination of Darlan,
  224–26, 229 n.29; in Darlan's
  administration in Africa, 196;
  Darlan's relations with, 184, 188–
  89; and North African armistice,
  187–88; and Operation TORCH,
  164–66, 167, 172, 177; United
  States' support of, 222
Godfroy, René-Emile, 82–84, 203
Göring, Hermann, 138, 140–41
Gort, Lord, 72
Great Britain. *See* England
Greece, 37, 62
Greenslade, Admiral John W., 149

Halifax, Lord, 44
Henri, Count of Paris, 207, 209–12,
  222
Henry-Haye, Gaston, 148
Herriot, Edouard, 75
The High Seas Force, 48
Hitler, Adolf: and Germany's
  withdrawal from World Dis-

About the Author

GEORGE E. MELTON is Professor of History and Department Chair at St. Andrews Presbyterian College in Laurinburg, North Carolina. His research in several American and French archives supports his interest in French naval and diplomatic history of World War II and the interwar period.

ISBN 0-275-95973-2

EAN

9 780275 959739

HARDCOVER BAR CODE